CHINA:
The People's Republic,
1949–1976

The Pantheon Asia Library

New Approaches to the New Asia

CHINA:
The People's Republic,
1949–1976

Jean Chesneaux, Director

With the assistance of J. Bellassen,
A.-M. Dubois, F. Le Barbier, J.-F. Olivier,
J.-P. Peemans, and N. Wang

Translated from the French
by Paul Auster and Lydia Davis

PANTHEON BOOKS, NEW YORK

Library of Congress Cataloging in Publication Data

Chesneaux, Jean.

  China: the People's Republic, 1949–1976.

  (The Pantheon Asia Library)
  Translation of La Chine
  Includes index
  1. China—History—1949–1976.   I. Title.
DS777.55.C44572313   951.05   78–51797
ISBN 0–394–42873–0
ISBN 0–394–73623–0 pbk.

Grateful acknowledgment is made to the following for permission to reprint previously published material:

Victor Gollancz Ltd. and Random House, Inc.: Extract from *The Other Side of the River* by Edgar Snow. Copyright © Edgar Snow 1962, published by Victor Gollancz Ltd. Used by permission.

Holt, Rinehart & Winston and Neale Hunter: Excerpts from *Shanghai Journal: An Account of the Cultural Revolution* by Neale Hunter. Copyright © 1969 by Frederick A. Praeger, Inc.

G. P. Putnam's Sons and Jonathan Cape Ltd.: Excerpts from *Birdless Summer* by Han Suyin. Copyright © 1968 by Han Suyin.

3456789

Contents

Contents

Maps

Preface

The year 1949 marks a radical break in the historical development of contemporary China. It also marks the beginning of a completely new historical approach to that development.

There are new types of source materials to be dealt with: for the most part these are documents which have come directly or indirectly from the Chinese authorities and include information from the national press, the local press when possible, official publications and materials, as well as the accounts of visitors who have been allowed to enter China. No matter how rich and diversified it might be, this type of information is tightly supervised and controlled.

New types of problems have also come into being as a result of the development of a communist society in China: these problems are different from those in the West and from those that existed in China prior to 1949. In China today questions of "line" and of theoretical analysis are all-important. Concrete historical facts are considered only in relation to more general political ideas which are used to describe those facts and demonstrate the limits of their application. Knowledge of the "diachronic" development of a particular province or area of society, for example, is not considered to be a legitimate goal of a historian's work: the Chinese do not consider such knowledge to be an end in itself. There is no equivalent in China of E. Vogel's book on Canton from 1949 to 1970, which is a typical product of the Harvard universe. Even the author himself confesses that such a book has no more than a very uneven hold on Chinese reality. In China the study of history is not seen as an attempt to resuscitate the past in the manner of Michelet, but as a way of integrating the past with a political thought that is *rooted in the present*.

How do the Chinese experience and think about the history of their country since 1949? Their relationship with the past is intense and deeply collective, but they do not see it as a neat, chronological story. Not only is their history filled with crises and sudden shifts, it is read *backward*, constantly being revised and reinterpreted as these crises and shifts occur.

It took the Soviet challenge to Stalinism in 1956 to reveal that the Chinese Communist Party, even before 1949, had forbidden the celebration of birthdays of important leaders and had not allowed their names to be given to cities and factories. For obvious reasons this decision had remained secret, since it was an implicit criticism of Soviet practices. By the same token, the crises that led to the elimination of Liu Shao-qi, Lin Biao, and Deng Xiao-ping retrospectively unmasked—at least partially—the cracks hidden by the CCP's facade of unanimity in the fifties and even the forties. The history of Chinese communism is seen in the country today as a series of jolts and internal struggles (see Chapter 7). It is no longer reduced to a reassuring chain of glorious revolutionary battles (the civil wars against the militarists of the North and the Guomindang, the national struggle against Japan and the American penetration) as was the case before the Cultural Revolution.

Because of these changes in approach, the history of the People's Republic of China is no longer available to interpretation according to the methods of foreign historians. The Chinese authorities have deliberately taken their own history in hand. It is they who control its rhythms and stages as options develop and changes occur: the Five Year Plan, the Great Leap Forward, the Cultural Revolution. It is they who decide which aspect of the past should be made public for political consideration and which aspect of their experience should remain hidden as a state secret. For example, they have never given any explanation of the short life of the cooperatives that came into being in 1954–1955 and which since 1958 have been based in the people's communes. They have never published a systematic report of the first Five Year Plan, even though such a critical report would seem to have been the logical precondition for the radical shift in 1958 (see Chapter 4). The Lin Biao affair was only belatedly and incompletely made known to the public; it remains a dark and confusing incident. And who reinstated Deng Xiao-ping in 1972–1973—and why—has never been answered.

The Chinese Communists have always contended that "it is the masses who make history." And indeed the participation of the masses has been very significant in widespread popular movements such as the agrarian reform of 1950, the Great Leap Forward, and especially the Cultural Revolution. However, we have become aware of this participation only through the materials and analyses provided to us by the leadership of the People's Republic. The only version we ever see is the one that has been dictated from above. Nevertheless, some attempts have already been made in China to give the workers a role in the writing and interpretation of their history, to allow them to "take their past in hand." An example of this was the "five histories" that were written between 1962 and 1964 by individual workers and peasants, factories, villages, and communes (see Chapter 5). Another example was the Red Guard campaign to seize the "black papers"—the secret dossiers of the state leadership (see Chapter 6).

Whether controlled by the leadership or to some extent created with the help of the workers, the history of China since 1949 has always been written as a collective political act; it has not been written by professional Chinese historians, who no longer have primary responsibility for it. It is undoubtedly this fact that is most confusing to Western historians when facing the situation. The object of their study, China, has become an active subject which in itself defines the restrictions and approaches that determine the area in which they must think and work.

Of course, there is still some room for speculation and interpretation for the Western historian. We can, for example, wonder about why the rhythm of 1958 was disrupted (see Chapter 4), or why the "struggle between the two lines" which had gone on for so many years suddenly turned into a major crisis in 1965–1966 (see Chapter 6). But this margin of speculation remains narrow, for it is defined by the information given to us by the Chinese themselves, which means that the questions we ask are in some sense predetermined. This is the situation, whether one likes it or not. Since 1960, for example, China has deliberately abstained from publishing production statistics in absolute values.

Few people today would still agree with Fénelon's statement that "the good historian does not come from any time or country." We write the history of China limited by our basic options and limited also by the problems of the society in which we live. Thus, the crises in education and university instruction in the West today have made us much more sensitive than twenty years ago to what is said and done in China concerning "open door teaching" (see Chapter 7), or discussions on the relation between manual and intellectual work. No book on China written in the West is neutral. This does not mean, however, that we can abandon the demands of rigorous objectivity, for this is the only guarantee against simplistic imagery and naive illusions, which are just as dangerous to the author as to the reader.

Critical reflection on historical knowledge has recently become an important subject in France, and the authors of this book have been deeply involved in it. The essential question is: What is the social function of history? Should knowledge of the past progress independently of the present—and can it? Are professional historians by right the privileged interpreters of the past, cut off from us in the name of the science of history?

This book does not enter into these debates on historical knowledge and historical writing; its essential aim is merely to present an outline of Chinese development since 1949. It is perhaps the expression of an unalterable situation: for even if we question the finality of the technical instruments of historical knowledge, the study and teaching of history continue by and large to rely on those instruments.

CHINA:
The People's Republic,
1949–1976

Chapter One

China in 1949

In 1949 the Chinese Communists took power over the whole of China except Taiwan. This was the culmination of twenty-two years of revolutionary wars that had gradually tipped the political balance in China from the Guomindang to the Chinese Communist Party (CCP). This taking of power, however, was not a revolution in the classic sense of the term; in China it is usually referred to as the Liberation, in order to emphasize the things that united the great majority of Chinese people during this critical period and the new things the new regime had given the people—excluding a tiny minority that had been stripped of its privileges. "Never again will the Chinese be an enslaved people," declared Mao Tsetung, the new President of the Republic, on October 1, 1949, before an immense crowd in Peking's Tienanmen Square.

The problems confronting China in 1949 were very diverse. Some of them were the direct result of the revolutionary struggles; others had been inherited from a century of foreign domination; still others stemmed from the distant past, both ideologically (for example, Confucian conservatism) and economically. To solve these problems the Communist Party and the leaders of the new state could rely upon their own considerable historical background and the definite support of the masses[1]—even though their experience had only partially prepared them for the tasks ahead and the unity of their views was somewhat fragile.

[1] See document 1 at the end of the chapter.

The Communist Party Takes Power:
The Political and Ideological Stakes

In 1949 both the Chinese people and the rest of the world marveled at the ease and suddenness of the success of the Chinese Communists during the last phase of the civil war (see Volume 2). It was only much later, during internal and external crises such as the Cultural Revolution and the Sino-Soviet break, that the rifts and uncertainties of the CCP during this period became known.

The CCP: the social and political bases of its influence

In September 1949 the Communist Party had four and a half million members (as opposed to 1,200,000 in 1945). Seventy-two percent were poor and middle-poor peasants ("middle-poor" being the lowest level of middle peasants), 2 percent were workers, and 25 percent were rich peasants and members of the urban middle class.

The prestige of the party, as well as its military and political authority, were a direct result of the role it had played in the Chinese revolution. The People's Liberation Army was a considerable force; it had resisted the Japanese and defeated Tchiang Kaï-chek's troops. It was a political army, based on conviction, discipline, and a determination to support the population in which it had the confidence that "a fish has in water." The presence of millions of PLA soldiers ready to take on the tasks of production, management, and political control, in addition to defense, was a major advantage for the Communists at the decisive moment when power was taken. They were thus able to dispense with the dilemma that proved to be a handicap to Lenin in 1917: whether to withdraw the best workers from the factories at the risk of diminishing production or to show confidence in the old administration.

The PLA was largely composed of peasants, as was the party itself. The victory of 1949 was a victory of a strategy that fundamentally equated the Chinese peasant movement, which had a rich secular tradition, with the political and military struggle of the Communists. The agrarian reform of 1947, which came into being because of the situation in the "old liberated zones" that were then held by the PLA, gave the land to the peasants; for them it became

identified with the revolution itself, with their desire to overthrow
the old agrarian regime of exploitation and misery.[2] The Chinese
peasants, at least those from the regions that had had a prolonged
experience with the Japanese occupation and the civil war, had
bitter memories of the repression of the Guomindang police, the
despotism of the landowners, and the unspeakable conditions that
had forced them to live in caves. The peasants from the village of
Liulin in North Shenxi told such a story to the Swedish sociologist
Jan Myrdal in 1962. More generally, by 1949 the Chinese peasantry
had become a revolutionary class in the full sense of the term. Its
political experience qualified it to participate actively in the building of a new society: this was another radical difference from the
Russian situation in 1917.

The fact that only 2 percent of the Communists were workers
was due to the special nature of the party's history. Based on the
struggles of the workers until 1927, the CCP gradually shifted the
focus of its attention to the countrysides. It had been removed
from the large cities for twenty-two years. Its ties with the working
class had become weaker, and by 1949 its experience with workers'
problems was infinitely less rich than its experience with the peasant
world. This was a paradoxical situation, since for reasons of
principle the Communist Party had decided to build modern socialism in China by calling on heavy industry to play a major role. This
fundamental disparity between the concrete political situation in
1949 and the economic strategy for the future would have a lasting
influence on the development of the People's Republic, manifesting
itself in the mechanical imitation of the Soviet model in the early
fifties—because there was no clear-cut Chinese frame of reference
for industrialization—or, in reaction to this, in the radical innovations of the Great Leap Forward and the massive appeal to the
peasantry for industrialization. In 1949 the reunion of the CCP and
the working class was not a foregone conclusion.

On the other hand, in 1949 the party was deeply tied to the
Chinese national movement. A product of the great enthusiasm
created by the movement for "national salvation" (*jiuguo*) in 1919,
the party was a major factor in the struggle against Japan; it had
represented the hopes for renewal of the country during the
Guomindang's corrupt and discredited regime. There were many
people, particularly from the middle classes, who supported it and

[2] See document 2.

had confidence in it, even though they were unfamiliar with Marxist principles and the revolutionary struggle the party represented.[3]

The historical experience of the CCP

In 1949 the Communist Party had the very original experience of the liberated zones behind it. Its leaders had not been in prison, exile, or the underground, as had been the case with the Bolsheviks in 1917, but in vast regions (with over 100 million inhabitants in 1945) where they had established their power, in some instances as many as ten years before. The political experience of managing the liberated zones was considerable, but nevertheless unequal. It functioned with great success in the areas of agricultural production, management of the base, political education, human relations, mutual aid, and popular culture—in short, in all that the Yanan heritage represented. Yanan, a city in the Northwest, had been the principal guerrilla base for the Communists after the Long March ended there in 1935. The Yanan heritage was founded on the "mass line," on the desire to link the cadres and the people, on patient discussion and persuasion, and on the preference given to minute political and ideological analyses over authoritarian directives. On the other hand, the Chinese Communists had much less experience in the areas of state diplomacy, large-scale financial and economic management, central state organizations, modern technology, higher education and scientific research, and the creation of a cultural elite. These were the very areas in which Soviet influence was greatest between 1950 and 1955, which became the so-called black line between 1960 and 1965 and then were known as the private kingdoms during the Cultural Revolution.

The Northeast was an exception. The Communists had held this former Japanese industrial stronghold since 1947. There they had administered large cities, had acquired a certain familiarity with heavy industry, and had cooperated with the Soviet technicians who had come at the request of Gao Gang, the principal leader of the CCP in the region. It was in the northeastern city of Harbin that the Seventh National Congress of Chinese Workers' Unions was held in 1948 (the last congress had taken place in 1928). The special experience in the Northeast was therefore ambiguous. It could have been the point of departure for an enlargement and en-

[3] See document 3.

richment of communist strategy concerning the major industrial centers, or it could have represented a radical reorientation, a divorce from the whole experience of Yanan.

Chinese Marxism

In 1949 Chinese Marxism was a living reality, a mode of thought that had become part of the political horizon for hundreds of thousands of people. Its influence had been limited in the twenties, and even the thirties, to several small circles of intellectuals and militants, and Marxist writings had been available in only a few classic texts that had been only partially translated and at best incompletely assimilated. With the wars of liberation against Japan and the Guomindang Marxist thought spread as a concrete method of analysis, for the most part through the writings of Mao and the Central Committee, in which Marxism was used to define the contradictions and class relations that were seen as part of the immediate political and military strategy, but also through the daily discussions in the villages and by guerrilla groups concerning questions of how to determine which class a particular peasant belonged to or what the political priorities were in regard to a particular action. William Hinton's book *Fanshen* is very rich in details of this kind.

The substance of Marxism had been absorbed by the people as well. They had gone beyond simply repeating the analyses of Marx and Lenin. Marxism was enriched by a whole series of new experiences and ideas; these were to be found in a condensed form in Mao's writings, which were widely distributed in the liberated zones before 1949 and which included texts on the principles of revolutionary war, theoretical notions such as "practice" and "contradiction," general strategic formulations such as the New Democracy, and attempts to define Chinese socialism. Nevertheless, this creative enrichment of Marxism was much more concerned with the peasants and the countrysides than with the working class and the cities. There is a glaring difference in the emphasis given to these two social groups in Mao's writings before 1949.

The rapid spread of the influence of Marxism was no doubt also due to the fact that its two basic ideas, materialism and the dialectic, had for many centuries been part of Chinese cultural traditions, if in a somewhat primitive form. The term "contradiction," for example, which is so important in Marxist theory, is in most languages a rather technical term fashioned by intellectuals. In China, however, the Marxists had only to say *mao-dun* (shield-sword)— which refers to a well-known legend—to illustrate the idea of contradiction.

The strength and cohesion of Marxism also stemmed from the fact that the CCP almost completely identified itself with it. It did not have to deal with left-wing national Marxism, social democracy, Trotskyism, or any other of the marginal varieties of Marxism. These currents, which were present by 1940 in Colombo, Saigon, Tokyo, and Delhi, touched only a tiny minority of individuals in China, most of whom had emigrated by 1949.

The intellectuals

There were three major currents among the intellectuals. First, there were those among whom the traditional culture was very much alive—the adherents of Confucianism (see below), who held a classic conception of the intellectual as a person deserving of prestige because of his knowledge. This type of traditional intellectual was to be found particularly in the small and middle-sized provincial cities.

Others, especially in Shanghai and the large modern cities, had been influenced by intellectual currents from the West since the nineteenth century; they were followers of scientism, evolutionary theories, pragmatism, liberalism, and the social values and life-style associated with these ideas. They were concerned with personal careers, technological progress, money, individual freedom, and disinterested culture. Engineers, professors, doctors, judges, and journalists, they had long envisaged a future China based on a Western model. The limited but deeply rooted influence of Catholicism and Protestantism was historically part of this same admiration for the West. In 1949 the several million Christians in China were deeply torn between their national allegiance and their special ties with the West.

There were also those intellectuals who belonged to the revolutionary movement, but they were very few in number. Marxism was practically nonexistent in the universities and among scientists and technicians. Very few intellectuals had come from the liberated zones, and the harshness of the struggle there had pushed cultural problems to the background. Only a few rare artists and writers had begun to work according to the line established by the Yanan

Forum (1942) and to join the popular struggles in any concrete way.

On the other hand, there were only a few intellectuals tied to the Guomindang and the United States who had emigrated to Taiwan in 1949. The great majority of intellectuals supported the new regime, but without much conviction; the CCP estimated that 90 percent fell into this category. Their attitude was one of mixed caution and hope concerning the regime's ability to bring about a renewal. The problem of the intellectuals would weigh heavily on the whole development of Communist China.

New democracy in action

The Common Program adopted in September 1949 by the Advisory Political Conference made use of the major ideas outlined by Mao in 1940 in his treatise "On New Democracy": they would not yet attempt to build socialism, but rather a society of transition in which the common aspirations of the four revolutionary classes (the industrial proletariat, the poor peasants, the middle classes, and the national capitalists) could be realized. This alliance among classes was reflected in the political forces present at the conference: Communists, small centrist liberal parties, Guomindang dissidents, people without party affiliation, as well as civilian and military organizations. The principal aim of the Common Program was to guarantee a return to order and prosperity: "a policy that is concerned with both private and public interests, that benefits both the bosses and the workers, that encourages mutual aid between the cities and countrysides and the exchange of goods between our country and foreign countries in order to develop production and bring prosperity to the economy" (Article 11). The realization of agrarian reform through the expropriation of feudal lands was essential if this policy of development and prosperity was to be successful.

A victory that was too sudden

Socialism "came to our country too suddenly," Mao declared in July 1957 during a campaign against the right wing. Somewhat later he added: "In 1949 our armies crossed the Yangzi, but our ideology did not cross the Yangzi." In other words, the very suddenness of the Guomindang's defeat (until 1948 the Communists had been expecting a much longer resistance) created a political void, at least in the South and in the large cities. Of course, direct opposition had disappeared; there were only a few networks of Taiwan agents left, many of which were tied to the old secret societies that the police patiently dismantled in 1950–1951 during the "campaigns to eliminate the counterrevolutionaries." But the shifts in loyalty had been too massive and sudden to build a solid foundation for the regime, and the popular forces in the South had not had enough time to entrench themselves and develop solidly as had been the case in the North where the struggle had gone on for a long time. It was even necessary for the military command to issue a directive on April 25, 1949, asking unsympathetic civil servants to remain in place, defeated soldiers to reenlist, and the personnel of the capitalist-bureaucratic enterprises (belonging to the "four great families" of the Guomindang) to continue working and to take care of current business. In the last phase of the civil war whole army divisions had surrendered without fighting, entire cities and provinces had fallen in a matter of weeks. All this was a tremendous burden on the new regime—especially the three million civil servants who had worked for the Guomindang.

Among these new adherents to the regime there were naturally many who hesitated. They shirked and criticized. In Mao's speech of June 30, 1949 ("On the Dictatorship of the People's Democracy"), he tried to answer their reproaches. For they were the ones who were saying to the Communists: "You are leaning to one side" (the socialist camp), "we need British and American aid," "you are setting up a dictatorship," "why don't you do away with the power of the state?", "why aren't you more benevolent to the reactionaries?" . . .

However, it was among these groups that new cadres had to be recruited, since there were not enough veterans of the revolution and the People's Army. According to a survey made the day after the Liberation, out of 6,000 cadres of the new regime 2,500 came from the middle classes; 1,150 were former civil servants, soldiers, and policemen from the Guomindang; 400 were members of the liberal professions; 150 were from the privileged classes (landowners and capitalists); and only 140 were workers.

In 1949 the Communists knew that they had to turn their attention to the cities[4] and that this would be one of their most

[4] See document 4.

important actions. But they also knew that the difficulties involved were just as great as the possible rewards.

Canton

Canton, the largest city in the South, is a good example of the problems that faced the CCP when it turned its attention to the large cities.

This city of 1,170,000, which had only been liberated on October 13, 1949, was packed with refugees who had arrived during the Guomindang defeat. The railroads and ferryboat lines had been cut, and communications with the rest of Guangdong were impossible; wandering gangs pillaged houses, supplies were running out, and inflation was rising. Canton had played a rather militant role during the republican revolution at the beginning of the century, but in the thirties and forties it had become more of a business center. The bourgeoisie was closely tied to the bourgeoisie of nearby Hong Kong; many families had relatives who had gone overseas to the European colonies of Southeast Asia and had come back with Western ideas and influences. The intellectuals also looked more toward the West than their traditional colleagues from Peking. Unemployment had been endemic at least since the Japanese occupation and had led to banditry, sampan prostitution, and opium traffic. The nearness of Hong Kong offered advantages to Guomindang agents and their sympathizers. The secret societies involved in rackets and smuggling were very influential, especially among the dockworkers, boatmen, and sailors.

The Communist cadres who had to deal with this difficult situation were very few in number. In addition, they were a heterogeneous group, made up of the underground militants from the Communist urban networks, who had never really recovered from the December 1927 massacre after the defeat of the Canton Commune and who numbered no more than a hundred in 1949; the cadres sent from the North with the new mayor Ye Jian-ying, who in most cases could only speak the Chinese spoken in the North and not the local languages (Cantonese, Hakka); and finally, the guerrillas from the small revolutionary bases that had been established in the interior of the province in the twenties, who were quite small in number and strongly particularist in their leanings.

This list would be extremely discouraging if we limited it to its local elements. The counterbalance was found elsewhere, on the pan-Chinese level; because the ties between Canton and the rest of China were ultimately very strong, the city was able to integrate itself into the Chinese socialist society as the other large cities had, in spite of the initial difficulties.

The Confucian heritage in 1949

Confucianism disappeared as the ideological structure of state power in China at the beginning of the twentieth century: even before the end of the empire, civil servants were no longer required to take Confucian examinations based on their knowledge of the canonical Four Books. As an ethical and philosophical system it had also been on the wane for a long time. In 1949 only the intellectuals of the old school were still familiar with the Confucian writings in *Wenyan*, the classical language which was studied only superficially in the schools.

But Confucianism was still an active influence on general ideology and behavior in numerous areas of social life. It remained the basis for the rigidly hierarchical relations between parents and children and the even stricter relations between men and women. In the villages women had to accept a life of docile obedience, and the status of a family was measured according to the number of male children it had. The prestige that continued to be given to learning was a result of Confucianism, and its influence could be found in the authoritarian and routine teaching methods that still prevailed, the respect for intellectuals, the book, and tradition, as well as the scorn for manual work. This accounted for the secular influence of the bureaucracy: civil servants considered their privileges and authority as a natural right, and the people passively accepted these privileges and this authority. Confucianism was also at the root of a number of social principles such as *cai* (talents), which affirmed the inequality of natural gifts among men and the necessity of choosing an elite of superior people; *ren* (virtue, benevolence), which reduced social relations to relations between individuals independent of social situations; and *tianming* (heavenly mandate, destiny), which led to a passive acceptance of fate, particularly concerning the natural world—climate, fertility, distribution and use of resources.

All these mental habits remained very deeply rooted, and in 1949 they continued to play a major role in the family and schools. They were not systematically challenged until the seventies, with the campaign of *pi Lin pi Kong* (against Lin Biao and against Confucius).

Chinese communism and the USSR

In 1949, at the height of the cold war, the victory of the Chinese Communists was seen throughout the world as an enormous and sudden coup for the Soviet Union and the other countries in the socialist camp. Nevertheless, relations between China and the Soviet Union were extremely complex, and had been so even before the break in 1960. The differences between these two major forces of world communism went very deep: in 1927 Stalin's obstinate support of a revolutionary strategy that favored an alliance with the Guomindang had left the Chinese Communists totally unprepared for Tchiang Kaï-chck's turnaround in April; in 1931–1935 Moscow had installed its team of "28 Bolsheviks," which replaced Mao and his friends at the helm of the CCP, and had led the "Chinese Soviets" to defeat; in August 1945 the Soviet Union had signed a friendship treaty with the Guomindang just at the moment when the CCP was in a position to take a leading role in China because of the part it had played in the defeat of Japan;[5] and again, in 1949, Stalin had shown open hostility to the CCP's taking of power over the whole of China. He frankly discouraged Mao and would have preferred a compromise between the Guomindang and the Chinese Communists.

But in 1949, and for many years to come, the Communists in Peking remained discreetly silent about these disagreements. They preferred to talk about the "priority of internal factors" and the support that the mistaken Chinese policy of Moscow and the Comintern had received from the CCP. They preferred to distinguish themselves from the Soviet Union in concrete practice rather than by taking an explicit stand. In 1949, for example, a resolution of the Central Committee forbade giving the names of leaders to cities, streets, or factories, and forbade the celebration of leaders' birthdays. This measure was not made public. It was only much later that Peking allowed a number of leaks on these subjects.

For identical reasons, the Soviet Union also showed considerable reserve, at least until 1960. When the Chinese Communists took

[5] See Volume 2 for descriptions of all these episodes.

power in 1949 Mao's writings were not made accessible in Russian, nor were the ideas developed at Yanan made known: the political capacities of the peasantry, the principles of people's revolutionary war, the antibureaucratic movements of 1941–1942, and New Democracy.

In 1949 China entered the socialist camp in an unorthodox manner: neither as a result of a proletarian revolution based on the model of October 1917, nor because of the arrival of the Red Army as had been the case in Eastern Europe and North Korea, but after a prolonged armed struggle, simultaneously directed against feudal exploitation of the peasants and foreign domination. The victory of the Chinese Communists was at once the culmination of the secular struggles of the peasantry and the modern struggles against Western and Japanese control of China. Thus in two ways China was part of the vast cycle of peasant movements for national liberation that shook Asia and Africa following the Second World War. In 1949 Communist China was extremely popular in the Third World.

The cold war and Liberation

This popularity, however, did not extend to the West. The Liberation of China in October 1949 took place in an international climate dominated by the cold war and fear of the Iron Curtain. With very few exceptions the Western countries had gathered around the United States in forming the Atlantic Pact. At the UN Latin America was part of the automatic pro-Western majority. The decolonization movement was just beginning in Africa and Asia (India, Burma, Ceylon, and Indonesia), and the war in Vietnam was growing more intense. The socialist camp was digging in, and the Korean War was approaching.

The People's Republic of China therefore entered the international scene under rather ambiguous circumstances, almost against the current. It was not in a position to pursue the broad and open diplomatic alliances that logically would have followed from the spirit of the New Democracy and the Common Program. The timid overtures the CCP had made in this direction came to nothing—for example, taking part in the governmental delegation sent by Nanking in 1945 to the United Nations Charter Conference, or the attempt to establish special relations with India after it had gained its independence in 1947. In 1949 the People's Republic ran straight into the iron curtain of opposition in the West, and this was unquestionably a disappointment to the Chinese leaders.

The CCP: united or divided?
The two lines after 1949

The Communist Party came to power by the route it had set out for itself in 1945 at its Seventh Congress: armed struggle, broad political alliances under the aegis of the New Democracy, and agrarian revolution. The party seemed to be headed by a prestigious team, which had come to power in January 1935 at the Zunyi Conference[6] in a time of crisis and which had led the Long March, waged the struggle against Japan, and defeated the Guomindang. This team had lived through the armed struggle, had managed the liberated zones, and had undergone many crises over the party and its direction. It included Mao Tsetung, the chairman of the party, whose skill at theoretical analysis had won him a special place; Zhou En-lai, the negotiator and organizer; Liu Shao-qi, the party man; and military leaders such as Zhu De, Chen Yi, Lin Biao, He Long, and Liu Bo-cheng, all of whom were very popular.

But were the heads of the party as unified as they seemed to be? The crises that later developed in 1955, 1959, 1967, and 1972,[7] and which led to the elimination of several of the most important leaders, became occasions for retroactive criticism of all their activities, including activities before the Liberation. The war leadership of Peng De-huai and Lin Biao, the management of Manchuria by Gao Gang, and Liu Shao-qi's role in revolutionary strategy were all brutally reconsidered after these men were deposed.

At the time, however, none of these conflicts was apparent. Perhaps the most important thing to study is not whether a purged leader should have been charged retroactively, but to try to analyze what tensions and conflicts might have existed in the CCP in 1949, above and beyond the collective enthusiasm and show of unity that had been created by the victory. The very swiftness of that victory had led to a conflict between the scattered guerrillas who had fought for so many years and the necessity of reorganizing into more classic large battle units. And although the CCP had never completely left the large cities, the repression it had encountered in the

[6] See Volume 2, Chapter 9.
[7] See Chapters 3, 4, 6, and 7.

urban centers had limited it to a defensive, almost wait-and-see
policy. The former leaders of these white sectors, such as Liu
Shao-qi and Peng Zhen, had necessarily undergone experiences
quite different from those of the men who had been in the red
bases; they were men of order and organization. The crisis of
1941–1942,[8] on the other hand, had not truly resolved the situation
concerning the group most closely tied to Moscow, which was led
by Wang Ming. He remained a member of the Central Committee;
his influence was relayed through northeastern leaders, such as Gao
Gang, who had also established special ties with the Soviet Union
both through their political and military leanings and through their
experience with the heavy industry of this region. The tensions and
divergent tendencies within the leadership of the CCP were carefully hidden in 1949, nor have they been completely revealed since
then; but it is a fact that they existed. The Yanan experience and
the mass line were neither shared nor approved by everyone.

China's Historical Heritage:
Unequal Development and Misery

The Chinese Communist Party which came to power in 1949
wanted to build a New China (*Xinhua*). In order to do so it
simultaneously had to eradicate the economic and social consequences of the civil war, undo the damages that a century of foreign
domination and unequal treaties had done to the Chinese economy
and society, and finally, at a deeper level, eliminate the evils, injustices, and backwardness created by centuries of feudalism that
continued to weigh on the masses of peasants.

Economic stagnation

Economic stagnation was the inevitable result of so many years
of civil and foreign war. Inflation, which had become staggering in
the Guomindang zones during the last period of the war (see
Volume 2), also affected the liberated zones; in around 1948 the
authorities had begun printing bills made payable in *renminbi*
("people's money"), whose rates of exchange varied from one region
to another. The monetary confusion reached its height in the spring

[8] Or rectification movement. See Volume 2.

and summer of 1949. The Communist authorities began with-drawing the old devalued Guomindang bills as well as the monies from the different liberated zones and exchanging them at very variable rates against people's *yuan*: one people's *yuan* against ten "*yuan*-gold" in Peking in January; 2,500 in Nanking in the spring; and 100,000 in Shanghai in June. But the inflation continued all through 1949. The money brought in by the state represented only two-thirds of what it needed. Prices rose regularly; and at four different times—in January, April, July, and November—these rises had to be made official, which resulted in an overall rise of 700 percent for 1949.

Unemployment was widespread in the cities and was further aggravated by the massive displacements during the last months of the war. Millions of people, especially in the South, had left their homes to crowd into the large cities.

The instruments of production were in poor shape in both the city and the country. The railroads were used only very irregularly, and then mostly for the army; there was no general plan governing railway use, and the equipment had not been repaired or replaced for a long time. Almost the entire merchant fleet had taken refuge in Taiwan, Hong Kong, and Singapore; the same was true of large-scale capital; and many technicians had fled. Numerous factories had ceased operation for lack of raw materials. The machines were in poor condition, especially since the departure of the Japanese, and individual parts were not available. In the villages the dikes and canals had suffered greatly during the war from negligence and the instability of traditional institutions. Their poor condition, along with the hazards of the weather, were responsible for the natural disasters that ravaged China in 1949: floods and droughts affected 120 million *mou*[9] and 40 million people. According to Chen Yun, a former Shanghai worker who was in charge of economic affairs for the people's government, the situation was almost as serious as it had been in 1931 when 157 million *mou* and 52 million people had been affected. The agricultural reserves were very low.

In 1949, according to estimates by the Communist authorities, production had gone down 50 percent in relation to the previous best year for coal, 80 percent for iron and steel, 25 percent for cotton goods, 25 percent for grains, 48 percent for raw cotton, and 16 percent for livestock.

[9] One *mou* equals ⅙ acre.

The heritage of China
and foreign capitalism

In 1949 China was deeply marked by Western capitalism—in the structure of production, its relations with the world economy, and the definition of its social values.

There was a Chinese capitalist sector which was very active in banking, heavy and light industry, maritime and river transportation, and urban services. Because of the violent expulsion of the Westerners in 1949 and the Japanese defeat in 1945, traditional comprador capitalism was no longer a major factor. But private Chinese capitalism, called national capitalism, was very different from the so-called bureaucratic capitalism. Bureaucratic capitalism was based on the investments—often very speculative in nature— made since the thirties by the groups at the head of the Guomindang (the "four great families": the Tchiangs, the Songs, the Kongs, and the Chens), which were made possible by their dominant position in the state government. This foundation was expanded when Japanese goods and businesses were seized in 1945. In 1949 the financial groups tied to the ousted state bureaucracy controlled 35 percent of all mining industries, 65 percent of electrical production, 40 percent of textile manufacturing, and nearly all maritime and river transportation, which amounted to nearly a third of all industrial production. The national capitalists consisted of a small bourgeoisie that had been pushed out of the most lucrative areas by the Guomindang and which had collaborated with the United States to a much lesser extent than the four families; their political representatives had been approached by the Communists as early as 1948 and had participated with them in the founding of the People's Republic in October 1949.

Bureaucratic capitalism was an essential element in the dependent relations that still tied China to world capitalism in 1949. Because of the war, there were far fewer businesses directly controlled by foreign capitalists than in the twenties and thirties. But the Chinese economy was still profoundly dependent on foreigners. It imported its machines and parts, as well as its equipment, particularly for the railroads and electricity. It also depended on foreigners for the distribution of its raw products and minerals; the commercial balance, which was based on this unequal exchange, was typically colonial. China still depended on the West as a cultural, economic, and technical model. Technicians who had been trained abroad were at a premium. It was commonly admitted that the country could not hope to challenge these dependent relations, that it could not hope to develop on its own. As a result, mineral prospecting was very backward, particularly for oil. There were only two hundred competent geologists in the whole country. The People's Republic had to fight stubbornly against the economic pessimism that had been so widespread during the period of the unequal treaties.

Historically, the development of Chinese industry had been uneven and filled with imbalances, and the effects of this were a great burden in 1949. Heavy industry, and especially the industry of the means of production (metallurgy, cement, and machines), was far behind light industry. Mining industries operated mainly for export (coal, nonferrous metals). On the other hand, light industries often depended on imported materials (American cotton, for example). One region would export certain surplus goods, while another region would import those same goods from abroad: there was no Chinese national market.

On the regional level these imbalances were particularly striking. Modern industrial production was concentrated in a few out-of-the-way centers, far from the great mass of rural consumers: Shanghai and the Lower Yangzi, Wuhan, Shandong, Tientsin and environs, and especially the Northeast—in other words the regions that were considered in the nineteenth century to be the most favorable for foreign capitalism and maritime commerce with foreign countries. The network of modern transportation (railroads and steamships) was completely imbalanced. Most of the railroads were concentrated in the Northeast and around the major ports in the East; very active provinces such as Sichuan and Fujian had no railway connections whatsoever. The surplus agricultural production of Sichuan, for example, remained blocked during a period of famine from the regions that could have used it most.

In 1945 modern industry held only a very small place in national production (about 10 or 15 percent); it was far behind agriculture and even artisan work in absolute value. But the influence of capitalist relations was far greater than their role—which was small —in actual economic production. This capitalist influence was reflected in the very conception of wages, in the terms of the exchange of goods, in the evaluation of the worth of products, in the definition of the criteria of progress, and in the search for profits—in short, in the whole social fabric that would be challenged in 1975 under the phrase "the bourgeois right."

The burden of the feudal regime

In the thirties and forties the Communists defined the revolution as antifeudal in nature. In traditional Marxism the term feudalism designates social relations based on the exploitation of the peasants by a privileged minority of landowners in whom power and knowledge are concentrated—even if, as in China's case, the varieties of this exploitation were very different from those characterized by classical Western feudalism.

Except for those who had lived in the liberated zones and had benefited from the radical Agrarian Reform Law of 1947, the Chinese peasants in 1949 still lived in a state of dependence on the landowners. The tenant farmers had to pay considerable rent either in money or kind, as well as perform a whole series of special duties and traditional obligations. Even those who owned their land in name were still tied to the landlords through usury, since they had to go into debt each time there was a poor harvest. These "poor" and "middle-poor" peasants (terms given by the Communists) were at the same time politically dependent on the landowners, who controlled the local government, especially with regard to legal and financial matters; to be out of favor with them was fatal. Only the "rich" peasants, who were economically independent and able to produce for the local markets, were free of these bonds of feudal dependence. But they were no more than a small minority, especially active around the big cities.

Social dependence and economic stagnation went together. The Chinese peasant was inescapably trapped in a struggle for survival, bound by the nature of rural work and the seasons. His equipment was often in poor condition and his technical knowledge rudimentary. He lived in misery. He was at the mercy of a bad harvest, and his back-breaking work could not protect him from drought and flood, in spite of the complex network of dikes and canals that for thousands of years had collectively controlled water resources. Yields were low, and the number of crops grown was few. The double rice harvest, for example, was only practiced in the coastal provinces of the Southeast. Beyond a few rich peasants, no one was interested in agricultural expansion. The peasants did not wish to be in the position of having to give more money to the landlords; and the landlords were content with their profits from usury and feudal rent.

The effects of agricultural stagnation extended throughout the whole of society. The countrysides were too poor to furnish the cities with agricultural products and to buy the industrial products from the cities. Rural crafts survived, but at a very low technical level which produced equally low incomes. It was not enough to meet the needs of the peasants, who had to accept the high prices of the peddlers and other salesmen from the cities. The ascendency of the cities over the countrysides could be seen in the exodus of peasants to the cities each time there was a bad harvest.

The dependency of the peasants was also apparent in the realm of ideas and social customs: resignation to one's fate, the Confucian concept of the Heavenly Mandate; the obsession with male children as a sign of prestige and a guarantee of labor and prosperity; mistrust of women, who were destined to pass from the authority of the father to the authority of the husband. These conceptions of the family inherited from Confucianism went hand in hand with an unstable demography that was the result of a high birthrate and a high infant mortality rate. In 1949 it was generally assumed that the population of China was 400 million. In point of fact, however, this figure was much too low (see Chapter 8).

Regional imbalances, past and present

In 1949 China was marked by the historical contradictions that had shaped it—from the recent past as well as from the distant past.

The revolutionary struggle had been characterized by its unequal development in the different regions. There were the old liberated zones, concentrated in the North, and the new liberated zones. In the first, where the Communists had been established for the past ten or fifteen years, the peasant masses were aware of the situation and had become hardened to the problems, essential foodstuffs were being produced, the traditional cadres and the intermediary elements had had to choose between support and opposition. In the second, the people's power had been established with unexpected quickness and ease, but there were tremendous problems for the future. The political situation was unstable; the opponents were more numerous than the supporters, the masses were inexperienced politically, and production was disorganized. The large cities fell into this second category. In 1949 the difference between the old and new liberated regions was a fully recognized fact in matters of economic and political management. The Common Program made explicit reference to it.

U.S.S.R.

Lake Balkhash

MONGOLIAN
PEOPLE'S REPUBLI

○ Urumchi

XINJIANG-UIGHUR AUTONOMOUS REGION

Lop Nor

PAKISTAN

Xin

Lake Xinghai

XINGHAI

TIBETAN AUTONOMOUS REGION

○ Lhasa

NEPAL

SIKKIM

INDIA

Kunmi

YUNN

BURMA

**MAJOR ADMINISTRATIVE DIVISIONS OF
THE PEOPLE'S REPUBLIC OF CHINA**

.... borders of provinces, autonomous regions, and the
3 special districts of Beijing (Peking), Tianjin
(Tientsin), and Shanghai

○ provincial capitals

500 km

Other regional imbalances were inherited from the period of Western domination: the concentration of industry in several coastal centers, the problems with the railway network, the distribution of universities. To which was added the problem of the Northeast, which had been seized by the Japanese and used as the industrial stronghold of the country and was oriented toward a colonial-style economic expansion. It had been cut off from the rest of the country and subordinate to the needs of Japanese militarism. Even traces of the old zones of influence established by the powers at the beginning of the century were still visible; the rolling stock, for example, was French in some regions, English in others, German or Japanese in still others. The ports in which foreign concessions had been set up were even more different from each other. Generally speaking, the contrast between the immense interior, which was still largely traditional, and the few islands of modern life that were scattered throughout the country was a legacy from the period of the unequal treaties.

By the time of the Opium Wars China was already the product of a complex historical development. The North, which was the historic center of the Han people and the base of imperial power, paradoxically became much less developed than the South, which had been settled later, but which was favored by ideal conditions for river and lake navigation and which, as a consequence, underwent a spectacular urban and cultural development, with a richer and more diversified production of goods. The contrast between the North and the South was deeply embedded in the history of the country and was still apparent in 1949; it could be seen in the appearance of the cities and the countrysides, in eating habits, and most especially in terms of language. In the homogeneous North, everyone spoke *Putonghua*, the "common language" (the ancient Mandarin known to nineteenth-century Westerners); in the South, on the other hand, there was a great diversity of languages: Wu in the region of Shanghai, the languages of the Southeast, Canton, and Hakka in the interior.

All this was of concern only to the regions inhabited by the ethnic Chinese, the Han. But in 1949 the greater part of Chinese national territory was inhabited by minority populations, most of whom had settled in China centuries before, although some had arrived during more recent migrations. There were several dozen of these national minorities, accounting for tens of millions of people. They were very different in religion, customs, language, and social organization. The China of the Liberation was a veritable museum of modes of production and social structures, from the strict theocracy of Tibet, which was founded on the absolute power of the Dalai Lama, the living god, and a Western-style serfdom, to the nomadic feudalism of the Mongols, not to speak of the slavery practiced by certain small peoples of the Southwest, or the equalitarian tribal societies of other mountain groups in the same region.

The largest minority groups were the Lamaist Tibetans, the Mongols (who were also Lamaists), the Uighurs from Xinjiang in the Northwest (Chinese Turkestan), and the Koreans from the Northeast. The Hui and the Zhuang were special cases; the former were Chinese Muslims from the Northwest and Southwest whose unique religion stemmed from certain national traits that were not widely known; the latter were proto-Indochinese from Guangxi in the Southwest whose language and ethnic characteristics had long been hidden by the Chinese policy of assimilation—to such a point that they, too, were completely unknown. In 1949 there were many other national minorities, both large and small, scattered through the West, the South, and the Southwest. In spite of their diversity, however, they had all undergone the same conflicts and had lived through the same history of exploitation by the Chinese government, whether imperial or republican, and by the Chinese merchants who had been hungry to buy the rare products from their forests, their mountains, and their steppes as cheaply as possible. The multinational diversity of China was a difficult and complex political problem in 1949.

China as a nation

All these regional imbalances, all these inequalities of historical experience and economic development, nevertheless took place within a remarkably coherent historical space, absolutely unique in relation to other countries: China, the "Middle Kingdom" (*Zhongguo*), the "central culture" (*Zhonggua*). This Chinese cohesion was the result of collective customs and traditions, of a national consciousness of art and life. It was expressed in cooking and the calendar of public holidays, in the makeup of the orchestra and the subtleties of calligraphy, in the unspoken codes of conversation, and in the way food was displayed by merchants.

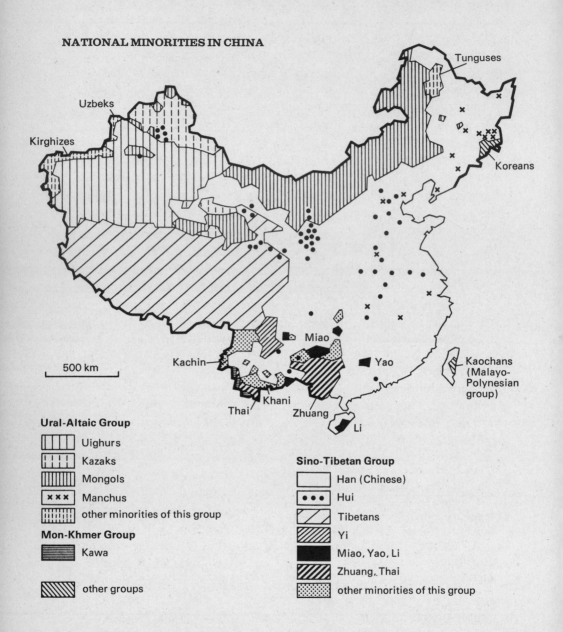

NATIONAL MINORITIES IN CHINA

Tunguses

Uzbeks

Kirghizes

Koreans

500 km

Kachin

Miao

Yao

Kaochans
(Malayo-
Polynesian
group)

Thai   Khani   Zhuang   Li

Ural-Altaic Group

⊞	Uighurs	
⊞	Kazaks	
⊞	Mongols	
×××	Manchus	
⊞	other minorities of this group	

Mon-Khmer Group

≡ Kawa

⧄ other groups

Sino-Tibetan Group

▭	Han (Chinese)
•••	Hui
⧄	Tibetans
⧄	Yi
■	Miao, Yao, Li
⧄	Zhuang, Thai
⸬	other minorities of this group

Mao Tsetung's *Selected Works*, which became the bestselling
Chinese book after the Liberation of 1949, attests to the richness
of this collective national tradition. Mao's writings abound in
political and cultural references that are well known to all Chinese
but incomprehensible to a foreigner: proverbs and quotations,
distant historical situations and episodes from the revolutionary
struggle, popular legends, and literary allusions and anecdotes.
They evoke the sage Zhu Geliang who fooled his adversary by
having two old soldiers sweep the open gates of a city empty of
troops and unable to defend itself; the crafty Sun Wukong, the
tireless Monkey King, the intrepid traveler over the Himalayas;
Wu Song the indefatigable, who was strong enough to kill a tiger
with one blow of his fist; the old "madman" Yu Gong who claimed
he could move mountains and who managed to do so through the
labor of his descendants, generation after generation; the plum tree
flowering alone under the hostile snow; the Plague King who was
sent away for good; and Kunlun Mountain, at the top of which you
must have a soul strong enough to brave the unleashed elements . . .

This sharp sense of Chinese continuity, of the uniqueness of
China, was not incompatible with the deep feeling that a break in
historical time had taken place in 1949. A new era (an almost
cosmological term) was beginning; a New China was about to be
built.

DOCUMENTS

1. A FRENCH JOURNALIST WITNESSES THE VICTORY MARCH IN SHANGHAI.

Source: Robert Guillain, *Le Monde*, July 9, 1949.

(Shanghai, July 7) The people of Shanghai celebrated the liberation of
their city and the victories of the Communist armies with an enormous march
which authorities said included 70,000 civilians and 250,000 soldiers. . . .

All activity in the city stopped in the afternoon. On the quays of the
Huangpu River, in the streets below the famous skyscrapers and tall buildings, the demonstrators gathered by the thousands. The demonstration, which
extended from the old Chinese city to the neighborhoods formerly held by
the Japanese, was extremely captivating, not only because of the intensely
vivid Chinese crowd dressed in festival colors and carrying hundreds of
banners and red flags, but because this crowd represented a new political
image of the city whose five million inhabitants had already been reorganized
by neighborhoods, social classes, factories, and trades, all arranged and
orchestrated by the militants.

Then came the indispensable instruments of popular enthusiasm: Chinese gongs. Shanghai, which had been suddenly awakened from the torpor of recent days, stayed up until late in the night, frenetically shaken by the insistent noise of the metal gongs, made even louder by the crashing of cymbals and drums and the tom-tom beat that worked so well on the spirits of the Chinese. . . .

The Liberation Army was extremely impressive. Drenched to the bone and yet impassive, marching without any noise of boots, for this army wears slippers, these battalions from the heart of the Chinese countryside were impeccably dressed in light olive cotton uniforms and carried brand-new equipment. Not only were the rifles, machine guns, and light artillery American made, but also—and this was the first time that Shanghai had seen such things—for almost an hour there was a parade of tanks, amphibious tanks, armored cars and trucks, and ultramodern antitank devices, all of them also American and freshly painted with big red stars. . . .

The civilians at last began to march. Giant portraits of the leaders waved above the multitude as in Moscow marches, but here the pictures were exclusively of the two great Chinese leaders, Mao Tsetung and Zhu De. In the middle of the crowd, trucks carried pyramids of shouting students. Carnival floats carried bamboo-framed pictures painted in wild colors: Tchaing Kaï-chek run through with the bayonet of a brave red soldier, Uncle Sam plotting with an old Japanese soldier, a Chinese worker breaking his chains. A hundred-yard-long dragon carried by fifty men moved along crazily, undulating its orange and gold body.

Then it was noticed that a good half of the military parade had remained behind. These delayed battalions were simply allowed to spill out into the avenue where the civilians were marching. The throng was then twice the size as night transformed the retreating marchers into a file of torches and lanterns. Over ten kilometers of the long Shanghai avenues, which had once borne the names Edward VII and Joffre, there was nothing but a slow procession of demonstrators drenched to the bone but still shouting official slogans: "Let's take Tchaing Kaï-chek alive," "Down with foreign imperialism," "Develop production," "Support the Russo-Chinese alliance," "Down with the American occupation of Japan," and so on.

2. THE CHANGES AFTER 1949 IN THE LIFE OF PEASANT LI HAINAN OF LIULIN VILLAGE IN NORTH SHENXI PROVINCE

Source: Jan Myrdal, *Report From a Chinese Village* (New York, Pantheon, 1965), pp. 112, 114.

. . . I had Father's debt, so I was compelled to stay behind in Hengshan. I married and we had children—we worked hard. We had eleven children. Ten of them died. [He weeps.] Our eldest daughter died when she was eight. The others when they were seven, four, five and three. They all died. We were poor and we couldn't afford to have the doctor. Doctors weren't for people like us. The only one to survive the illness was my son. But it made him deaf and dull-witted. He went to school for four years. Now he's fifteen. He mostly gathers firewood. He's the only one of my family left now. Things were difficult for poor people. Hard work and big debts and nothing but hunger and illness all the time.

In 1945, I had a letter from my aunt, Li Fong-lan; she is Dong Yang-zhen's grandmother. In that letter my aunt wrote: "If life is hard for you, you should know that things are better here. If you come here, the communists will help you. There's land here. I'll help you and the communists won't let anyone who is willing to work starve." But, of course, I had these fifty taels of silver to pay back, so I couldn't do anything. Ma Zu-zhuan had died, but his family was still there. Debts did not vanish so easily.

In the end, my aunt sent me an ox from Yanan. Oxen fetched high prices then. In that way she paid my debt and I became free. In the month of March according to the moon calendar of the year 1948 I went down to Yanan. When I got there I had a talk with my aunt. She said: "I'll see you have a cave and food." I was given some abandoned land and a pig. That was a very difficult year. Ma Hai-xiu was leader of Liu Ling village then, and it was he who arranged that I got twenty mu of hill land. I didn't have to pay anything. I myself owned the land. In July that year my wife and son came here. They walked. All that we possessed then and had brought with us from Hengshan was an old quilt. We had had to sell the rest because of the debt.

Later, in the year 1949, everything was settled about my land in Liu Ling. I was given a stamped certificate and everything. . . . It was the first land we had owned. No one had cultivated it before. We were very happy. Before that we had never even dreamed of having our own land. Why should we? We didn't dream of anything. And if we didn't have quilts enough to keep out the winter's cold, we couldn't long for land of our own. That's how it was. But now that we had got land of our own, Father came to me and said: "You should be grateful to the communists. Without them you would never have got this land." . . .

3. A CONSERVATIVE CHINESE ENGINEER DECIDES TO REMAIN IN THE COUNTRY IN 1949

Source: Han Suyin, *Birdless Summer* (New York, Putnam, 1968), pp. 55, 57, 77.

. . . I suddenly *want* to write down my life, to write down everything that happened. Many of us now have this urge, for we feel we have lived through a great change. For a Revolution is not impersonal events moving helpless human beings about. It is made by man, and it also is an inner process, it changes us. I feel as a pond that has been dredged, mud gone, bottom stone seen. As I left my Department that day, spring had begun. . . .

Our world was changing, faster and faster, a great wind would blow down upon us, sweep away these structures, denude us of the apparel of ceremony, render our classical education useless. A new world would be born, in pain and suffering. I knew it not, but one thing also saved me in the end: my mother's deep, tenacious passion for the earth, for this our soil, for the things that grow in this earth of ours, this universe of poverty, torment and despair which was to be reborn, remade one day into something human and good.

And that is why when Liberation came, and some of my friends committed suicide and others died because they could not change, they could not understand, they went madly on, plotting to restore the terrible yesterdays, I needed no such stubbornness, craved no other heaven or earth than to see once again the fields grow their rice, the magnolia flower in its spring, and the brown sun of a pickle jar's belly was sun enough for me. There was much that was new, strange and painful to learn, but had I not, all my life, suffered these wrenchings? . . .

So I remained, while the stranger, my love, left me, taking away the crucifix that had hung its sad narcotic visage above me all those years.

And all this was part of the Big Change that had been in preparation even before my birth.

I had a stroke two months before Liberation, and the blood froze in my head and my left side became useless. As I lay on my bed, unable to move, I could see them pack, my wife and my Second Daughter, hastily picking up things all through the house and flinging them into their suitcases. They were going away. I knew they were frightened, frightened because the Communists were coming. But I was not frightened. I had been expecting them for so long, so long . . . in fear and hope, in doubt and wonder, for nothing could be worse than what we had undergone, yet who knew what the new era would bring?

Chapter Two

The Period
of Reconstruction:
1949–1952

The policy of the Communist authorities in the years following the Liberation was aimed at taking care of the most urgent business, getting the basic machinery of the economy and administration running, and initiating certain socially progressive measures. In spite of its popularity, the new regime was fragile. The leaders were deeply aware of their own inexperience and the novelty of the problems they had to deal with. The conflicts that had probably existed among them since Yanan, and which would be brought out into the open in the sixties, were hidden behind a facade of common agreement and only discrete allusions were made to them.

However, because there were so many pressing fundamental questions during this reconstruction period, it was also a time for making a number of basic decisions: China entered the socialist camp and based itself on the Soviet model. And yet was this alignment compatible with the Yanan heritage and the mass line, which remained a vital influence in agrarian and family matters, as well as a source for the antibureaucratic mobilization of 1951? This contradiction, however, remained undiscussed and did not become an issue until 1958–1960.

The Communists Take Power

The Communists took power during a serious international crisis which imposed certain military, political, and economic priorities that were rather authoritarian in nature. The Common Program of 1949 and the principles of New Democracy continued to be the essential guides for political and social reconstruction. From this period on China would present a profile considerably different from that of the people's democracies in Europe, where Communist parties had also come to power and which were in the same socialist camp China had just entered.

The Korean War

For China the Korean War was totally unexpected and came as a heavy burden—politically, economically, and militarily. The Chinese would later let it be known that Stalin had skillfully seized this opportunity to bind them more tightly to the socialist camp.

In June 1950, when war broke out between the two Koreas, the United Nations condemned the North and sent an expeditionary force that was for all intents and purposes American. American troops were also sent to Taiwan and the Seventh American Fleet anchored off Fujian in order to protect Tchiang Kaï-chek's government. It was almost a declaration of war by the United States against China. The embargo of May 1951 forbade all trade between the United States and China.

In the fall of 1950, General Douglas MacArthur, the American commander, arrived at the Yalu on the Chinese border. China reacted by sending volunteer divisions to fight in Korea. After 1951 the front stabilized. A long and murderous war of position began, a type of war that was completely foreign to the experience of the Chinese guerrillas. It ended in July 1953 with an armistice that acknowledged the division of Korea.

The commander of the Chinese troops was Peng De-huai, a former Guomindang officer who had gone over to the Communists in 1930. He was in favor of a well-equipped professional army. In order to deal with this conventional front war, China had to create a heavy artillery, as well as build road and air transportation services—for which Russian aid was indispensable. Aviation especially, with the Migs, was a completely new and highly technical area in the Chinese army, something completely outside the tradition of people's war established at Yanan.

China's military effort took a heavy toll in matériel and men and held up the work of reconstruction. The matériel was Russian, bought with the loan credits of January 1950 (see below). Later, during the public controversy of 1963–1964, China declared that it had paid for these arms sales in the form of merchandise, which made up a large part of Chinese exports to the USSR. The human losses were no less heavy: 700,000 soldiers were engaged in Korea at the same time, most of them qualified industrial workers—which meant that civilian production suffered greatly. Hundreds of thousands were killed and a proportionate number were wounded. China also bore the burden of the war in terms of diplomacy: it was isolated, condemned as the aggressor by the UN, and had to give up its hopes of contact with the West which had been kindled in 1950 when England and the neutral European countries had given diplomatic recognition to China.

The Chinese watchword of the period, *yi bian dao* (take sides with a camp), was doubtless little more than the acceptance of an already given situation. In February 1950 Mao signed a mutual aid and friendship treaty with Moscow, but the benefits for China were rather meager: 300 million dollars in credit—which was less than Austria had received from the United States after the war—and Soviet help in developing Chinese civil aviation, the port of Dairen-Dalny (Liuta), the Northeast railroad (the ex-Trans-Manchurian), as well as prospecting for the oil and nonferrous metals in Xinjiang, an area that had been occupied by the Soviets in the thirties and forties.[1] This mining would be undertaken in common by the same system of mixed companies that Stalin had created after the war in order to tap the natural resources of Poland, Rumania, and North Korea. This amounted to a disguised seizure by the Soviet Union of certain areas of the Chinese economy. To these economic ties were added financial ties that linked the *yuan* with the ruble; and to the military ties created by the Korean War were added ideological ties. The Association of Chinese-Soviet Friendship, which was headed by Liu Shao-qi, had eighteen million members, which was three times the size of the Communist Party; it distributed newspapers, brochures, and films. Russian became the first foreign language taught in the schools. Chinese libraries abandoned the Dewey

---

[1] See Volume 2, Chapter 10.

decimal system, which it had copied from the U.S. Library of Congress during the Guomindang period, and adopted the system used in Soviet libraries.

The new political and judicial system

The territorial basis for the People's Republic of China had been stabilized. The liberation campaigns had continued after October 1, 1949, and the Communist armies had occupied Hainan, the Tachen islands off Fujian, and Tibet in the spring of 1950 (this last by means of a political agreement between Peking and the Dalai Lama that recognized Tibet as a "local government"); it was provisionally established that because of the uniqueness of the Tibetan situation Chinese reforms would not be applied to Tibet. The Guomindang was left with Formosa (Taiwan), the Pescadores, and the islands of Quemoy and Matsu off Fujian.

Civil war was therefore a distinct possibility. The high command was the most solid branch of the new society and was given the task of setting up the political institutions. The result was a system of six political and military regions that divided up the various provinces as follows:

Regions	Provinces	Command
Northeast	Liaoning, Heilongjiang, Jilin, Jehol	Gao Gang
North	Hebei, Shanxi, Chahar, Suiyuan, Peking, Tientsin	Liu Lantao
East	Jiangsu, Zhejiang, Anhui, Shandong, Fujian, Nanking, Shanghai	Chen Yi, then Jao Shushi
South Central	Hubei, Hunan, Henan, Jiangxi, Guangdong, Guangxi, Canton	Lin Biao
Southwest	Sichuan, Guizhou, Yunnan	Liu Bo-cheng
Northwest	Shenxi, Gansu, Ningxia, Xinjiang	Peng De-huai

In these regions civilian and military powers were combined. The leaders were well-known personalities from the top of the CCP hierarchy. But this system, which would last until 1952, was by no means the beginning of federalism. Rather, it represented regional delegations from the central power, which had become more closely tied to the provinces.

The central power was organized gradually on the basis of the Common Program and the decisions of the Advisory Political Conference which had proclaimed the birth of the new state in September 1949. This conference was maintained both as a provisional parliament and as a constituent assembly (its efforts led to the constitution of 1954). Non-Communist parties were overrepresented in it. The conference defined the executive power structure and its branches. This central people's government, which was headed by Mao Tsetung, was responsible for internal and external policy. It enacted laws and ratified the budget. But the real management of affairs was handled by a Council of State Affairs, which was headed by Zhou En-lai and included the major ministries.

The foreign minister, the Commission for Chinese Abroad, the security services, and education were all under the direct control of the prime minister. Judicial and military institutions, which were organized around the Supreme Court and the Revolutionary Military Council, were tied to the central government.

This system represented the desire of the Chinese Communists to move on from a de facto political-military power to stable judicial institutions, which would have the added benefit of reassuring the public. But it was a difficult process, one which ran the risks of formalism and the creation of a swollen bureaucracy. In fact, many of these new organizations functioned in the void, the important decisions still being made by the party and the army.

This complex state structure enabled several important positions to go to non-Communists. At the lower levels, millions of adherents to the old regime had rallied behind the new government. There were many conflicts between these competent civil servants and the old militants from the guerrilla bases who were inexperienced in matters of nonmilitary management. The transition took place gradually, under the control of the party.

The Communist Party and
mass organizations

The CCP had five million members in 1950. After a severe purge in 1951 its membership continued to grow; about a million members had been expelled during a tense period of the cold war—the first year of the Korean campaign, when it appeared likely that there would be a direct confrontation with the United States. The party's authority was considerable: it had been the major factor in the victory of the revolution after so many years of struggle. It declared itself Marxist-Leninist, but without turning its back on the originality of its political experience—the essence of which was to be found in Mao Tsetung's *Selected Works* (*Xuanji*), now officially published in an edition of several million copies. The social base of the new regime continued to be defined as an alliance of the four revolutionary classes (workers, poor and middle peasants, petty bourgeoisie, and national capitalists); it was the CCP that had organized and brought this historic bloc together.

The party's influence was extended through the mass organizations which had already been important at Yanan and which now were multiplying in all areas of social life: unions, women's organizations, youth groups, professional intellectual organizations, and friendship clubs with the Soviet Union and other socialist countries. In Leninist tradition these "transmission belts" were part of a hierarchy organized outward from the central level to the base. They were very active and in close touch with the concrete problems found in each social category; at the same time they attempted to explain and win approval for the line and decisions that came from above. In 1952 the women's organization had 76 million members, Democratic Youth had 7 million members, the Federation of Students had 1,600,000 members, and the unions had 6 million members.

The smooth, unbroken functioning of the state and party apparatus, along with the mass organizations, was no different in the China of the reconstruction from the system of institutions in the European socialist countries. But at the same time the rhythm of political life was marked by discontinuous jolts, which was a strictly Chinese phenomenon, a result of the Yanan heritage: the mass movements (*yundong*). These sudden and disruptive mobilizations were an attempt to link the masses to the important decisions of the moment, to give them an active role, and to consolidate new ideological values through campaigns of spontaneously written posters (*dazibao*), through discussion meetings, and through enormous marches. Examples of this were the 1951–1952 "Aid to Korea and Resistance to the United States" movement, the campaign in late 1951 for "increasing production and being more economical," the 1952 antihierarchical movements called the "Three Antis" (*sanfan*) and the "Five Antis" (*wufan*), as well as, most importantly, agrarian reform itself.

Intellectuals, information, and education

In 1951–1952 the ideological reshaping of the intellectuals was the occasion of another mass movement. Intellectuals were asked to rid themselves of the elitist tradition of Confucianism and the individualist tradition of the English and Americans, both of which were very strong. Debates and study groups were organized around these subjects based on the classics of Marxism and the *Xuanji* of Mao; they were asked to study the history of the Chinese revolutionary movement, which many of them did not know very well. They were put in contact with peasants and workers, and for most of them this was the first time they had ever met these people as equals; the workers and peasants described their life to them under the old regime. The intellectuals were also asked to write their autobiographies, which amounted to political self-analyses in which it was thought they would be able to understand how privileged their position had been in the past.[2]

The struggle against the old ideology was organized around several choice targets. One was Hu Shi, a veteran of the May Fourth Movement (1919)[3] and the campaign for the propagation of the spoken language in literature, who maintained considerable prestige among liberal intellectuals in spite of his siding with the Guomindang in the thirties, his ties with American universities, and his departure for Taiwan. He was denounced and criticized everywhere. The same thing happened to Wu Xun, a picturesque figure from the lumpen intelligentsia of the nineteenth century who had devoted his life to popular educational works, but on an apolitical foundation and with respect for the established order; a film shown in 1950 which hailed his role as positive was strongly denounced by the authorities. Another victim was Liang Shu-ming, also a May Fourth veteran, who had remained in People's China along with many other moderate intellectuals (he was one of the leaders of the Democratic League), but who was accused of hostility toward socialism and Marxism. He was forced to engage in severe self-criticism.

It was also during the reconstruction period that a solid structure for the dissemination of official political information was established. From now on the daily *Renmin Ribao* (the People's Daily),

[2] See the story by Han Suyin's father (Chapter 1, document 3).
[3] See Volume 2, Chapter 3.

and the news dispatches from the *Xinhua* (New China) agency would provide the basic political references and present the official point of view in the most important controversies. Following these publications is as indispensable to the Chinese cadres as it is to foreign observers, even though it is a highly allusive kind of coded information that is always presented in a conventional style.

In the area of education the emphasis was placed on reorganization, with the accent on popular education and the importance of scientific and technical studies. Literacy campaigns were organized in the villages, factories, and the poor sections of the cities. The number of students doubled between 1949 and 1952 (from 24 to 51 million primary school pupils and from 1 million to 2½ million secondary school students). An Academy of Sciences, directly inspired by the Soviet model, was established in 1949 under the directorship of the poet Guo Moruo, an old party fellow traveler; it kept the traditional name Academia Sinica.

The desire for cultural continuity went hand in hand with the effort to create an ideological break. The study of Marxism became compulsory at all levels in the schools and universities. Manuals and editions of classic Marxist texts were widely used in the reeducation campaigns for intellectuals. As a result, most of the new positions that had been created in all areas of society were given to intellectuals, who had an advantage because of their academic backgrounds and their superiority in oral and written expression—and who seemed to have assimilated Marxism, at least in a bookish way —rather than the workers, who found it more difficult to study and express themselves clearly. This policy of promoting reformed intellectuals adopted during the reconstruction period contributed greatly to the elitism of the cadres of the regime during the fifties and sixties and was not seriously questioned until fifteen years later with the great antihierarchical movement of the Cultural Revolution.

The spread of Marxism did not prevent an emphasis on the richness and originality of the Chinese cultural heritage. The traditional opera was encouraged everywhere, to the great pleasure of Chinese as well as foreign audiences. Character writing was kept, even though its outright suppression had been envisaged by the Communists in the thirties and forties. The only changes made were the codifying of certain characters that had already been simplified in practice. This policy of deliberately honoring Chinese culture applied to the area of medicine as well. Acupuncture, moxibustion,[4] mineral and plant pharmacopoeia, and pulse techniques were systematically encouraged in specialized research institutes and in city and village hospitals.

Women and the family

The marriage law (1950) was one of the most radical measures of the reconstruction period.[5] Along with the abolition of the feudal regime and agrarian reform, it was one of the most important undertakings of the new society, one which most clearly distinguished it from the old China, which had been traditionally based on the subordination of women to men. Through the institution of marriage, which from now on was based on equality and free mutual consent, the position of women in society was vastly improved. This advancement, however, did not take the form of increased opportunities for individual and career choices, as it had with the Westernized bourgeoisie of Shanghai and the famous trio of Song sisters during the period of the Guomindang.[6] Rather, it was a question of a collective advancement, which included the participation of women in productive work and social responsibilities equal to those of men.

The marriage law was also a law for the defense of children. The killing of children was forbidden—a common practice in the old China, particularly for girls; it became illegal to sell children, which had happened frequently among the Chinese peasants during the famines of 1921, 1931, and 1943; and finally, it became illegal to marry off young girls against their will to become domestic slaves subject to the despotism of their mothers-in-law.

The immediate result of the marriage law was a wave of divorces: all women married by force or against their will asked for annulments and were supported by the women's organizations. Some women appeared before the judge holding in their arms a very young child to whom their families had sold them, well before their future husbands had come of age. But the effects of the law in regard to social responsibility were much slower to bear fruit. Women did

---

[4] The placing of combustible cones on the body; the burns produce a counter-irritation.
[5] The main articles of the law appear in document 1 at the end of the chapter.
[6] See Volume 2, pp. 195, 269–70. One of the sisters married Sun Yat-sen, another married the wealthy financier H. H. Kung, and the third married Tchiang Kaï-chek.

not attain high positions until the large movements of collective mobilization such as the Great Leap Forward and especially the Cultural Revolution.

The rehabilitation of women also included the abolishing of prostitution. In the big ports such as Shanghai and the old urban centers such as Peking the pimps were arrested and the bordellos were closed; the prostitutes were given medical care and emotional support and were reeducated politically. At first grouped together in special units of production, they gradually reentered society.

Social order and repression

Prostitution was only one aspect of the social disease of old China that had been denounced by the British and American missionaries in Shanghai in the past. In confronting all these illegal activities, the new regime defended the principle of human dignity; at the same time it was eager to remove the abscesses from the big cities that included all sorts of secret businesses and rackets run by a shady element traditionally connected with the Guomindang's secret police. The peddlers of opium and other drugs were hunted down; the reeducation and cure of opium addicts was organized; games of chance and public gambling were outlawed. The picturesque headquarters of these illegal businesses were closed—including the Dashigie ("High Society") of Shanghai, the Tianqiao ("Heaven's Bridge") of Peking, and the floating city of unused sampans in Canton, anchored in the River of Pearls and used by gangsters as a hideout. These gangsters were severely punished, often after popular trials.[7]

Political repression—under the direction of the ministry of security (*Gonganqu*, "bureau of public order"), headed by General Luo Rui-qing and helped by an efficient and discreet secret police—therefore had a curative aspect. It struck at the centers of these illegal businesses, which were also centers of political opposition. More generally, this repression was defensive in nature. The Guomindang, which had taken refuge in Taiwan, continued to rely on a network of secret agents who were well equipped with radio transmitters and weapons. These networks tried both to consolidate while waiting for the "liberation"—solemnly announced each year in Taiwan by Tchiang Kaï-chek—and to survive, while at the same

[7] See document 2.

time trying to maintain a state of insecurity—both physical and emotional—through sabotage, circulating false rumors, and infiltrating the ranks of political life. These networks of adversaries collaborated particularly with the remnants of the old traditional secret societies, some of which were still very active, especially in Peking and Shanghai—for example the *Yiguandao* (the Way of United Landowners) which had collaborated with the Japanese in the forties. The members and cells of the *Yiguandao* were hunted down and broken up in 1950.

The movement (*yundong*) for the elimination of counterrevolutionaries begun in 1951–1952 by the police in conjunction with popular vigilance was directed against the agents of the Guomindang networks, the secret societies, cases of sabotage, and overtly hostile behavior to the people's government. But it also indiscriminately attacked numerous persons suspected of being uncommitted politically who were not necessarily active or resolute adversaries. This was the period in which the Korean War was dragging on indefinitely, in which the long-anticipated reconstruction was being slowed down, and in which the Communist Party itself underwent a severe purge. The zeal of the special organizations of repression, which were often trained and advised by Soviet technicians, with their tendency to make security an end in itself, no doubt aggravated things. Some sympathetic observers estimate that there were 800,000 victims of this campaign to eliminate opponents—in the form of executions, arrests, detentions, reeducation work, and various sanctions. During this period an autonomous apparatus of repression was organized in China, with special services and places of detention and corrective work. This apparatus was solid and durable, even if it did not attain the size and harshness of the Soviet Gulag.

Economic Reconstruction

The objectives of economic reconstruction were limited, for both material and political reasons. Because destruction and upheaval had been so widespread, a return to order was the most that could be hoped for in the short run. In addition, the political balance in 1949 (the four classes) meant that progress toward socialism had to be slow. It has even been said that the reconstruction period was a second Golden Age for the Chinese national bourgeoisie—after

that of the First World War.[8] Even though it was not known until
much later, it seems that this period saw the beginning of serious
differences between the moderates and the radicals of the leadership
group over the extent and length of the concessions necessary to
appease the national capitalists in the interests of the reconstruction.

Overall economic objectives

The economic reconstruction was part of the Common Program
of September 1949: there was no question, therefore, of socialism,
but of New Democracy reforms which would pave the way for an
economic recovery that would be mutually beneficial to the peasants,
the workers, the petty bourgeoisie, and the national capitalists, and
detrimental to the landowners, the bureaucratic capitalists tied to
the Guomindang, and foreign financial interests. It was felt that
the conflicts of interests that might exist in the democratic bloc—
for example between poor and rich peasants or between workers
and management—were secondary in comparison to the things
that united them against their common adversaries. In particular,
maintaining the political alliance with the national capitalists
seemed essential during this uncertain transition period, even though
certain groups would necessarily have more privileges than others
for the time being.

The structure of the economy reflected this complex base. Officially, there were five sectors: (1) the state enterprises, including
those confiscated from the four great families of the Guomindang
and from foreigners, those that had already been nationalized
before 1949 (like the railroads), and those that had been newly
created (for large-scale and international commerce); (2) the
private enterprises of the national capitalists; (3) the state capitalist
enterprises, whose mixed status derived from the fact that they
belonged both to the national capitalists, who kept their shares, and
to the old bureaucratic capitalists, whose shares were transferred to
the state; (4) the cooperatives, which had already become numerous in such areas as agriculture, urban crafts, and small businesses;
and finally (5) the small private individual businesses, which were
still common in the cities (boutiques, street stalls, workshops, and
crafts), and which had increased to a dramatic extent in the countrysides because of the agrarian reform. Among these five sectors,

[8] See Volume 2, Chapter 2, p. 49.

whose methods and means were very different from one anotl only the state could coordinate the whole in the form of a gen yearly plan, which necessarily meant that the private sectors hww had to submit to certain controls.

Finally, the economic undertakings of the reconstruction were never separated from social objectives, even in the short run: to raise the standard of living, particularly in the countrysides; to improve hygiene through health education campaigns; and the war against parasites, rats, and epidemics. A great effort was made to set up clinics, child-care centers, and nursery schools. By 1950–1952 the streets and villages of China began to present a less sordid, more welcoming appearance.

Agrarian reform

Agrarian reform was the keystone of the whole economic reconstruction: in a country like China the needs of the farming population and farm production demanded top priority. The hope was to achieve the aims of the revolutionary struggle that had been waged for the past twenty-five years in the countrysides by once and for all doing away with feudal relationships and the power of the landowners (*dizhu*), relieving the peasants of their secular burden, and by freeing their productive capacities, to the benefit of the whole economy. But agrarian reform also took into account the very particular political and economic factors of the reconstruction. At the national level the *dizhu* had already been defeated, power had changed hands; but priority was given to increasing production, and all economic potential compatible with the new regime had to be preserved.

That is why the Agrarian Reform Law of June 1950, unlike that of 1947,[9] divided up the rural lands and goods of landowners without indemnity, but left them in possession of their city properties and businesses (while these urban goods had been confiscated in 1947). As for the rich peasants, who had been hit hard in 1947 as political accomplices of feudalism and the Guomindang, they were allowed to keep their lands and holdings, consideration being given to their productive capacity and the needs of the cities. Between 1947 and 1950, then, priorities had clearly been altered. But there was no moving backward, and the more flexible measures of

[9] See Volume 2, Chapter 12.

1950 applied only to the new liberated zones which the Liberation Army did not yet have control of in 1947. In the old liberated zones the 1947 measures remained in effect.

The law of 1950 therefore divided up the properties of the land-lords among the poor and middle peasants without indemnity. Tenant farming—with payments both in kind and in cash—was abolished, which represented 300 million hundredweights per year, a quarter of the country's agricultural production; also abolished were forced labor and other feudal services traditionally demanded of the peasants. The approximately 300 million peasants who bene-fited from the reform divided up about 700 million *mou*. China became a gigantic conglomerate of tiny agricultural holdings just big enough to meet the basic needs of the peasants. All the bene-ficiaries of the reform became full owners of their land: they could sell, buy, and rent. But the reform was not equalitarian: the rich peasants retained their lands, which were larger and of better quality. Three changes were made in the basic Agrarian Reform Law, clarifying the criteria for distinguishing classes (rich, middle, and poor peasants), defining the powers of the poor and middle peasant associations that had been set up to enforce the reform, and establishing people's courts in cases of conflict.

The reform, which was temporarily delayed in the ethnic minor-ity regions, was a political measure, a collective *yundong*. It abolished the feudal system of landed property and the exploitation of the peasants, but at the same time it also abolished the political power, the prestige, and the ideological ascendency of the *dizhu*. Out of the peasant associations—which were dominated by poor peasants and advised by cadres sent from the villages—there arose a dawning consciousness and a political mobilization at denuncia-tory meetings and public trials of the most hated landowners. These were the people who had been responsible for the misery of the peasants—which until then had been accepted with fatalism, passivity, and a feeling of technical inadequacy. By overthrowing the authority of their secular adversaries, the peasants gained confi-dence in themselves, and this was all the more important since the 1950 reform applied to the regions which had been the last to be occupied by the Communists, the regions in which the traditions of radical agrarian struggle were the least solid.

In the short run the agrarian reform greatly contributed to an increase in agricultural production. From 113 million tons in 1949 cereal production went to 164 million tons in 1952, surpassing the

150 million tons that had been the best prewar year (in China "cereals" also include tuber plants, which are counted at one-fourth their weight). But this progress had its own limits. Once rid of the burden of tenant farming, the small individual holdings that came into being because of the reform were forced to languish at a fairly low level because only mediocre equipment was available. They could not undertake the hydraulic projects necessary to further progress. In 1951 and 1952 "mutual aid" teams started to be formed, which was the first timid step toward the creation of true cooporatives. But during these same years the dominant tendency was toward free competition among the small peasants, which led to the eviction of the poorest by the richest. The campaign of increased cooperation of 1954–1955 tried to fight this phenomenon of social polarization.

Agrarian reform also helped to animate the life of the villages[10] by changing their physical aspect: health and literacy campaigns conducted by the peasant associations, activities by women's groups (especially concerning application of the marriage law), and young people's activities.

Entering the factories . . .

Since 1927 the Chinese Communists had been cut off from the country's major industrial bases; this was a political disadvantage which also hurt them where matters of the economy and technology were concerned. Not only did they have very little experience in managing large enterprises and with the industrial sector in general, but they had almost no influence in the factories, where their only support came from a few Communist veterans who had escaped the repression, some enthusiastic but inexperienced young workers, and some sympathetic cadres who backed them for patriotic reasons.

The situation was made all the more delicate by the fact that management and the national bourgeoisie were in a very solid position. Their traditional adversaries (foreign groups and bureaucratic capitalists) had been evicted. They were now in control, especially in the area of light industry; they represented nearly two-thirds of all of industrial capitalism, and the state had majority holdings only in the very underdeveloped area of heavy industry (70 percent of coal, 90 percent of steel, and 78 percent of elec-

[10] See document 3.

tricity). The national bourgeoisie's strength lay in its economic and technical knowledge, its experience of the market, and the indispensable political role it had played in the Liberation. Its position was further consolidated by the Korean War and the 1951 embargo declared by the United Nations: it became all the more indispensable because the outside sources of industrial products had dried up.

The Communist authorities therefore had to compromise, at least temporarily. They had to content themselves with running the machinery of the economy, dealing with such things as price controls, the distribution of primary materials, and state orders. To gain a firm foothold in the factories the Communists called upon both their own experience and the Soviet model: on the one hand the army, on the other hand the union "transmission belt." Immediately following the Liberation the army was given numerous tasks concerning the rural economy, notably the reconstruction of the hydraulic network, the dikes, and canals (which could not have been done by individual peasants, even in mutual-aid teams). The army was also often entrusted with the management of the large factories confiscated from the Guomindang as well as the management of priority services (rail and road transportation, supplying basic foodstuffs). On the other hand, in order to offset the tens of thousands of industrial cadres and technicians who had been slow to support the new regime and who were politically indifferent in the best of cases and often linked to the bourgeoisie of the national capitalists, union structures based on the Soviet model were very quickly organized. This was the 1950 law concerning labor unions. Along with the marriage law and the Agrarian Reform Law, it was presented at the time as the third basic building block of the regime. Nevertheless, it was quite different from the other two laws because it did not reflect an already very dynamic mass movement, as the women's and peasant movements did. The CCP organized a vast and complex network of union sections in factories, city federations, provinces, and branches of industry, which were all part of the General Pan-Chinese Union. The structure was quite rigid, and its role was to oversee factory social services, organize literacy campaigns, and to win acceptance for often heavy production norms in the state enterprises and compromises with management in private enterprises, for example concerning salaries; the unions were much less preoccupied with expressing the aspirations of the workers and mobilizing the workers politically. The president of the General Pan-Chinese Union was Liu Shao-qi.

In spite of all these political and social problems, industrial production rose sharply between 1949 and 1952. Its total value rose from 10 to 27 billion *yuan*, and its percentage of all production went from 23 to 33 percent:

PRODUCTION	1949	1952
Steel (tons)	158,000	1,350,000
Coal (tons)	32,430,000	66,490,000
Crude oil (tons)	121,000	436,000
Cement (tons)	660,000	2,860,000
Electricity (KwH)	4,310,000,000	7,300,000,000

But rural and urban craftsmen continued to fill the great majority of needs, particularly in the areas of household equipment, clothing, preparation of food products, and material for transportation and navigation (poles, yokes, baskets, wagons, and sampans).

Transportation, finances, and commerce

The railroad system, which was in very poor condition, was gradually repaired, largely due to help from the army. An effort was made to remedy the system's lack of balance and to improve service in the western and southern interior. Lines were constructed and opened for traffic from Chongqing to Chengdu (Sichuan), from Tianshui to Lanzhou (Gansu), and from Laipin to the Vietnamese frontier. An entire industry for the production of railroad material was created from scratch. By 1952 the railroad network had increased from 21,715 to 24,232 kilometers.

River ways and roads, which were particularly extensive in the South and West, were also repaired; they were used almost exclusively by traditional means of transportation: sampans and junks with sails or oars, carts pulled by both animals and people. Two large roads were started to link Lhassa and Tibet with Yunnan on the one hand and Gansu on the other.

Two measures of financial stabilization were taken by the People's Bank of China, which had been created at the end of 1948. It was the only institution that distributed money, and it controlled the private credit establishments that still existed. Chen Yun, the minister of finance, sought to fight the still rampant inflation by putting the policy of the three balances (the national budget, trade, and the circulation of money) into practice in February–March 1950. Taxes were simplified, victory bonds at 5 percent interest were sold to the wealthy, foreign currencies and precious metals had to be turned in to the authorities, and the capital and goods of people who had gone abroad were seized. All these measures helped to stop inflation after 1950 and to balance the state budget.

Wholesale trade gradually passed under the control of the state: the private sector, which controlled 76 percent in 1949, maintained control of only 36 percent in 1952. State commerce had the effect of regulating trade and controlling prices. State companies handed over orders to the private sector both for the processing of raw materials and for the production of fixed quantities of goods.

The public control of trade was also organized through commercial cooperatives, which began to grow after 1950. These supply and sale cooperatives, which received state credits, primarily benefited the state trade network for the distribution of merchandise. They were often able to sell products for 10 to 20 percent less than the market price, and their members in this way could buy clothing, food, and farming equipment less expensively. From 1950 to 1952 private retail trade dropped from 83 to 58 percent, the remainder being taken over by the cooperatives and the state stores, which were just then coming into being.

Political options of the reconstruction

During this period of inexperience and groping, opposite political tendencies were already forming and social tensions were surfacing in both the cities and the villages.

In the cities the national bourgeoisie, which was given an official place by the Common Program as a beneficiary of the Liberation, profited equally from the economic situation and the embargo. Cases of clandestine hoarding of rare materials, speculation, as well as production of only certain goods for large profits because of shortages and not in response to social needs were not uncommon in 1951 and 1952. The question was what attitude to adopt concerning this rise in capitalist activity. It seems that some of the leaders, followers of Liu Shao-qi, were in favor of appeasement and compromise to help increase production. They closed their eyes to the demands made by management on the working class, who were asked to accept low salaries and long work hours (up to twelve hours per day). Liu Shao-qi seems to have followed out this policy personally in the region of Tientsin[11] where he went in September 1959 to lead a conference between management and workers that called for class collaboration. In his speech of May 1950 as a union leader he again called for cooperation between capital and labor. In July 1951 at the Marx-Lenin Institute he asked the cadres to abandon their "peasant mentality" so that they could become good modern administrators and adapt to urban life.

In the countrysides, the options were no less clear. Once the agrarian reform had been instituted and the feudal exploitation of the peasants had been eliminated, the question was how to define the future of Chinese agriculture. One tendency—again advocated by Liu Shao-qi and his followers—emphasized the priority of technical equipment and mechanized agriculture; they felt it was therefore necessary to wait for industrial progress before the rural areas could achieve socialism: no cooperatives without tractors. In the short run, this meant a laissez faire policy concerning the growing social polarization in the countrysides, which profited the most productive people and hurt the poorest and least experienced. The left, led by Mao, did not confront these problems until 1954–1955 with the "rising tide of socialism in the countrysides" (see Chapter 3).

The twin movements of the *sanfan* (Three Antis) and the *wufan* (Five Antis) in 1952 represented the first attempt to defeat these bureaucratic tendencies and the new rise of capitalism. These movements, despite their modest objectives, were part of the continuity of antihierarchical initiatives that stretched from Yanan to the Great Leap Forward and the Cultural Revolution. It would seem, then, that they were the work of Mao and his entourage, although we do not know for certain whether the political rifts in the CCP leadership were already so clear-cut.

The *sanfan* movement was aimed at the cadres and functionaries who profited from their privileged position to practice corruption wastefulness, and authoritarianism. The *wufan* movement attacked the capitalists who took bribes, engaged in fiscal fraud, stole goods from the state, practiced deception on state contracts, and illegally obtained secret economic information. The joining of the *sanfan* and the *wufan*, the fight against the bureaucracy and the fight against the bourgeoisie, was not an accident; it gave the first hint of the originality of certain theoretical analyses of the CCP concerning the risk of the reemergence of a new bourgeoisie of privileged

[11] See document 4.

cadres after the taking of power. But what would be stated much more clearly after the break with the USSR and the Cultural Revolution fifteen years later was at this point only faintly sketched out, perhaps not even very consciously.

Wufan and *sanfan* were people's campaigns. Of course it was the authorities who issued the sanctions, who dismissed or imprisoned the cadres (at the same time a purge was taking place in the party itself), who levied fines on the capitalists and confiscated their goods. But the investigation of the cadres and capitalists was done collectively, in public, with the participation of the population. Thus, in the first six months of 1952, 450,000 businesses were inspected in seven major cities. Seventy-six percent were found guilty of infractions.

However, the *sanfan* and the *wufan* did not seem to substantially change the options that would lead to the technical and management priorities of the first Five Year Plan.

DOCUMENTS

1. THE MARRIAGE LAW (1950)

Source: *Marriage Law of the People's Republic of China* (Peking, Foreign Languages Press, 1950), pp. 1–7.

Article 1

The arbitrary and compulsory feudal marriage system, which is based on the superiority of man over woman and which ignores the children's interests shall be abolished.

The New Democratic marriage system, which is based on free choice of partners, on monogamy, on equal rights for both sexes, and on protection of the lawful interests of women and children, shall be put into effect.

Article 2

Bigamy, concubinage, child betrothal, interference with the remarriage of widows and the exaction of money or gifts in connection with marriage shall be prohibited.

Article 3

Marriage shall be based upon the complete willingness of the two parties. Neither party shall use compulsion and no third party shall be allowed to interfere.

Article 4

A marriage can be contracted only after the man has reached 20 years of age and the woman has reached 18 years of age.

Article 7

Husband and wife are companions living together and shall enjoy equal status in the home.

Article 8

Husband and wife are in duty bound to love, respect, assist and look after each other, to live in harmony, to engage in production, to care for the children and to strive jointly for the welfare of the family and for the building up of a new society.

Article 9

Both husband and wife shall have the right to free choice of occupation and free participation in work or in social activities.

Article 10

Both husband and wife shall have equal rights in the possession and management of family property.

Article 11

Both husband and wife shall have the right to use his or her own family name.

Article 13

Parents have the duty to rear and to educate their children; the children have the duty to support and to assist their parents. Neither the parents nor the children shall maltreat or desert one another.

The foregoing provision also applies to step-parents and step-children. Infanticide by drowning and similar criminal acts are strictly prohibited.

Article 15 .

Children born out of wedlock shall enjoy the same rights as children born in lawful wedlock. No person shall be allowed to harm or discriminate against children born out of wedlock.

Where the paternity of a child born out of wedlock is legally established by the mother of the child or by other witnesses or by other material evidence, the identified father must bear the whole or part of the cost of maintenance and education of the child until it has attained the age of 18.

With the consent of the natural mother, the natural father may have custody of the child.

Article 17

Divorce shall be granted when husband and wife both desire it. In the event of either the husband or the wife insisting upon divorce, it may be granted only when mediation by the sub-district people's government and the sub-district judicial organ has failed to bring about a reconciliation.

2. A PEOPLE'S COURT SENTENCES PEKING GANGSTERS TO DEATH
Source: Paul Tillard, *Le montreur de marionettes* (Paris, Julliard, 1956).

The author wrote this novel based on accounts given to him while he was a correspondent in Peking shortly after the Liberation.

. . . A low square platform about thirty feet wide had been set up in the western part of the Heaven's Bridge* in a place more or less empty of barracks. The soldiers of the regular army stood impassively, their faces seemingly dead, their machine guns against their chests. Liu and Sun arrived just as four prisoners, [their hands tied behind their backs] and surrounded by other soldiers, were climbing onto the platform . . . . No one had ever seen them before. Evidently such extraordinary characters did not show themselves to the people. The general surprise increased when a soldier stepped to the edge of the platform and declared that these four men were dangerous criminals: "These four drinkers of blood are called the Dominators of Heaven in the North, the South, the East, and the West. Their time has come to an end. No man has the right to dominate the people."
. . . At the other end of the platform some other men soon appeared, also under soldiers' guard. Everyone knew these men, everyone had seen them beat people who couldn't pay their protection money, and each one of them had been responsible for the death of three, four, or five jugglers, perhaps even more. One-Eyed Horse was with them, along with Limping Tiger, Mule Head, Tailless Lizard, and a dozen others. They seemed to be terribly afraid. But they were looking for their friends, and the crowd also seemed to be afraid.
. . . The soldier pointed to the four kneeling Dominators. "The money they extorted from you," he went on, "helped them to live as parasites, and to organize prostitution and drug rings. They worked for the Japanese bandits and then for Jiang's bandits—to whom they denounced Chinese patriots. They are responsible for the deaths of hundreds of your brothers. That is why the people's army tribunal has sentenced them to death; they will be punished."
. . . One-Eyed Horse, Mule Head, and the others looked out at the crowd. No one dared move. No mouth opened to accuse them. How could one speak out against crimes that were so common that everyone had become used to them? Were they really crimes? Hadn't there always been bandits of this sort who had been called lords before the arrival of the Communists?
. . . Liu, his mind tossed about like a sampan in the whirlpools of the Yellow River, was filled with terror. Old Yupi, standing on her wooden legs, whispered into his ear: "You didn't come only for your son." His

---

* "Heaven's Bridge" (*Tianqiao*) was the neighborhood of Peking's jugglers. They were the constant victims of a whole hierarchy of gangsters and racketeers. Old Liou is a puppeteer whose son was denounced by One-Eyed Horse as a Communist and killed by the Guomindang.

courage returned. "He killed Michiteh," he shouted. Michiteh had been a Communist and also the best sword juggler in Heaven's Bridge. His swords were like lightning from Heaven in his arms. Everyone was afraid of him because of his swords, and also because of his strength. One-Eyed Horse himself was afraid of him. One day Michiteh refused to pay his protection money. One-Eyed Horse came back with five of his men at his side.

"Death," shouted Yupi in Liu's ear.

3. PEASANT LI GUIYING BECOMES THE LEADER AND DIRECTOR OF A CO-OPERATIVE

Source: Jan Myrdal, *Report from a Chinese Village* (New York, Pantheon, 1965), pp. 218–22.

In 1951, we were told that the party school in Yanan was having a training course for female ganbus. It was said that as half the population consisted of women, trained women were needed as well. Our labour group for mutual help was now to be turned into a farmer's co-operative. It was Father who forced that through. It was the first of its kind and it was an experiment. The labour group for mutual help told the party school about me, and I was accepted and sent off to attend the course and study for six months. Ever since I had been small, I had dreamed of being able to learn to read and write. I had dreamed day-dreams of becoming a student. . . .

That time at the party school was the decisive time of my life. It was then I realized what I must do with my life. I came back to Liu Ling in July 1951. I could then read and write, and I took part in the autumn harvest and, in the winter, I began organizing the women to study. . . .

That winter I taught ten women to read and write a hundred characters each. That isn't enough to be able to read a newspaper or such, but it is enough to be able to write simple accounts and receipts and to keep notes. They have gone on with it since, but it has been difficult for them. . . .

There were three labour groups in the farmers' co-operative in 1953. Two of men and one of women. I was chosen leader of the women's group. At the meeting, the women said: "She is young and hard-working and she can read." So I thought that, if they had such faith in me, I must show that I was worthy of their opinion of me. That I must work much harder than before. I wanted to get the women as a group moving. . . .

. . . It had now become quite usual with our generation for husband and wife to discuss the family's problems and decide about them together. Women now no longer work just in the house; they also work in the fields and earn their own money. But the men of the older generation still say: "What does a woman know? Women know nothing! What's a woman worth? Women are worth nothing!" In such families the men decide everything and their wives say: "We are just women. We are not allowed to say anything."

We won. Gradually the others were voted down and persuaded and got to agree. I was elected a member of the committee of the East Shines Red Higher Agricultural Co-operative. . . .

4. MANAGEMENT AND WORKERS UNDER THE NEW DEMOCRACY: THE TIENTSIN
AFFAIR (1949)

Source: Han Suyin, *Le premier jour du monde* (Paris, Stock, 1975), pp.
63–65.

*The author, who often stays in Peking, echoes the criticisms made retro-
actively after the Cultural Revolution concerning industrial management
following the Liberation and Liu Shao-qi's supposed role in it.*

The unions were organized in 1949. They followed the Soviet model and
their existence gave rise to a dilemma. In order to play their role as representatives of the working class, the workers had to be given a political background as well as a background concerning industrial management and
business power. But at the same time the imperatives of production demanded
discipline and obedience to orders from above . . . .

Factory rules for establishing "normal relations" between capital and
labor were promulgated at Tientsin: continuation of the "normal" twelve-
hour day with two days off each month, but only for union members!
Factory occupations and worker power were also strictly proscribed. Behind
the slogan "Production first" was almost always hidden the power of the
director or boss. He remained the sole judge of a worker's abilities. The
system of apprenticeship was maintained (five years of work without
salary). In arbitration over differences between workers and management
the rules provided for recourse to "traditional practices."

The report on a conference held in Tientsin on September 7, 1949, gives
an idea of the restrictions imposed on the workers:

—the capitalist keeps the right to fire workers (if they are not indispensable to production),

—the workers must observe strict discipline,

—schedules remain "faithful to custom,"

—no pay raises. Exaggerated complaints will not be accepted,

—salary for women and children equal to that of men if the work is equal,

—customary vacations: seven days a year on public holidays.

These rules, which were published with the approval of the local section
of the CCP, caused a deep discouragement among the workers. On April 6,
1950, an article obviously inspired by Mao entitled, "We Must Have
Confidence in the Masses for Factory Management," emphasized the place
of the proletariat and its role in running the factories and the country. The
article called attention to "the deplorable incidents at Tientsin and other
cities where, in the name of production, members of the party have totally
given in to the demands of management without worrying about the workers'
interests," and recalled the existence of a "bureaucracy that has changed
nothing of the old system."

The law of June 29, 1950, established unions in all factories, mines, and
workshops. Worker's insurance was created. The workers must "participate
in the management of nationalized businesses and have a say in work

conditions in the private sector . . . ." No doubt the life of the workers improved, but their hopes of participating in state decisions—"no money, but power," as one workers' slogan said—would remain unsatisfied until 1958.

Chapter Three

The Five Year Plan:
1953–1957

In 1953, reconstruction work seemed far enough along and the level of economic activity high enough so that a five year plan could be started. This was the period in which China most clearly modeled itself on the Soviet Union, economically as well as politically. Yet even at this time, China already differed from the USSR in its approach to agriculture and in its ideological analysis of socialist society—the theory of "contradictions among the people" (1956). The political and economic tensions that had been latent within the classicism of the years 1953–1955 came out into the open with the disruptions of 1956 and 1957, disruptions that corresponded to a serious crisis in the socialist camp outside of China. China's development, then, was irregular and hesitant, and in the end did not achieve the stability and continuity that in 1953 seemed to lie ahead. Was this a result of inexperience or was it caused by the tensions that at that time secretly divided advocates of the two lines in the leadership?

The Soviet Economic and Political Model

By choosing the Soviet Union as an economic and political model, China was really choosing a Soviet type of society. Planning techniques and economic priorities could not be dissociated from certain political concepts and structures that favored bureaucracy, order, continuity, and initiative from above.

56

The Five Year Plan

In 1953, a "general program of transition to socialism" was adopted, and the Five Year Plan was its concrete instrument; the general arrangements and mechanics of the plan were based on principles that were not challenged until much later. Priority was given to economic growth as an end in itself, and as a consequence specialized technology and management strictly planned by the higher authorities were encouraged too. The success of the plan, therefore, depended mainly upon an elitist class of technocrat-managers whose privileged political and material status showed what an indispensable role they played. These highly specialized cadres made concrete decisions and wielded power at every echelon: this was the system of "one-man management," a Soviet formula. The workers hardly participated at all in setting up programs, researching technical innovations, and supervising. When they were called upon at all, it was to compete with one another on an individual basis, with a complicated system of points and quotas inspired by Russian Stakhanovism. The plan, then, was intended as a specifically economic program of development, but its operation involved a precise *political* organization of social relations.

In principle, the plan favored heavy industry, particularly that of the means of production, in the great tradition of Stalin. At the same time, it favored the heavy units, the "extranormal projects": there were 694 of these projects (giant factories, mining centers, civil engineering works, etc.), almost all located in the large cities. Besides being a slavish imitation of the Soviet model, the plan reflected the Chinese leaders' desire to break with the rural tradition of the guerrilla bases where they had lived for twenty-two years, or at least their conviction that such a break was necessary: they had to make China into a modern country. The slogan words that were popular now were "regularize," "systematize," and "rationalize." As for Marxist theory, the dominant interpretation—and the one that was to mark the Eighth Congress of the CCP in 1956—was that the principal contradiction was between an "advanced" social system and "backward" production forces ('backward," therefore, was thus applied to the masses who were the agents and active participants in production). This was the conviction shared by great administrators like Liu Shao-qi, Bo Yi-bo, Minister of Finance Chen Yun, and Deng Xiao-ping. The other line, which advocated a high level of political awareness on the part of the masses and the need to mobilize them and remove obstacles to that mobilization, was followed by a minority of the people at the time of the first Five Year Plan and was perhaps not even clearly formulated. Mao later described how ill at ease he had been at that time, faced with so many new problems.

The Five Year Plan: its objectives and its implementation

The plan was not officially adopted and promulgated until the beginning of 1955, but it covered the whole period from 1953 to 1957 and so included the temporary economic programs of 1953 and 1954. Its beginnings, then, were slow and uncertain: was this a sign of inexperience, or were internal differences already taking their toll?

Essentially, the plan aimed at doubling industrial production by an annual rate of increase of 14 percent. Of the 42 billion *yuan* allocated to the Five Year Plan, 58 percent was to be spent on industry and only 7 percent on agriculture. Each year the accumulation fund would absorb 22 percent of production, a very heavy burden. Eighty-eight percent of the spending would be allocated to the heavy industry of means of production, in keeping with the plan's orientation.

The main effort was directed toward regions in the interior, whereas in 1952 three-quarters of the industrial potential was still concentrated on the coasts for historical reasons. Of the 694 large projects, 472 were in the interior.

The arrangements of the plan were determined by China's privileged ties with the Soviet Union. Integration into the socialist camp depended on what its basic options were. Priority was given to the sectors in which cooperation was both easiest and most necessary: heavy construction, advanced pinpoint building projects, advanced technologies, and mechanical or electrical precision industries. Out of 694 extranormal projects, 156 were to be carried out with Soviet equipment and technicians (the number reached 211 in 1956). Evidence of this integration was the fact that the Soviet Union supplied parts and sent numerous experts (10,000 in 1956) and that Chinese technicians were required to study Russian.

The published results were spectacular; in general they surpassed the plan's expectations:

Production	Best Previous Year	1952	1957
Steel (tons)	900,000	1,350,000	5,400,000
Coal (tons)	62,000,000	66,490,000	130,000,000
Electricity (KwH)	6,000,000,000	7,300,000,000	19,000,000,000
Oil (tons)	320,000	436,000	2,000,000
Raw cotton (bales)	848,000	3,600,000	4,500,000
Cotton cloth (meters)		3,300,000,000	5,000,000,000
Grain (tons)	(?) 150,000,000	163,000,000	170,000,000

The diversification of products was as important as these figures. In 1957, China manufactured electrical, mining, and railroad equipment, special alloys, pharmaceutical products, watches, and pens for the first time.

The progress of the railroads (nearly 5,000 kilometers of new tracks were laid down) and the roads (14,000 kilometers were new) created a much larger circulation of agricultural and industrial products. Provinces like Sichuan and Fujian had now been opened up. China was in the process of changing from a number of regional markets to a unified national market.

The progress of agriculture was much slower. The balance sheet was not really positive except in the domain of large-scale agricultural projects carried out with heavy equipment and experts brought in from Eastern Europe: these included state farms and tractor stations, large dams and networks of canals, and bands of protected forest. The Yellow River "project with many aims"—for example, dams, canals, and power stations—was a symbol of this preoccupation with large-scale works like those in Siberia. In its 1955 form the Yellow River project was later simply abandoned.

A technological and production-oriented culture

The political options of the plan—and this is not really the paradox that it seems—were even more clearly reflected in China's culture than in its economy. Emphasis was placed on technical specialization, institutional structures, and the quantitative aspect of cultural and educational activities. It was during this period that "industrial construction palaces," built by Soviet architects, sprang up in the larger cities all over China. Their style of ornamentation, with heavy wedding-cake decorations artificially plastered over urban facades, went hand in hand with their technological orientation: the point was to impress the so-called backward peasants with a display of advanced techniques.

At that time China had an unwieldy centralized administrative network of research institutes, libraries, professional groups (writers, architects, journalists), and various different cultural institutions, often very unimaginatively based on Soviet models. In scientific research what was emphasized above all was the need for planned centralization, expressed in 1955 by a program for scientific development in twelve points; only specialists were involved in this—no one drew upon the ideas and experience of the workers.

In education, the emphasis was on quantitative growth, discipline,[1] and increasing the number of graduates. Between 1953 and 1957, the number rose from 48,000 to 56,000 at the university level, from 454,000 to 1,299,000 at the secondary school level, from 118,000 to 146,000 in technical and professional studies, and from 9,945,000 to 12,307,000 at the primary school level. In 1955, a Cantonese educator frankly compared a university-level institute to a diploma factory: its technical equipment was the means of production, the teachers were the technicians, the new students were the raw material, and the graduates were the finished product. "We must," he said, "standardize the raw material in order to obtain a good product. . . ."

The party and political life

As in the USSR, the political system in China was based on the hierarchies of party and state. The country was run by the party; ruled by democratic centralism, in each cell as well as in the Central Committee, the party performed at every echelon a complex function combining initiative, protection, competition, and control over the whole machinery of social life. According to the 1954 constitu-

---

[1] See document 1 at the end of the chapter.

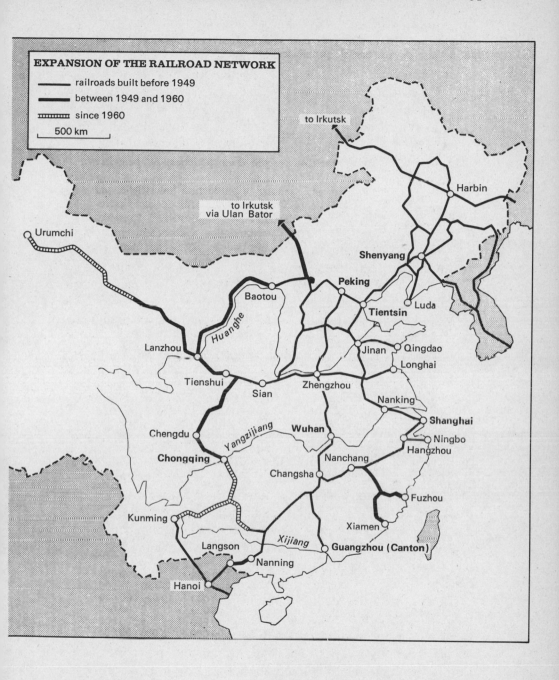

EXPANSION OF THE RAILROAD NETWORK

—— railroads built before 1949

━━ between 1949 and 1960

▭▭▭▭ since 1960

500 km

to Irkutsk

to Irkutsk
via Ulan Bator

Urumchi

Harbin

Shenyang

Luda

Peking

Tientsin

Baotou

Huanghe

Lanzhou

Jinan

Qingdao

Longhai

Tienshui

Sian

Zhengzhou

Nanking

Shanghai

Chengdu

Yangzijiang

Wuhan

Ningbo

Chongqing

Nanchang

Hangzhou

Changsha

Kunming

Fuzhou

Langson

Xijiang

Xiamen

Nanning

Guangzhou (Canton)

Hanoi

tion, whose chairman was Liu Shao-qi, the state was run by a
National People's Assembly, ministers forming a Council on Affairs
of State, and a President of the Republic (Liu Shao-qi) assisted
by vice presidents. The same type of apparatus, with certain differences, existed at the level of the provinces, the districts (*xian*), and
the rural cantons (*xiang*). The only exception to this cumbersome
classical system was the Supreme State Conference, a flexible con-
sultative body of doubtful status which Mao used several times (for
example in 1957) to appeal against the inertia and ill will of the
official apparatus.

Still associated with the party and the state were the mass
organizations (of women, unions, and youth) and democratic
parties. The former were "driving belts" in the Leninist style, spreading the influence of the Communist Party to every echelon in the
hierarchy; the democratic parties, leftovers from the Political Pact
of 1948 and the Common Program of 1949, had no real political
existence except in Peking among intellectuals or the old bourgeoisie
who still believed in the prestige of the revolutionary Guomindang
and the Democratic League.

This whole system was based on an immense army of cadres. Not
only had party membership grown tremendously, but the members
now had a totally different function. The militants had become
functionaries, managers, technicians. These cadres (*ganbu*) were
classified into eight hierarchic echelons, the same number as in the
old Confucian bureaucracy. The system was further weighed down
by the practice of pluralism in the central and provincial echelons:
one leader could simultaneously perform several dozen different
functions, half real and half honorary, in different bodies of the
party, the state, the administration, and the mass organizations. The
machinery of public life had grown faster than the number of "sure
and tested comrades." Ten years later, this situation was to make
the aged "multi-dignitaries" particularly vulnerable to the Red
Guards.

China's political structures were just as much a part of the international apparatus of the socialist camp as its economic machinery.
Exchanges were made between the federations of women, young
people, and writers in China and their counterparts in Eastern
Europe. China belonged to international organizations whose center
was the Soviet Union—the Peace Movement, the Worldwide Federation of Unions, etc. China and the other socialist countries frequently exchanged government delegations, groups of artists, and

cultural and scientific missions. This well-oiled, ponderous official machinery was prominently featured in the press; it also took up a considerable amount of time, personnel, and funds. Political life appeared to be the concern of a privileged group of specialists.

The army

The army, too, was becoming increasingly professional and specialized. The Korean War, during which the Chinese army had fought in a conventional manner along a front, relying on its heavy arms and moving beyond its frontiers, had facilitated the break with the Yanan tradition ("fish in water"). The great military laws of 1955, the work of Peng De-huai, minister of war and former commander of Chinese troops in Korea, were intended to shape the army into a professional army of the Soviet type. Recruitment was carried out administratively, using a selective draft which raised the size of the army to two and a half million. The army's territorial structures (military regions) were dissociated from civilian provinces. These laws also prescribed decorations, honorary titles (marshalships), and prestige uniforms copied from the uniforms of the Soviet army. The militia still existed, but it remained in the background, as did the organs of the party within the army (the political committees and political commissaries). More generally, relations between the army and the civilian population seemed to deteriorate at this time because of the privileges the military enjoyed and because of their superior material condition—which was perhaps some kind of compensation for a certain disaffection on the part of the civilian population toward the military institution after so many years of war.

During the Five Year Plan, the emphasis was on modernization, specialization, technical development, and heavy equipment. Here again, these options went hand in hand with strengthening technological ties with the Soviet Union; Peng De-huai and his staff were counting on the USSR to provide equipment for aviation, heavy artillery, logistical infrastructures, and eventually nuclear armaments. It provided prototypes, parts, and technical advice. In this way, the army became a self-contained body and ceased to have anything to do with political work and the support of production, which had been among its duties in the Yanan period and would be again during the Great Leap Forward and especially during the Cultural Revolution.

The national minorities

The ethno-linguistic map of China is complicated. The 1953 census, taken before the elections for the first National People's Assembly, put the minority population at 35 million as compared to 547 million Han (ethnic Chinese). These people were all spread out along the edge of the country or in the mountainous regions of the South and Southwest (see Chapter 1).

The 1954 constitution defined China as a Multinational Unified State; it accorded all its peoples territorial administrative autonomy at different levels. Certain regions were autonomous at the same level as the provinces: for example, Xinjiang, Ningxia, and Guangxi became the autonomous territories of the Uighurs (1955), the Hui (1957), and the Zhuang (1957). Other smaller or more scattered groups were autonomous at the level of the prefectures or the districts. This system was both more flexible and more realistic than the semi-federalism of the Soviet Union. It did not attempt to maintain a second chamber (called the chamber of nationalities) or to recognize the minorities' hypothetical right to secede (Multinational Unified State). The rights of the nationalities were handled on a local level. There was respect for minority customs, culture, and language, and minorities participated in public organizations on an equal basis.

The policy of promoting minority regions at the time of the Five Year Plan was certainly beneficial: improvements were made in hygiene, transportation, cultural equipment, and the training of local cadres, and exchanges and production were increased. But the fact that this policy was condemned again and again both before and after 1957 as representing at once "petit-bourgeois nationalism" and "great-Han chauvinism" bore witness to how far back the mutual distrust and prejudice went.[2]

Tensions and Crises Between 1953 and 1955

Even at a time when a Soviet-type socialist classicism seemed to dominate all of Chinese political life, there were tensions and imbalances. Sometimes they turned into crises that seemed cyclical, like the Gao Gang and Hu Feng affairs. At other times, when

[2] See document 2.

economic and social development were involved, they took a much more diffuse and disguised form.

Imbalances in the Five Year Plan

The original positions of the "Chinese way" (see Chapter 8), as they were later defined, implied a radical criticism of the options of the first Five Year Plan. Yet this criticism was never systematically presented in Peking, at least not publicly. Perhaps there was some hesitation about challenging the Soviet model in its Stalinist version, criticisms of the USSR being limited to revisionism after 1960. And doubtless too because among the team of leaders in office during the first plan, not all positions had been defined. At that time, there was more emphasis on fumbling and inexperience than on divergencies and errors of direction. Only general remarks and allusions were made, most often through official spokesmen like Han Suyin. She described the first plan as "a number of large front line units cut off from the masses of troops in the rear." In fact, the imbalance between the large production units and the small and middle-sized industrial units, between heavy industry and light industry, between regions of advanced development and average regions, and between cities and rural areas became more pronounced after 1953. Mao's speech in 1956, "On the ten major relationships," enumerated the main imbalances in Chinese society, and could pass for a systematic critique of the economic philosophy of the first Five Year Plan. But it was an indirect critique, and significantly enough, it did not become public until much later.

The fact was that the intensely administrative and production-oriented tradition established by the first Five Year Plan remained very strong; it became dominant again and again in the sixties and seventies, particularly just before and after Mao's death.

On the other hand, many people hostile to China viewed the first Five Year Plan—especially after 1960—as a "reasonable" period in contrast to the later "disorder." It is undeniable that between 1953 and 1957 China's economy made spectacular if uneven progress. However, the growth rate it attained (15 percent per year for industry) did not take into account the demographic growth (11 percent). In relation to the population, the growth rate of agriculture over five years was not 23.5 percent but 9 percent. It had been necessary to continue and systematize the rationing—begun at the time of the reconstruction—of the three principal expendable items—grain, edible oil, and cotton cloth. According to the interpretation of Marxist principles dominant at the time, there was no question of limiting population growth.

Because of its overall options, the Five Year Plan had to be heavily centralized; it favored vertical administrative apparatuses, industrial ministries, and economic commissions at the expense of local and regional initiative. It encouraged the growth of an often excessive managerial staff who had only weak ties to the base and sought prestige above all and spectacular but fragile successes. For example, in Canton, these cadres were later criticized for having devoted only 10 percent of the 300,000 square meters of new construction raised during the plan to actual production. The Cantonese were particularly bitter about this because many of the most important decisions had been made by cadres from the North who did not speak the local language and because they had been instructed to carry out a general policy which had not designated Canton as one of the favored growth centers.

Mao later declared that the absolute priority given to heavy industry had been given "without regard for people's lives." In fact, the plan's production-oriented policy required accelerating the pace, lengthening the workday, extending the piecework salary and profit bonuses, and tightening discipline. In 1954, Li Fu-chun, one of the officials who drew up the plan, declared that between 1953 and 1955 industrial productivity increased 42 percent while the average salary increased 15 percent and the real salary (buying power) only 7 percent.

All these imbalances contributed greatly to the sudden turning point in 1958, when the five year plans were replaced by the Great Leap Forward and the "general line."

The rural areas

The rural areas were sacrificed in the first Five Year Plan. They actually only benefited from a minimal share of the planned investments, which made agricultural production lag even farther behind industrial development. Agricultural prices were fixed centrally and were kept low, much lower than the prices of industrial products: the worker was still being fed cheaply for the sake of industrial priorities, but the peasant was paying more for expendable items and agricultural equipment which he bought in the city, for the sake of profitability. In addition, the quotas of obligatory sales to the state (between 16 and 25 percent of the harvest) were quite high. This caused a widespread tendency among the peasants to resist passively, and there were sporadic incidents. One cadre declared (*Renmin Ribao*, May 10, 1955) that grain buying was "the dirtiest work."

This was particularly true because in 1951–1952 the effect of the agrarian reform had been a distinct rise in the peasants' standard of living because of the abolition of tenant farming. The spontaneous operation of economic forces and the rivalry between poor and rich peasants hardly contributed to the progress of agricultural production. Many peasants resorted to subsistence farming. The mutual aid teams and the first cooperatives did not substantially help raise production either. These cooperatives were "of an inferior type"; the poor peasants, who were not able to contribute much material or equipment, had to work more. Inexperienced cadres fixed norms that were too high, and they preferred to support the rich peasants, who seemed to them more dynamic. Faced with these difficulties, some of the leading cadres (Liu Shao-qi was later implicated) chose to dissolve these first cooperatives and revert to the parceling up of rural farms, as long as the industrial infrastructure did not allow for mechanizing the countryside. In 1954, 15,000 cooperatives were broken up in Zhejiang province alone.

Mao and the other leftists reacted to these agricultural problems by accelerating the agricultural cooperative movement in 1955 in order to resolve the crisis through a more widespread political mobilization of the peasants.

The political crisis of 1954–1955

This crisis affected both the intellectual circles and the leadership.

The campaigns of 1951–1952 had not been enough to rally most intellectuals to Marxism and socialism, and the influence of Western liberalism was still strong. The leading cadres responsible for intellectual problems, especially Zhou Yang (who in 1935 had already come into conflict with Lu Xun with the support of the CCP apparatus), had to resort to the authoritarian methods which Zhdanov had used in the Soviet Union at the end of the Stalinist period. The literary community was called upon to choose between bourgeois idealism and socialist realism, the scientists had to choose between bourgeois science and proletarian science. In 1954, an important controversy over the great eighteenth-century classic novel, *Honglou Meng* (*The Dream of the Red Chamber*), resulted in a severe criticism of literature professor Yu Ping-po and in his public self-criticism. Yet the uneasiness spread, and at its center was the writer Hu Feng, an old fellow traveler of the CCP, who denounced the methods used by Zhou Yang (with whom he had been at odds since the thirties). He rebelled against the cultural bureaucracy, but in an ambiguous manner. Far from opening the way to a truly popular culture, as would happen in the sixties, his protest concerned only the individual rights of the writer. When Hu Feng actually challenged China's choice of socialism, he was arrested and publicly denounced as a counterrevolutionary.

Politically, the economic priority that the plan gave to large regions concerned with heavy industry—both the old ones, like the Northeast, and the new ones, like Shanghai—resulted in tendencies to dissidence in the provinces. Gao Gang and Rao Shushi, two veterans of the CCP, the former a party official in the Northeast and the latter an administrator in Shanghai, came into sharp conflict with Peking and the political choices made by the leadership. For a long time Gao Gang had maintained privileged relations with Moscow in the Northeast, since at that time Moscow was not content with the generally pro-Soviet orientation of Chinese politics and was seeking direct support in China. With the help of the Soviet Union, and using it as a model, Gao Gang had organized the development of this region on a more or less particularist basis. In Shanghai, Rao Shushi too had tried to work out an independent line of regional economic development, apparently based on a policy of moderation toward the bourgeoisie which had remained influential in the Lower Yangzi. The Gao-Rao alliance and its political bases are still obscure, but the crisis occurred in 1954, when Stalin's death gave the Chinese authorities more room to act. Gao Gang killed himself, Rao was arrested and put into prison, and ten other important regional leaders were punished. The affair was not revealed to the public until 1955, a year later.

Foreign policy during the Five Year Plan

China still maintained special ties with the Soviet Union, because this was the logic of the political and economic options of the plan. But China's relationship to the Soviet Union was less subordinate and more flexible than it had been before Stalin's death. The mixed companies formed in 1950 for civil aviation and mining in Xinjiang were dissolved in 1955, and the railroad and maritime installations of the Northeast, including Dairen, were returned to China. Soviet aid to China was increased considerably, the number of projects undertaken by Moscow was raised in 1955, and thousands of new Soviet experts arrived in China.

After the end of the Korean War (with the Panmunjon Conference in 1953) and the war in Indochina (with the Geneva Conference in 1954), Peking began to take part in international affairs on an equal footing with Moscow, as a responsible partner. At the Bandong Conference of uncommitted countries, one further step was taken. The Soviet Union, a white power, did not participate, but Zhou En-lai appeared, along with Nasser, Nehru, and Sukarno, as a leader of the former colonial countries fighting against old and new forms of imperialism (1955).

Early Breaks in the Rhythm: *1956–1957*

During 1956 and 1957, the validity of the economic and political options of the first Five Year Plan—that is, the validity of the Soviet model—began to be questioned, and this was the preparation for the radical turning point of 1958. The questioning was slow, confused, and full of setbacks. The struggle between the two lines was certainly already a factor, but so was inexperience and uncertainty—aggravated by the delayed effects of the death of Stalin and by the crisis that shook the entire socialist camp in 1956.

Acceleration in the formation of agricultural cooperatives (1955–1956)

The imbalances of the Five Year Plan were most clearly apparent in the agricultural sector. It was there that the advocates of the radical line launched their offensive in July 1955 by establishing agricultural cooperatives everywhere. The central apparatus resisted this "rising tide," which was openly supported by Mao and appealed mainly to provincial cadres: it was an anti-centrist movement. At the same time, emphasis was placed on class struggle, on the militant initiative of poor peasants, and on the fact that since the reform of 1950 the rich peasants had been favored by the natural workings of the economy.[3] Cooperatives became widespread very quickly: there were 35,000 in Jiangsu in July 1955, and 191,000 in October. In 1956, virtually all Chinese villages had been integrated into cooperatives and were suddenly confronted with completely new problems having to do with such things as management, the establishment of production plans, and the criteria for remuneration by work points. These problems were even more complex in semi-socialist cooperatives (ones which took into account the initial contribution in land or equipment by each member of the cooperative), than in the truly socialist cooperatives, which were fewer in number and already solid enough not to take that kind of contribution into consideration. In 1955 and 1956 the new cooperatives were set up, and the problems they posed were generally confronted with active and dedicated support by the poor and middle peasants. The party apparatus was mobilized in the villages to help appoint the gigantic army of rural cadres that would be needed from then on. Yet these cadres were often inexperienced and therefore inclined to advocate planned economy and to inflate statistics: one cartoon widely published during the criticism movement of 1957 shows peasants leaving the village in early morning; ten turn to the right toward the offices of the cooperative, and only one turns to the left toward the fields! From then on there was a constant risk that rural life would be bureaucratized, and this risk marked all the later Chinese campaigns: the communes, the movement for a socialist education, the Dazhai movement, etc.

The cooperatives that came into being during the rising tide of 1955–1956 were exceptionally short-lived: in 1958 they were replaced by communes. Although they constituted a necessary stage, they did not satisfy certain basic economic needs. They formed an economic space that was too limited to meet the demands of the Great Leap Forward, in particular the need for a liaison between agriculture and industry outside the cities; nor had they put an end to the rural exodus (see below). Politically, they were perhaps also too restricted, and the social unwieldiness within them threatened more and more to favor a few cadres with weak ties to the peasants and strong ties to a central apparatus that was often conservative.

In 1956, a Twelve Year Plan for Agricultural Development was adopted. It emphasized both technical innovations and the political mobilization of the peasants with a view to their participation in the

[3] See document 3.

planning and management of agriculture. Thus the autonomy of the rural sector, which had been a poor relation during the Five Year Plan, would be reaffirmed. Agriculture would then cease to depend on production in the cities (of agricultural machinery), on technology, or on the philosophy of the "forces of production." This was a clear break with the principles of the Five Year Plan, and the advocates of these principles apparently did all they could to slow down the adoption and diffusion of the Twelve Year Plan, which Mao worked actively to support.

Just as much of a departure from the Soviet model was the adoption in 1956 of the principle of birth control and its practical application—at least in the cities.

The "three socialist transformations" (1956)

In 1956, the slow and gradual progress of the Five Year Plan was not only disrupted in the agricultural sector, but also in the sectors of crafts and industry. In large and small cities, the craftsmen's stalls and workshops, the tiny fixed and moving businesses, and the various street occupations were gathered into cooperatives on the neighborhood level. As for the national capitalists, so important during the period of reconstruction, it was decided that their goods and enterprises would simply be transferred to the state. But out of regard for their past as political allies, which dated back to the end of the Guomindang, they were accorded a substantial indemnity in the form of a fixed interest in proportion to the goods they had transferred, to be paid for seven years. By 1956, then, crafts, agriculture, and industry had all undergone "the three great socialist transformations."

Not only were these measures surpassing the cautious expectations of the Five Year Plan (according to which collectivism would not even be achieved by 1957), but they were being enacted in a new style, a political style: the transition to collective or public management had not been the result of an administrative decision from above but a mass movement with processions through the streets, gongs, streamers, and firecrackers. The public participated fully in these demonstrations, as did the workers involved—they were symbolic of the collective takeover of the economy.

This was the beginning of the radical change that prepared the way for the Great Leap Forward in 1958. In 1955 and 1956 a whole series of internal debates at different echelons took place, in which people scrutinized the new tendencies, tendencies that emphasized popular initiative rather than informed economic planning—production with a view to "more, faster, better, and more economically." Yet the effects of the contradictions and ambiguities of the Five Year Plan continued to be felt. In 1956 the peasants seemed even more inclined to leave the countrysides, both because of the lower standard of living in the villages and because of the sometimes authoritarian methods by which the first cooperatives were formed. In 1956, 500,000 peasants immigrated into Shanghai, and during the fall of 1956 and the winter of 1957, 300,000 peasants immigrated into Canton, according to the figures published by the press during the public debates in the spring of 1957. In the cities, where inflation still existed and prices continued to rise, salary scales swelled, particularly because of the production-oriented policy followed since 1953 (including the spread of piecework salaries). The question was whether these problems should be handled through technical measures (production norms, salaries, prices, etc.) or confronted directly; should their political roots be exposed, should the contradictions of a developing society be accepted as an inevitable burden? In 1956 and 1957 the leaders of the People's Republic adopted both these attitudes, sometimes alternately and sometimes concurrently. Two tendencies emerged, neither of which was really dominant, and already they began to take shape around the figures of Mao Tsetung and Liu Shao-qi.

The Hundred Flowers (spring 1956)

The Hu Feng affair had shown what problems the regime had in dealing with intellectuals. According to an official estimate made in 1956, 40 percent of them supported the new regime more or less actively, 40 percent supported it without taking any active part, 10 percent went along with it reluctantly, and 10 percent were openly hostile. As the society underwent socialist transformations and as people lost confidence in the automatic assurances of a good "economist" management, it became more and more indispensable to rally the intellectuals to the new regime and to ensure their active participation in economic development and political mobilization. This was what Zhou En-lai explained to a Central Conference of the CCP on intellectuals in January 1956: it was necessary to help them progress, both by improving their professional skills and by increasing their political awareness; they had to be brought closer to the CCP.

To accomplish this, it was necessary to help them to express themselves, to have confidence in themselves. This was the meaning of the slogan "Let a hundred flowers blossom, let a hundred schools of thought contend," which was publicly launched in May 1956 with Mao's personal support. For example, film directors and writers were encouraged to produce works that were more personal in orientation and style, less directly controlled by the administrative services responsible for cultural affairs. Items appeared in the newspapers favoring the discussion of ideas.

But the movement was ambiguous. Was the emphasis where people in the West believed it was at the time—on free self-expression as an end in itself, after the fashion of the Petöfi circle in Budapest? Or was the emphasis on opening the way for a kind of criticism whose immediate target would be the bureaucracy but whose final aim would be to free the creative energies of the intellectuals and thus bring them closer to the workers? The same kind of ambiguity had already characterized the Hu Feng affair, and in 1956 the answers as well as the motives of those involved in the Hundred Flowers were contradictory. In the fall, as the Eighth Congress of the CCP approached, advocates of a more conventional, less audacious policy took advantage of this ambiguity to gain ascendancy; the movement of the Hundred Flowers was over, at least for the time being.

China and the crisis in the socialist camp (1956)

The Hundred Flowers movement in 1956 corresponded to a tendency on the part of the entire Communist world to move into a "thaw." But the same ambiguity existed outside of China: was this thaw elitist in its effect, benefiting intellectuals whose privileges were not threatened? Or was it one stage of an inevitable antibureaucratic critique in which the masses would sooner or later become the principal agents and the principal beneficiaries?

The political tremors grew more violent. In February 1956 the Twentieth Congress of the CPSU was held and Khrushchev made his secret report, vigorously denouncing Stalin—though only for his concrete practices—and proposing to the worldwide Communist movement a strategy of moderation in both domestic and foreign affairs. There were violent chain reactions in the Communist parties of the West and even more in Eastern Europe—the riots in Poznań (April), "Polish October," and, worst of all, the Hungarian crisis which began with critical discussions among the intellectuals and ended in massive riots, the infiltration of Western agents, and the sudden arrival of Soviet tanks.

How did China react? Here again two attitudes were adopted almost at the same time, and neither one was clearly dominant.

One reaction was to search for the deeper causes of the crisis. For example, two official texts were published in Peking in April and October on "the historical experience of the proletariat"; according to these texts, Stalin made serious mistakes, but also played a positive role. What mattered was the fact that the class struggle always existed in a socialist regime and that Stalin's reaction to the problems it posed was to try to solve them from above. Mao's influence on these two texts was obvious. They constituted one more argument in the CCP's long-standing criticism of the Soviet model, criticism which had begun in Yanan and which had remained internal for tactical reasons. "In 1956," said Mao shortly after, "all socialist countries learned a lesson."

The second reaction was to take the tremors of 1956 and their dangers as a warning that imprudent developments and innovations could only lead to a crisis. Therefore the party apparatus with its traditional authority had to be strengthened, and the experience and the customs of the classical period had to be retained. This was the attitude that later prevailed at the Eighth Congress of the CCP, where Mao was pushed into the background.

Zhou En-lai's trip to Russia and Poland at the end of 1956 was proof of China's growing authority in the Communist world, but Zhou did not choose between these two opposing interpretations of the crisis.

The Eighth Congress of the CCP

For the first time since the Liberation, the supreme authority of the party made a general assessment of the changes that had occurred: revolution had been replaced by organization; 1,210,000 militants had been replaced by 10,340,000 elite functionaries. Because of this trend, along with the troubling events taking place in Budapest at that very moment, the organization men, the ones belonging to the party apparatus, led the Congress: they were Liu Shao-qi, Secretary General Deng Xiao-ping, and Bo Yi-bo, the central planning official. Mao was staying in the background, and hardly said a word. Liu explicitly criticized the "leftist deviation" and declared that the class struggle between the bourgeoisie and the proletariat had been resolved; from now on what mattered was the contradiction between the advanced nature of Chinese socialist society and the backwardness of the forces of production (in other words, the masses). Emphasis was placed on technical skill and on management of the economy. The Congress adopted a second Five Year Plan which the bodies of the state were then supposed to ratify and which the Great Leap Forward later rejected. The second plan favored heavy industry and specialized applied research— steel production was to be tripled, for example, and the railway network doubled—but agriculture remained very much in the background as far as the allocation of funds went. This return to economic classicism had the effect of slowing down the "three great transformations." During the summer, Liu had arranged for a partial reestablishment of the agricultural free market, an extension of private plots of land, and a raise in salaries that particularly favored the higher working class. This priority given to growth goals and this production-oriented thinking were to be toppled by the Great Leap Forward.

Behind the unified facade of the Congress, then, there were feelings of antagonism. The revised statutes eliminated references to "Mao Tsetung thought" which had been defined at the Seventh Congress in 1945 as the Chinese expression of Marxism; they established the Permanent Committee as the collegiate leadership of the Politburo. In the atmosphere of 1956, these appeared to be nothing more than preventive measures against the cult of personality criticized everywhere in the world by Communists. In fact, these measures worked against the original options and the mass political line which Mao tried in vain to defend during the congress.

The second *zhengfeng* ("rectification")

At the beginning of 1957, for reasons that are not very clear, the balance of power was reversed again. Phrases like "red and expert" and "socialist education for the cadres" circulated, which represented a considerable shift from the position of the Eighth Congress.

In March criticism of "one-man management" in industry resulted in the establishment of workers' assemblies locally endowed with real powers of control. In February, in a speech before the Supreme State Conference, Mao analyzed the "contradictions within the people" and their "just solution": they were normal and in fact necessary, he said, even after the taking of power, and they had to be dealt with politically, not by force. This text, which ran counter to Soviet practice, was amplified in March at the National Conference of Propaganda, during which the political passivity of the management cadres was attacked. But these ideas were in some sense being imposed from outside on the reluctant central party apparatus. Mao's two speeches, in February and March, were delivered before ad hoc bodies, not statutory ones. The February speech was not published until June, in a very expurgated form. The March speech did not appear until the Cultural Revolution. As was later learned, Mao vainly denounced this policy of secrecy and "the newspapers which are in the hands of the dead."

April marked the official beginning of the campaign of political rectification (zhengfeng, a term adopted from the 1941–1942 movement at Yanan).[4] Its targets were bureaucracy (guanliao-zhuyi), sectarianism (zongpaizhuyi), and subjectivism (zhuguan-zhuyi), in other words the "three scourges" (san hai). This frontal attack by the left occurred in a tense social climate; strikes had broken out because of overly strict administration imposed for the sake of production, and Mao said that they had to be confronted without panic;[5] employment as a result of the uncontrolled exodus from rural areas was a burden on the urban economy, as was the rise in prices.

But the rectification movement contained the same ambiguities as the slogan of the Hundred Flowers. The conservative cadres mistrusted it; sometimes they resisted, and sometimes they passively let things proceed, though not without ulterior motives. The motives of those who supported the zhengfeng were full of contradictions. Was it a matter of freeing collective initiative and the energy of the people, which had been restricted by cadres who were slaves to routine? Then should the criticism be carried on with open instead of closed doors (within the established structures) as the cadres would prefer? Or was the point to criticize bureaucracy in defense

---

[4] See Volume 2, Chapter 11.
[5] See document 4.

of individual freedom and pluralism? This was what certain circles of students hoped for, as did certain political cadres from the small centrist parties formed in 1949. There was a great deal of agitation on the campuses in April and June, particularly in Peking. Criticisms that were sometimes very radical were heard alongside demands directly inspired by the West. Certain organs of the press, like the *Guangming Ribao* (*The Light*) opened their columns to liberal intellectuals who frankly called into question again the very principles of China's socialist options. Was China about to follow in the footsteps of Nagy's Hungary?

Anti-rightist tendencies (June)

On June 6, an editorial in *Renmin Ribao* ("Why All This?") abruptly stopped the criticism and debates. From now on the "rightists" were under attack, and the main slogan was "Without the Communist Party, there would be no People's Republic" (*mei you Gongchandang, jiu mei you renmin Zhongguo*). Why this abrupt switch? One explanation has been that it was a sly attempt to trap the opposition in order to punish them later. Yet it certainly appeared that the initiators of the movement, and even Mao himself, were surprised by the unexpectedly large opposition within broad sections of the middle class and among the intellectuals. It could be that the suddenness of the switch was only an expression of the ambiguities of the Hundred Flowers and rectification movements. For the Maoist group, the principal aim of the movement was to free the masses from the yoke of the bureaucracy so that they could make greater progress. But another aspect of the situation had gradually become dominant, that is, a Hungarian type of liberalization from which certain intellectuals had amply benefited, including veterans of Yanan like the novelist Ding Ling, while the conservative cadres became alarmed. In fact, the anti-rightist campaign brought party machinery men like Deng Xiao-ping back into the limelight, while Mao remained in the background because he had not really been able to master the contradictions in the situation.

All summer long, the anti-rightist movement (*fan youpai yundong*) continued, with public hearings, accusations and self-criticisms, lists of rightists published in the press, and changes in the personnel of the cultural services, often at a high level. Ding Ling and the editor in chief of the *Guangming Ribao* were ousted. Hundreds of thousands of intellectuals and cadres were sent into villages to be reeducated through work; this was the *xiafang* movement ("dispersal to the base"). But only a few were sent to prison.

Mao in Moscow (November 1957)

On the occasion of the fortieth anniversary of the October Revolution, an International Conference of Communist Parties was held in Moscow to assess the recent crisis. Mao went there in person: this was his second and last trip outside China. He spoke up on questions of foreign policy, questions that would later be instrumental in causing the Sino-Soviet split: among them were the strength of Third World movements, war and peace, and East-West nuclear parity. But it was still a time for compromise, and the compromise took the form of an ambiguous Declaration in 64 Parts coupled with a nuclear agreement guaranteeing China the protection of the Soviet umbrella. Mao's visit to Moscow, at a time when the Great Leap Forward lay immediately ahead, no doubt sharpened his perception of what he considered to be the traps and illusions of the Soviet options.

ADDITIONAL BIBLIOGRAPHY

René Dumont, *Révolution dans les campagnes chinoises* (Paris, 1957).
Merle Goldmann, *Literary Dissent in Communist China* (Cambridge, Mass., 1967).
L. Lavallée and P. Noirot, *L'économie de la Chine communiste* (Paris, 1957).
Roderick MacFarquhar, *The Hundred Flowers* (New York, 1960).
Siwitt Aray, *Les Cent Fleurs* (Paris, 1973).
Richard Walker, *Communist China: The First Five Years* (London, 1956).

DOCUMENTS

1. RULES OF CONDUCT FOR STUDENTS, PROMULGATED BY THE MINISTRY OF EDUCATION IN FEBRUARY AND MAY 1955

Source: Theodore Chen, *The Chinese Communist Regime: A Documentary Study*, Vol. 2 (California, Asian-Slavic Studies Center, 1965), pp. 113–114.

> 1. Endeavor to be a good student; good in health, good at study and good in conduct. Prepare to serve the Motherland and the people.

3. Obey all the instructions of the principal and teachers. Value and protect the reputation of the school and of the class.

6. Be orderly and quiet and assume a correct posture during the class. When desiring to leave the classroom, ask the teacher's permission first.

7. During the class, work diligently and listen attentively to the teacher's instruction and the questions and answers by your classmates. Do not talk unless when necessary; do not do anything else besides your class work.

8. During the class when you want to give an answer or to ask a question, raise your hand first. Stand up and speak when the teacher allows you to; sit down when the teacher tells you so.

9. Carefully complete in time the after-class work assigned by the teacher.

11. Respect the principal and the teachers. Salute your teachers when the class begins and again at the end of the class. When you meet the principal or the teachers outside the school you also salute them.

12. Be friendly with your schoolmates and unite with them and help each other.

13. When going to school or returning home, do not delay on the way so as to avoid accidents.

14. Respect and love your parents. Love and protect your brothers and sisters. Do what you can to help your parents.

17. Do not tell a lie or cheat people. Do not gamble. Do not take away other people's things without their permission. Do not do anything that may be harmful to yourself or to others.

18. Take care of public property. Do not damage or dirty tables, chairs, doors, windows, walls, floors or anything else.

19. Eat, rest and sleep at regular hours. Play and take exercise frequently to make your body strong.

2. INTRODUCING THE JINGPAW PEOPLE OF YUNNAN TO THE ECONOMIC VALUES OF SOCIALIST COOPERATIVES

Source: A Winnington, *The Slaves of the Cool Mountains* (London, Lawrence and Wishart, 1959), pp. 194–195.

"Our custom," Lela said, "is to look down on people who haggle over what one person does for another. We think it shows a bad heart. I may help you to build a house or open a field. But afterwards I forget it. You are not obliged to do the same for me. You don't owe me something. What grows on my land is mine but you are welcome to come and eat it as my guest.

"If several families work on a piece of land, we do not add up what each does, or calculate that this person is strong while this one is only a child and that one an old man, or whether this person worked ten days and that one fifteen. We never heard of dividing the crop unequally and giving people who worked harder more grain, and we never had regular working hours. Our way is that more people shorten the work and the time goes better with the talk. It's not so tiring. Counting work done seemed nonsense to us and rather unfriendly."

One very old Jingpaw, an obvious opponent of co-operatives, broke in at this point. He had been fretting and fuming while Lela was talking and now he reproduced almost the identical argument I had heard among the Wa. "It's all new-fangled nonsense," he said. "Life isn't like that. I was a child, then a man and now I am old and weak. That's life and we are all the same. I don't agree with these work-points. One day I feel like working, another day I want to have a drink or sleep. In a lifetime everyone does about the same. So I say share alike and never mind what a man does on this or that day." Having got that off his chest he went back to his bubbling bamboo water-pipe.

Lela had been a leading figure in trying to get the co-operative going from the moment the idea was put out in 1955. Other people had said this was just a cunning Han trick to get the Jingpaw to grow things for them. Lela had not believed that. "They seemed to be sincere people, giving us things. They knew more than we knew and I believed them when they said co-operatives would help us." He in turn helped the work-team to persuade eleven out of Lungjun's twenty-five families to form the first co-operative there in 1956.

One of the many vexed questions which the co-operative was to meet came up immediately over planning their crops. As Lela explained: "What we Jingpaw have are all the same things. We grow the same things—what we need—and don't buy or sell among each other. If we have nothing we eat with others and if everyone has nothing we sell things from the jungle to people below on the plains.

"We think it madness to plant things we don't want, just to sell them. We prefer to plant what we want ourselves."

3. THE POPULAR MOVEMENT FOR RURAL COOPERATIVATION IN A DISTRICT OF THE LOWER YANGZI

Source: *Socialist Upsurge in China's Countryside* (Peking, Foreign Languages Press, 1957), pp. 46–49.

After the land reform in Xixu Township was completed in the spring of 1951, the enthusiasm of the peasants, particularly that of the poor peasants and farm labourers who had received land, was greatly increased. At that time, the local Party branch began organizing the peasants into labour mutual-aid teams. The rich harvests in 1952 and 1953 brought the yield of the land to the pre-war level, and the life of the peasants greatly improved. In spite of all this, class differentiation continued to take place in the rural areas. The rich peasants and speculative merchants stopped at nothing to line their own pockets. Dai Hui-bo, a rich peasant, paid only five pecks of rice to get back his three *mou* of land which had been requisitioned during the land reform; and, as if forgetting himself, he said: "Anyone who needs money may come and borrow from me." Guo Hui-ru, a well-to-do middle peasant, bought nine *mou* of land less than a year after the land reform. By 1953 there had already been 11 new rich-peasant households. Among the nine Party members in the township, five did some business and four bought land. On the other hand, the life of a large number of peasants was getting worse. Figures for 1953 showed that 39 households sold their land, 57 households borrowed money from usurers and two poor peasants had to hire themselves out as farm hands. . . .

The first thing was to concentrate upon running the productive work well. It was true that when the co-ops were first set up, the members' feelings varied. While the poor peasants were in high spirits, the middle peasants wavered. But they had a common desire to make a first-rate job of their productive work. In the spring, the Party branch led the members to build and repair such irrigation works as dikes and ditches and to accumulate manure. The Jibu Co-op, for instance, accumulated enough manure for 267 *mou* of land, several times more than before the co-ops were formed. An average member in a co-op could accumulate enough manure for 1.7 *mou*, while a man working in a mutual-aid team could only accumulate enough manure for 0.6 *mou*. This fact fortified the members' confidence and stunned the middle peasants outside the co-op.

Field work was done chaotically in spring; the members scrambled for work to do like a hive of bees, while the cadres themselves were too busy to give directions, and consequently all were dissatisfied with this state of affairs. The system of short-term responsibility for work was introduced during summer harvesting and sowing, but because the group leaders didn't know how to allocate manpower, chaos, though on a smaller scale, still prevailed and labour efficiency remained low. The chaos was removed in autumn when a plan for short-term field work was drawn up by the production groups which were again subdivided according to the nature of the jobs to be done. It was after a long period of trial and error, coupled with an arduous ideological struggle, that good order in productive work was brought about. The poor peasants and the lower middle peasants on the one hand and the well-to-do middle peasants on the other, for instance, had reacted quite differently to the system of fixed responsibility for a specified job. The former gave positive support to it, while the latter were loud in crying that the work was too heavy and that they couldn't stand it. It was only when the well-to-do middle peasants were brought to realize that labour was glorious and increased yield was impossible without hard work that an agreement in viewpoint was reached.

4. "Don't fear troubles" (Mao Tsetung, January 1957)

Source: Mao Tsetung, *Selected Works of Mao Tsetung* (Peking, Foreign Languages Press, 1977), pp. 371–374.

. . . In socialist society the creation of disturbances by small numbers of people presents a new problem which is well worth looking into.

Everything in society is a unity of opposites. Socialist society is likewise a unity of opposites; this unity of opposites exists both within the ranks of the people and between ourselves and the enemy. The basic reason why small numbers of people still create disturbances in our country is that all kinds of opposing aspects, positive and negative, still exist in society, as do opposing classes, opposing people and opposing views. . . .

With respect to the way people think, subjectivism and seeking truth from the facts are opposed to each other. I believe there will always be subjectivism. Will there be no trace of subjectivism ten thousand years from now? I don't think so.

Opposing sides exist in a factory, an agricultural co-operative, a school, an organization or a family, in short, in every place and at every time. Therefore, disturbances by small numbers of people in society will occur every year. . . .

. . . We should adopt an active, and not a passive, attitude towards disturbances by small numbers of people, that is to say, we should not be afraid of them but be ready for them. Being afraid is no solution. The more you are afraid, the more the ghosts will haunt you. If you are not afraid of disturbances and are mentally prepared for them, you will not be put on the defensive. I think we should be prepared for major incidents. When you are thus prepared, such incidents may not happen, but when you are not, disturbances will occur. . . .

. . . Problems give rise to revolution and after the revolution other problems crop up. If a big nation-wide disturbance flares up, I am sure the masses and their leaders, maybe we ourselves or maybe others, will certainly come forward to clean up the situation. Through a big disturbance of this kind, our country will emerge all the stronger after the boil has burst. Whatever happens, China will march on.

As for small numbers of people creating disturbances, in the first place, we do not encourage this, and in the second, if some people are bent on creating disturbances, then let them. . . .

Chapter Four

The Great
Leap Forward:
1958–1962

Beginning at the end of 1957, the Great Leap Forward (*Da Yuejin*) broke with the economic priorities of the Soviet model; it laid down what would from then on, in spite of oppositions and setbacks, constitute the basis of Chinese socialism. The advocates of this new direction analyzed the Soviet failures, particularly the agricultural failures, and the difficulties of the first Chinese Five Year Plan; they affirmed the need for a radical change in outlook. It was necessary, said Mao and his supporters, to engage all the people's energies in combating backwardness and attacking its roots in the countryside. It was necessary to depend on each man, on his capabilities when equipped with just political principles. The Great Leap Forward was thus an economic answer to the crushing preponderance of agriculture and the small amount of accumulated capital. But it was more than a fresh case of planning. It was a fundamental and original *political* choice: through "the struggle against complacency, superstition, prejudice, and bureaucracy . . . it would reshape the land of China, remake Chinese man" (Han Suyin).

By the end of 1957 and the beginning of 1958, Chinese leaders were disillusioned. They were no longer optimistic about the USSR, and Mao's trip to Moscow had confirmed their criticisms. At the

end of the first Five Year Plan, in spite of its positive aspects, there
were clouds on the horizon, there were dangerous imbalances. The
general impression was that it had been an uncontested economic
success but had not constituted the takeoff point for a developing
economy, as had been anticipated.

Difficulties, disappointments, doubts: an analysis

These disappointments confirmed the views Mao expressed in
1956 in his speech "on the ten major relationships," which was the
fruit of months of discussion within the party. "Ten questions, ten
contradictions," said the text, which contained the critical bases of
the Great Leap Forward. Some of these ten points concerned international or domestic policy—relations between "the party and those
who are not in the party," between Han and minorities, between
revolutionaries and counterrevolutionaries, between "the just and
the mistaken" (how to deal with "those who have made mistakes"),
and between China and foreign countries. Others touched on problems of bureaucracy and economic questions: the relations between
the different sectors of production, between the different regions,
between the state and the producers, between the central government and the regions. The text emphasized the significant imbalances that had appeared between heavy industries and light
industries (which were lagging behind), and the regional inequalities resulting from the fact that the industrial capacity of the
coastal regions—Fujian and Guangdong—had been underestimated.
The priority of large industry had been misunderstood (the text did
not challenge it), so that part of the country's productive forces
had not been used or had been insufficiently used, while the rural
standard of living had gone down. And Mao concluded: "The uni-
lateral development of heavy industry without regard for people's
lives . . . brings discontent in its wake . . . and heavy industry cannot progress. This way, in the long run heavy industry develops
more slowly and not as well."

These criticisms went hand in hand with Mao's criticisms of the
entire administrative apparatus: that it was bureaucratic, exces-
sively centralized; that the central power, rigid and ill informed as
it sometimes was, allowed too little initiative to businesses, cooperatives, provinces, municipalities, and districts. "We need unity," said
Mao, "but also specificity."

A Chinese direction?

The left thus became aware of the negative effects of the plan: most of the people had submitted to the changes passively, without really playing a role in them. A large part of the human and material resources of the country had remained unproductive because the state sector had not had the means to integrate them actively into the development plan. Because of this, the left now sought a different direction. The break caused by the Great Leap Forward was the work of Mao and the party leftists. This fundamental change of direction toward the mass line posed the question of the *initiative* behind such an important redirection. Had it been a party decision? Merely a coincidence? Or had it emanated from the base   was it the maturation of a policy shaped and strengthened by certain leaders in accordance with the formula "from the masses, to the masses," a formula that was widely repeated during the Great Leap Forward? It really seemed that a movement of dissatisfaction had actually come into being among the poor peasants, while the middle peasants, who often had ties with some of the party cadres, had grown stronger; in the factories, the most aware and most active workers challenged the authoritarian management. No doubt the Great Leap Forward echoed these diffuse impulses of the popular masses.

The radical change in direction of the Great Leap Forward had been defined by the Central Committee at the end of 1957, then worked out in detail and confirmed in a series of conferences between provincial cadres of the CCP and members of the Politburo. Liu Shao-qi made the broader outlines public in May 1958 (at the time of the second session of the Seventh Congress).

China had little capital. But it possessed an abundance of that "most precious of all goods"—a people that was active, free of prejudice, animated by a just political orientation, and therefore capable of accomplishing in two or three years of exceptionally hard work "a general transformation toward better conditions in almost all regions of the country," and a qualitative and quantitative leap that would allow China to overtake the most advanced countries in Western Europe. "Overtake Great Britain in fifteen years," was one slogan. "Make steel production jump to ten or twenty times that of Belgium," said a text that appeared in 1958.

This massive investment of work had to be brought about by "walking on two legs" (*rang liang tiaotui zoulu*). Although industry would retain priority, the basis for all this had to be agriculture; its progress would ensure a balance between production and consumption, and a surplus for investment. Progress in agriculture would require the massive mobilization of energies that until then had been ineffectively used. This way great works would be accomplished, increasing profits and helping to promote industrial cultures and independent subsistence in the rural areas, without handicapping the cities. The countrysides would have to supply their own needs in the way of manure, agricultural tools, and the other industrial goods they used. All this would be possible if the economic organization was decentralized, if the burden of planning was eased, and especially if creative energies were freed, eliminating the peasants' old prejudices against industrial work. "Dare to think! Dare to act!" (*gan xiang gan gan*), said Mao. The peasants had to dare to take initiatives, fight against the waste of materials and ideas, and take pride in the skill they had accumulated over the centuries. Everyone had to be both "red and expert" (politically conscious and technically able), have confidence in the bases in spite of skeptical technicians, and follow the mass line in opposition to private or individual interests. These economic options were the result of a political choice, they were based on the class struggle, in which proletarians and poor peasants opposed champions of the old or new bourgeoisie.

These strategic options were part of an attitude that affected relations with the imperialist West and the concept of war. "The main factor is man, not weapons," and China's defense did not depend on a classical privileged army but on the mobilization of all the people and the capacity of each region to defend itself, which led back to the economic options of the Great Leap Forward. Confronted with the United States's sophisticated arms, people took up the 1946 slogan again—"Imperialism is a paper tiger" whose decline had already begun; for from now on "the east wind prevails over the west wind."

Against the wishes of the technocrats, who advocated the capitalist way, the Great Leap Forward therefore put "politics in command" everywhere. This provoked opposition within the CCP that was at first discreet but which grew more pronounced during the times of difficulty. Opposing Mao and the leftist line was a group of people who advocated the Soviet model as a rational choice, people who felt that the Great Leap Forward was unrealistic; their basic support lay among people like the wealthy peasants, whose interests were threatened by this turn of events. They denounced the originators of the Great Leap Forward as lovers of the past because they had spoken of the gains made at Yanan and the Paris Commune.

The Great Leap Forward in the Rural Areas: *The People's Communes*

The "three red banners"—the basis of the whole policy instituted in 1958—were the general line (or mass line), the people's communes, and the Great Leap Forward. This recurrent symbol appeared, for example, at the top of the pillar on the monumental bridge at Nanking. Even though the bridge was built after the Great Leap Forward, it was a perfect symbol of the spirit of those years.

The spread of the people's communes

The people's communes, which had been few and isolated, spread throughout China in 1958. Between April and July, several were formed at the same time in different districts of Henan, Hebei, Jilin, Liaoning, and Shandong. Were they formed spontaneously by the base? Whether they were or not, the initiative apparently came from the local cadres. The communes tried to solve problems posed by the cooperatives, both by providing a larger setting and by building structures in the countrysides that were more and more collective: in this way they put a stop to tendencies manifested by the cooperatives at the end of 1956 and the beginning of 1957. In the summer of 1958, Mao Tsetung visited some communes (which at that time were not yet called communes) in Henan and Shandong; the public approval he expressed led to the spread of what was now called the people's commune. By the time the CCP formed the Beidaihe Resolution concerning communes (August 29, 1958), more than a third of all Chinese peasants were already living in them. The way the communes formed, then, was gradual and complex, and expressed very clearly the special dynamics in which the local echelons of the party played a determining role: certain aspects of the communes (for example, the tendency to collectivize daily life) had existed in the cooperatives since 1956).

The resolution ratified and systematized the formation of the communes. They were formed by combining cooperatives on the basis of the *xiang*, or about 2,000 households (very occasionally several *xiang*, or up to 7,000 households). Land, equipment, dwellings, and livestock were the collective property of the members of the commune: whatever had been private property before was given up without interest and without compensation.

Yet there were still privately owned goods, small livestock and poultry yards, a few trees, and personal objects. The privately owned plot of land, however, no longer existed. Work was organized on the basis of teams (*zu*), which were in turn grouped into production brigades (*shengchan dui*), roughly equivalent to the old cooperatives. Payment was made within the team and was still a function of the work that had been done; the brigade was the basic accounting echelon. The communes had to make sure that a number of their members would be assigned industrial work, and had to do their best to raise their technical, cultural, and political level far enough to reach the level of the working class; women (a maximum of 30 percent) had to take part in production work. The commune had to make this possible by providing certain services: child care, the mending of clothes, communal meals, the upkeep and improvement of the dwellings, etc. In the future, vast communes were to be formed—10,000 or even 20,000 households—by creating federations of communes at the level of the *xian* (district). In general, the tone of the Beidaihe Resolution was calm and cautious: "We must not force things, we must not hurry, we must go at half speed. Each district must first of all try it out in one place, and then proceed to more generalized development." This prudence was particularly recommended in the area of private plots of land and "cooperative shares," compensation for the peasants' initial contribution: "We must not hurry," said the text, urging the adoption of transitional forms. "Fruit trees will remain private property for the time being. . . . As for the funds of the cooperative shares, we can wait a year or two." Finally, the resolution categorically dismissed the idea of forming state farms, "because state farms do not include workers, peasants, shopkeepers, intellectuals, and soldiers."

At the end of the year, the Wuhan Resolution (December 10, 1958) specified the role of the communes and how they would be run. At that date, there were already 26,578 communes in China, accounting for "99 percent of all the peasant families of all races in China." The recommended administrative system was described as "the system of a single administration and management by echelon" —overall administration at the level of the commune, but organization of production and financial management at the level of the base echelons. At the head of the commune would be a management committee drawn from an assembly of representatives of the commune elected for two years; the whole previous organization of the *xiang* (canton) was combined in these new bodies, along with a unified party organization at the level of the commune which would play a very important role.

The Wuhan text very clearly defined the functions and the role of the commune. "The people's commune," it said, "is the basic unit of the socialist social structure of our country, combining industry, agriculture, trade, education, and military affairs; at the same time it is the basic organization of the socialist state power." Undoubtedly its greatest originality lay in its versatility: it represented the local fusion of the state's administrative and economic apparatus. It absorbed and unified the old administration as well as the management bodies of the cooperative. Its powers, therefore, extended into all domains: teaching and culture, hospitals and hygiene, the administration of public thoroughfares and the police, scientific experimentation and the army (see below). Economically, it had to bring about transformations in agriculture, undertake the building of factories, train technicians. It had its own banking organization and could make agreements with urban businesses and other communes. Yet "the planning of the people's commune must be part of the national plan and be subject to state administration. At the same time, in working out its plan, the commune must develop its own individuality and spirit of initiative to the full." The creation of the commune, then, caused two apparently contradictory movements. It reinforced the tendency to centralization through the role of the local party organs, which in economic matters took precedence over state bureaucracy of the sector: this way, middle and lower cadres of the CCP became pivotal in the movement. But also the communes provided a setting for fresh initiative and for breaking down the barriers between industrial and rural workers and between manual laborers and intellectuals. It was the beginning of the challenge to the state bureaucracy: although the Twelve Year Plan had fixed the general norms for agriculture, each local echelon had the power to contest them and to obtain allowances for local conditions. A credit of one billion *yuan* was allocated to the development of the communes in 1958; but each locality, each collective had to provide the funds it needed for mechanization, unlike the Soviet collectives. So as to encourage the accumulation of the necessary capital, the agricultural tax was reduced from 15 to 10 percent of production. Although the communes did not have "all the power," at least they had important opportunities to act on their own initiative.

Was communism imminent?

The Beidaihe Resolution had shown great concern for practice: yet it was not always applied as prudently and realistically as had been anticipated.

During 1958 enthusiastic reports came from all the provinces. More and more great works, some of them begun at the end of 1957, were being carried out, including embankments, retimbering, and irrigation works. For example, the construction of three large reservoirs and about thirty small ones in the Linxian district (Henan) mobilized 40,000 workers from fifteen communes. Small industrial enterprises were springing up all over, sometimes with whatever means were at hand, always with a great deal of ingenuity, determination, and patience, applying the slogan: to produce with "quantity, rapidity, quality, and economy." Intended to provide agricultural needs, to furnish consumer goods to the inhabitants of the communes, and finally to produce an excess that could be sold commercially, their aim was also to create a "new economic man," who was both peasant and worker (and also, as we shall see, soldier). Their goal was to bring about a fundamental change in economic thinking, to organize the work in the same way industry was organized—in short, to enlarge the working class. "With the establishment of industry in the communes," wrote the *Hongqi* on December 1, 1958, "it is easier for the communes to model their agricultural production on production in a factory." The initial results were encouraging: Henan employed 80,000 people in the communal workshops and factories in September 1958, and Hebei 1.3 million in August. The *Xinhua* agency stated on June 22, 1958, that "all the provinces and autonomous regions except Tibet can produce tractors now." Relations were established with the factories in the cities in order to ensure the training of new workers. Special emphasis was placed on mineral prospecting and steel production: beginning in the middle of October, 600,000 small blast furnaces were put into operation, sometimes using traditional methods, and this occupied ninety million people.

This triumphant news, as well as the excellent harvest of 1958, along with certain difficulties which may have caused some of the local cadres to rush ahead, led to a radicalization of the movement in the summer of 1958 in spite of the caution advised by the central bodies of the party. In this leftist atmosphere, people began saying that the differences between the cities and the rural areas were disappearing, and that communism was at hand: in the people's communes, the buds of a communist society were beginning to emerge. People were becoming more and more versatile (in September, Liu Shao-qi insisted that the cadres had to participate in manual labor), and it was now possible to begin applying the principle of "to each according to his needs." Now there were brigades practicing the system of "half distribution, half salary"; in October, Shanghai workers recalled that in the Red Army and among the cadres at Yanan there was no question of salaries. Individualism was eliminated; during these months, daily life was collectivized, which made it easier to mobilize all the workers (particularly the women), and also clearly threatened the family structure, at least in practice. Collective kitchens were built which in many cases could accommodate several hundred people: for example, in the commune of Panyu, in Guangdong, a commune that numbered 276,358 members, there were 738 dining rooms; on the average, 375 people ate together. Various services (maintenance, cleaning, mending) greatly lightened the burden of domestic duties. Late marriages were encouraged, and "romantic relations" were frowned upon. Most important was to strike out the spirit of individualism at its roots, by socializing primary education as much as possible, because "if a child is given a communist education at school and a noncommunist education at home, the results are bad. . . . The weaknesses of education at home from this point of view are more and more obvious" (*Renmin Ribao*, October 4, 1958). Whenever they had the means to do it, the communes tried to set up live-in nurseries. The Chinese women emerged from the ancient seclusion of the home and entered into production in large numbers. But the vision of communism looming so close drove the cadres to demand (and perform) so much work that everyone was at the limit of his strength: examples of enthusiastic workers remaining on duty twenty-four or forty-eight hours at a time were widely publicized; in November and December, party directives called for moderation, for example in the employment of pregnant women. These directives were evidence of how great an effort was being made, but also of the excesses certain cadres were committing and the tensions growing within the communes.

Every citizen is a soldier

Finally, in addition to the various economic tasks assigned to the members of the communes, there were also military duties, to the extent that the commune, as a complete unit, also had military authority—and duties.

The military role of the commune was related to the new conception of the way the PLA functioned, a conception borrowed from Yanan, and in a more general way the Chinese Communist Party's attitude toward its international relations.

The Great Leap Forward intensified a struggle that had in fact begun in 1956 within and around the PLA. It accelerated the questioning of the 1954–1955 options and the "classical" army which resulted from them. Starting in 1956, criticism of this technocratic military model became widespread in the party as well as in the army itself. This criticism had the support of a number of soldiers and veterans among the cadres, but was probably unwelcome to many new officers who had graduated from recently founded military schools and to Peng De-huai himself; it had led to the revival of the mass line in the army through the "three democracies" (political, economic, and financial), the revival of soldiers' committees, participation in production work, and the choosing of cadres from the ranks.

The Great Leap Forward gave this process a new impetus. In August 1958, the *Renmin Ribao* denounced "the purely military views, the dujunism" (that is, the tendency of warlords to reappear) "and the dogmatism [which] have reappeared among a part of the personnel." The style of command was clearly being challenged. The effort to bring the army closer to the people involved suppressing certain material privileges that the soldiers enjoyed; participation in production work had to be increased, particularly during this phase of intense effort when there was great need of manpower. Thus, the army built eighty-two factories in 1958 and 1959, completed more than 20,000 hydraulic works of various sizes during 1959, and helped carry out agricultural projects and train peasants to be technicians. There continued to be internal changes in the People's Liberation Army: at the beginning of 1959, 150,000 officers, including seventy generals, had served in the rank and file for a time.

From a strategic point of view, the role of the army was to work alongside the people's forces, who would provide local defense and guerrilla activity in cases of aggression. In this sense, the changes in the army were complemented by the appearance of the militia in most of the communes.

The militia had actually existed for a long time: the *minbing* had been organized by the CCP during the war against Japan, and according to John Gittings 8 to 10 percent of the population belonged to them in 1945. After 1949 they helped keep the peace and provided one of the bases for military service; although the draft which was established in 1954 had nothing to do with the militia, later the militia and the reserve were combined: at the end of 1957, membership in the two together reached thirty million people. In 1958, the party started a movement to militarize the people, using slogans like "Every citizen is a soldier," first heard in August. Men and women between the ages of 16 and 30 were urged to participate actively; men and women between the ages of 30 and 50 formed a reserve corps. The militia, placed under the command of the authorities of the commune assisted by the army, was therefore clearly being managed by the party. In January 1959 it had 220 million members; 15 percent of them had undergone real training which varied greatly from one commune to another, no doubt reflecting some uncertainty on the part of the cadres as to how to apply the directives.

More generally, the production effort and the organization of work were conceived according to military schemes and references; slogans tended to compare the Great Leap Forward to a form of revolutionary war.[1] "Soldiers of the revolution," said a text published in 1958, giving as an example Korean War veterans struggling with the problems of setting up a small factory, "do not abandon the battlefield before the victory has been won. We must not stop fighting on the industrial front."

Transforming Urban Work

The people's communes movement was the most visible contribution of the Great Leap Forward. But the theories on which it was based implied an overall decentralization: they posed the question of power and competence in every enterprise, including the city factories, even the large ones. At the same time, because the com-

[1] See document 1 at the end of the chapter.

mune was conceived to be a model for all of China, it implied the creation of people's communes in the cities. There was an effort to create uniform conditions of life and work in cities and rural areas, and to draw all categories of urban workers into the on-going struggle.

The question of power in industry

This period marked the beginning of a general movement toward decentralization in industry. In 1958 enterprises run by central ministries were transferred to local authorities—provinces, autonomous regions, and special municipalities. Between 1957 and 1959 the percentage of enterprises under central control fell from 46 to 26 percent, while the percentage of enterprises under local control rose from 54 to 74 percent.

This change, which took into account the size and weakness of the railway system, aimed at giving a certain amount of self-sufficiency to the provinces and regions, particularly those that were notoriously underdeveloped industrially—Guangdong, Guangxi, and Sichuan, for example. With this end in mind, local authorities would be able to retain 20 percent of the profits realized by these transferred enterprises for investment purposes; the same was true of the revenue from a number of local taxes (on stamps, landed property, interest, etc.) For this reason, the party supported the small and middle-sized businesses, which were easier to organize and in which the workers' capacity for invention could have more free play. Yet the state did not stop building large units: 1,200 projects of this sort were completed in 1958, representing a capital of more than 17 billion *yuan*. Here as in rural industrialization, the emphasis was placed on steel, in the hopes—starting in August— of waging a war to win back Taiwan. This two-headed ax—large *and* small industries, modern technology *and* the use of already existing skills—was quite in keeping with the general spirit of Mao's *Ten Major Relationships* mentioned above.

Both small and large companies therefore gained a certain amount of independence from the central power. They could hire and fire workers on their own authority (except of course administrators and technicians) with the agreement of local party officials. They fixed part of their norms; in fact, the state had abandoned the five-year system and worked out plans for one year only, defining no more than four objectives (instead of the previous twelve): production, the number of workers, the overall figure for salaries, and the rate of profit; and as with agriculture, these objectives could be discussed.

Within the companies, the party increased its authority with regard to "pure" administrators or technocrats and urged the workers to participate directly in the management of the factory or workshop and to be inventive. Here too, the slogan was "Dare to think, dare to act." During 1958, the debate taking place in all the companies led to the spread of the system of "responsibility of the director under the administration of the party committee," and of the "two-one-three." This system involved a party committee elected by the members working in a company after consultation with the other workers. The committees varied in size but were not very large (for example, in a company employing 6,000 workers, the committee might consist of fifteen members); this committee took action in all major areas (planning, internal regulations, the appointment of cadres, payments, etc.). The director (assisted by management cadres) was appointed by provincial or ministerial authorities and was responsible to this party committee: he therefore had less initiative, as did the unions, apparently. The party also induced workers everywhere to bring about the "two participations" (the participation of cadres in manual labor and of workers in management), "one reform" (the reform of incompatible rules), and the "triple union" (workers-technicians-cadres) in overseeing, innovation, and reform. In practice, accounting and management duties were often transferred to work teams: these teams would discuss the objectives, see that they were accomplished, and to do this would elect officers from among their membership; they had the power of decision over the cadres. The latter were obliged to do varying amounts of manual labor.

Conversely, during this period manual laborers took part in conception and innovation to a certain extent. This was part of the general questioning of the educational system begun during the Great Leap Forward. Under Mao Tsetung's own impetus it had set out to break the monopoly of the schools and universities and the privileges of the degree-holding intellectuals. In a speech in January 1958, Mao Tsetung said with refreshing directness: "If the skin no longer exists, where will the hair be implanted? I was comparing the intellectuals to the hair which must be implanted in the skin of the working class, otherwise they will become 'gentlemen thieves.' " No intellectual could refuse manual labor. For reasons that were both political and economic, scholarly institutions also had to become production units. In a draft resolution, "Sixty Points on Work Methods" (February 1958), Mao wrote:

> All secondary technical schools and schools for technicians should, if possible, experiment in setting up workshops and farms to attain complete or partial self-sufficiency by engaging in production. Students should do part-time study and part-time work. Under favorable conditions, these schools can take on more students but should not at the same time cost the country more money . . . . The middle and primary schools of a village should sign contracts with local cooperatives to take part in agricultural and subsidiary production. Rural students should make use of their summer vacation, other holidays, and leisure time to work in their own village.

Conversely, it was important to recognize the workers' and peasants' intellectual capacities in all areas, from technical invention to poetry: if, according to Mao, the poetry of the "professionals" was uninteresting ("I myself would not read it unless I was given a hundred dollars"), "perhaps we will discover millions and millions of people's poems . . . and these poems will be easier to read than the poems of Du Fu and Li Bo" (March 1958).[2]

During 1958 and 1959, two million cadres, nearly three million students from secondary schools and universities, and one million intellectuals (including teachers) worked on construction sites or in the fields. Schools were established that combined work and study. Conversely, between the end of 1957 and the end of 1958, 23,500 half-time "universities" (with classes at nonworking hours) produced an army of engineers and technicians who had risen from the base. The Great Leap Forward was marked by a wave of inventing, from tinkering that was sometimes inspired by genius[3] to processes for increasing the profits of heavy industry. For example, a steel mill in Daye, in central China, invented a process by which the length of casting could be reduced by one hour while productivity was increased by 7.6 percent. A steel mill in Wuhan perfected a method by which 30,000 yuan per furnace of more than 1,000 cubic meters could be saved each year, while consumption of coke was reduced by 12 kilograms per ton of reduced metal. On a much more

[2] See document 2.
[3] See document 3.

modest scale, in thousands of workshops in cities and rural areas, innumerable practical gadgets were invented, not only in response to the imperative of production, but also out of a desire to improve working conditions.

According to the party, the spirit in which these different efforts were made necessarily represented a high level of political consciousness—it had nothing to do with material payment. The examples that were published emphasized self-denial in one's participation in the building of socialism, both as far as material contribution went (workers were urged to contribute their savings or their tools in trust or as loans to help create or develop businesses) and in the length of the working hours. There were debates in the factories about questions of payment and material stimuli. The latter, which were disputed, did not disappear completely. But two tendencies emerged: for one thing, in 1958 and 1959 bonuses were often allocated on a collective basis; and for another, ideological stimuli (stories of heroic workers) were encouraged. The scale of salaries was reduced somewhat.

People's communes in the cities

People's communes began to be established in the cities in the summer of 1958. They were supposed to be integrated units combining the functions of industry, agriculture, and commerce along the same lines as in the country. As it turned out, they conflicted with certain aspects of urban life and economy: they were rarely able to complement agriculture (this would have required a suburban zone), and, what was worse, many townspeople lived far away from where they worked. The only places the communes could be successful were near central economic poles—industrial or mining enterprises, state institutions (schools or hospitals), or more rarely a residential neighborhood—and between the summer of 1958 and the end of 1958 a number of them were formed in the larger urban centers. In residential neighborhoods, efforts were made to create small workshops in which housewives with no work outside their homes would be given an opportunity to contribute their ideas. But not much progress was made in producing uniformity in the cities on the model of the rural communes; besides, the project was interrupted at the end of 1958, and when it was resumed its nature was quite different (see below). In their first version, these "industrial zones which we are trying to make rural" (as Tsien Tche-hao put it) probably encouraged some of the recent immigrants from rural areas to return home—these were unemployed and dependent people—even whole families of peasants, whom one directive from 1957 tried to stop from blindly immigrating. However, these attempts were far from successful: the cities continued to attract people from rural areas.

Disillusionment and Readjustment: *The Struggle over the Great Leap Forward and the Swing Back to the Right: 1959–1962*

It is difficult to throw any light on the years 1959–1962. This was a period of apparently contradictory decisions, and coming as it did after the triumphs of 1958 it was marked by difficulties, defeats, and sometimes defeatism. What became particularly clear at this time was how great a gulf separated the two lines, as their positions and their adherents became better known. On the one hand, what emerged during these years was that in spite of the apparently unanimous decisions made by the state apparatus and by the party, the leftist line—whose positions were represented by the Great Leap Forward—temporarily had the support of the majority, but that this support was precarious and limited, as was evident as soon as the first difficulties arose. The influence and the vitality of the right—at the very moments when it was paying lip service to the Maoists (as Liu Shao-qi did)—became obvious in 1959, when the forecasts of the preceding year turned out to be overly optimistic: scarcity threatened and then became an actuality. The right was strong enough to attack Mao Tsetung personally. If this was true, when Mao relinquished the presidency of the republic to Liu (in December 1958), was he actually being ousted from office, or was this a deliberate transfer of activity away from the state apparatus? Yet it seems that this deep divergence was not simply a contradiction within the bureaucracy of the state and the party. The answer given by the different social categories in China revealed—and this was never merely a mechanical choice—that many cadres, technicians, intellectuals, and more important, a large number of middle peasants sided with the opponents of the Great Leap Forward (along with part of the working class, no doubt). Most poor peasants, however, in spite of their reluctance to go along with the very radical aspects of the developments that took place in the fall of 1958, seemed to see immediate advantages in the Great Leap Forward.

The disappointments that began in 1959 did not cause an official repudiation of the Great Leap Forward; its line was never formally abandoned. But these four difficult years were marked by more and more extensive measures of readjustment. These measures were complicated: some (starting in 1958) reflected the left's effort to correct leftist mistakes. Others—and there were more and more of them—represented successes for the right. The swing back to the right was evident not so much in the directives issued as in actual practice—practice that did not change the letter of the 1958 decisions but made them to some degree meaningless.

1959–1960: economic disappointments and growing tensions

The year 1958 was exceptionally good agriculturally—the autumn harvest in particular attained record proportions, at least according to the figures supplied to the state bodies. In fact, as it later turned out, these figures, which served as the basis for the grandiose forecasts of 1959, were not accurate. As Zhou En-lai said to Han Suyin, "The leaders were not given the correct figures": premature estimates were made, people were influenced by the ideological situation, and sometimes there were no instruments with which to take measurements. At the beginning of 1959 it became clear both that there had been extreme exaggerations and that production would fall short of what was needed. For example, in 1957 grain production rose to 170 million tons; an early estimate for 1958 was 375 million tons, a figure that had to be corrected down to 270 million. In January 1959 there were food shortages. Although it emphasized the exceptional successes of 1958, Zhou En-lai's "Report on Government Works" (presented to the National Assembly on April 18, 1959) contained a clear warning: it especially insisted on the need to raise productivity. "We are convinced," he said, "that if everyone applies himself seriously . . . our plan for the national economy for 1959 *can certainly be realized* and even surpassed." In fact, the harvest in 1959, which took place during disastrous weather conditions, was worse than mediocre: the food shortage was so bad that the peasants had to be allowed to suspend their sales to the state. The situation did not improve in 1960. Quite the contrary: in part of the country there was an unusually bad drought, undoing the peasants' unprecedentedly hard labor, while in the South there were catastrophic floods. Having affected only the cities the year before, scarcity (though probably not famine) was now widespread. China had to buy foreign grain. The country did not begin to recover and return to normal until 1961 and not fully until 1962—but the goal for grain production that year was only 250 million tons.

Industrial production suffered the same fate, though after a certain time lag. It made definite progress in 1959 and 1960, continuing to extend westward and southward as it had begun to do during the first Five Year Plan. But the abandonment of small-profit production caused a slack that was not overcome until 1963 and 1964 (see table below). The poor quality of a number of products was actually equivalent to outright waste. This was particularly the case for rural metallurgy products: in February 1959 it became necessary to close down blast furnaces in the country. What was more, there was wear and tear on machinery and transport equipment everywhere.

INDUSTRIAL PRODUCTION	1957	1958	1959	1960	1961	1962	1963	1964
Coal (millions of tons)	131	230	290	270	180	180	190	200
Crude oil (id.)	1.5	2.3	3.7	4.5	4.5	5.3	5.9	7.0
Steel (id.)	5.4	8.0	10.0	13.0	8.0	8.0	9.0	10.0
Chemical fertilizer (id.)	0.8	1.4	2.0	2.5	1.4	2.1	3.0	3.6
Cotton cloth (billions of m.)	5.0	5.7	7.5	6.0	3.0	3.0	3.5	4.0

In view of the hopes of 1958, how can this enormous catastrophe be explained? It was undoubtedly not only caused by the poor weather or by purely economic factors; in the last analysis, the disputed facts were essentially political. Of course, technical elements played a part in the situation—for example, the statistics and planning services quickly became disorganized and helpless in the face of all the problems that existed. External factors, too, played a considerable part: the break with the Soviet Union, for example, made things very difficult for China.

The Sino-Soviet crisis

In the summer of 1960 the Soviet Union announced that it was withdrawing its technicians (nearly 1,400 according to the Chinese, several thousand according to the Soviets) and ending its assistance. The USSR had originally agreed that in the course of the first three five-year plans it would provide China with 300 industrial installations and with technical training. Only 154 installations had been completed when it withdrew. This withdrawal was actually part of the ever-intensifying crisis that was dividing the two countries in spite of appearances to the contrary. The Chinese were disillusioned, and denounced the Soviets as revisionists; the Soviets were unfavorably critical of the Great Leap Forward and the people's communes; and all this was aggravated by serious international disputes during these years. Twice in 1958 the Soviet Union failed to back China: the first time was in August, during the Taiwan Straits affair, and the second was in the fall, during the conflict with India after the Tibetan rebellion. The CCP saw this as proof of the Soviet Union's growing compromise with American imperialism, confirmed for them by the Soviets' attitude in the Middle East in 1959 and, especially, in the middle of the year, by the meeting between Khrushchev and Eisenhower at Camp David. From then on there was no more than a fragile facade of an alliance (even less after the withdrawal of the Soviet experts). This facade was still maintained in November 1960 at the congress of eighty-one Communist and workers' parties. In autumn 1961, at the 22nd Congress of the CPSU, the conflict became open. It grew more intense the following spring and was marked by incidents on the border of the Ili.

Yet the sudden move on the part of the Soviets in the summer of 1960 was a source of considerable difficulty for China. "The steel mill at Wuhan closed down," wrote Han Suyin; "Anshan was 80 percent paralyzed. Until 1966 many factory buildings remained empty." This disorganization did not cancel the financial burden: in 1960 China's debt to the USSR rose to 1.5 billion dollars—a debt which China, in spite of its difficulties, managed to repay on time in 1964. The lesson that the CCP learned from this episode was the need to be independent at any price; China had to be "self-reliant" (*zili gengsheng*) and "not be afraid of ghosts."[4]

---

[4] See document 4.

Contradictions in the Great Leap Forward

Whatever its value in the long run, at least the Great Leap Forward was full of idealism. Starting in July 1959, Mao criticized overestimates in all areas, the party's bad judgment of people's capacities, and inexperience. These serious defects had led to a leftist direction; they had sometimes ended in an impasse, making a temporary retreat unavoidable.

Tensions arose in the people's communes, sometimes because a number of the peasants resisted sudden collectivization, and because many cadres came from the cities without any experience of rural life. Their task was made no easier by the fact that directives were not very precise. For example, should family savings be contributed to the collective, and even furniture and kitchen utensils? Everyone decided these matters in different ways. Sometimes savings were demanded as an "additive investment," which was actually a form of confiscation, a practice that was condemned in December 1958 but not followed by restitution. The same thing happened to poultry yards and family pigs.

In the leftist atmosphere of autumn 1958, the transition to communism seemed very imminent (within perhaps three or four years) because of the communes; therefore, people felt, the pace had to be accelerated. Some of the communes gradually abandoned the system of wage earning and introduced the free distribution of food, health products, clothes, haircuts, etc. But this proved to be expensive and wasteful. Despite the appeals of the CCP, poor distribution and overly long work hours caused serious imbalances. Some brigades employed up to 80 percent of the peasants in nonagricultural duties to the detriment of food production, which was left up to the women. Other mistakes included the harmful extension of industrial crops and the total disappearance of the family plot (which had provided a large proportion of the family's food), while collective production of fruits, vegetables, and meat was still not very large. People sometimes worked to the point of exhaustion (in December 1958 the party recommended that everyone get eight hours of sleep). And not all of the large works undertaken were justified: for example, wells were sunk in regions where there was no water table, because there had not been enough money to finance preliminary studies of the land. Harmful land clearing practices led to water runoff and soil erosion. In addition, during the Great Leap

Forward certain industrial crops, like cotton, had done spectacularly well, but not everywhere, mainly because of a lack of fertilizer. The small communal industries did not produce enough fertilizer and there was less natural manure because there were fewer privately owned pigs. Certain orders did not take into account what the peasants knew from first-hand experience: for example, birds were exterminated on a large scale in 1959 because they devoured seeds, and this left the land defenseless against insects.

Certain setbacks reflected class divisions in the peasants' attitude. The passive resistance of many of the middle peasants turned into aggression. They used up their reserves (food, clothing, household equipment, watches) rather than turn them in. They hid grain, sometimes in collusion with cadres or poor peasants (*Hongqi*, November 1958). They killed and ate their pigs. These cases of "bourgeois mentality, individualism, and pessimism" (*Hongqi*) amounted to an insidious form of sabotage; their opposition was also expressed by demoralizing criticisms and the denunciation of public distribution as an encouragement to laziness. There were instances of cadres being murdered. On the other hand, the Great Leap Forward was supported by most of the poor and middle-poor peasants: they could only gain from it. The measures enacted in 1956–1957 had lowered their income and benefited the well-to-do peasants; the latter, who had more active workers in their families and possessed tools, seeds, and animals, took advantage of the extension of the free market (until August 1957) and of the extension of private plots (10 percent of the arable land per person). But the poor peasants, burdened with children and lacking capital and reserves, could only hope for more and more complete collectivization; an investigation carried out in 1956 in Hunan showed serious food shortages among some of them. The same divisions intensified debate over wage earning, which the well-to-do peasants refused to give up.

In other cases, resistance was more ideological. The Great Leap Forward launched a massive attack against superstition, prejudice, and fatalism. In order to make cultivation easier, the graves that were still scattered through the countryside were leveled, and this was on the whole accepted fairly calmly. But many men, even among the poor peasants, were very much against the entry of large numbers of women into production and the abandonment of their traditional domestic duties (even though in many villages women had happily thrown their pots through the window as a symbolic gesture when the creation of communal dining rooms was announced).

The cadres were very unsure of how to deal with all these problems. In 1959 they were reproached for being at once overly equalitarian and overly authoritarian. Certain city cadres, jealous of their privileged positions, opposed the promotion of workers to positions as cadres and technicians. The insidious resistance of the intellectuals to the Great Leap Forward and to reliance on the workers' empirical knowledge became open and almost violent in 1961–1962.

The Tibetan affair

Of all the national minorities, Tibet was the only large region not yet promoted to the status of an autonomous region, a process which had begun with other national minorities during the first Five Year Plan. The Chinese army had gone into this remote, independent zone in 1955 and established a Committee to Prepare for Autonomy, gradually training social, cultural, and poltical cadres among the natives. But the theocratic institutions of Lhassa and the feudal regime were both still functioning. Discreet though it was, China's direct control of Tibet caused a certain amount of uneasiness among the Tibetans, and the aristocracy, anxious about its privileges, took advantage of this with the support of India. In March 1959, the religious and civilian feudal landowners started an armed revolt which was quickly crushed; the Dalai Lama fled to India. After his departure, reform was accelerated, concentrating on serfdom, forced labor, and high land rents.

1959–1960: uncertainties

The debate within the party became more intense during these difficult years. The crisis came out into the open in August 1959 at Lushan, during the Eighth Plenum of the Central Committee. Peng De-huai, minister of defense and an open adversary of the Great Leap Forward because of the technical imperatives of the army and the economy, was replaced by Lin Biao, and his supporters were removed from the leadership. The leftist line was reaffirmed, particularly where diplomacy and the army were concerned, but consolidation of gains and short-term adjustments were stressed. Mao gave a long self-criticism before the plenum.[5]

There were more and more calls for moderation starting in autumn 1959. The economy was more important than utopian ambitions. People were once again encouraged to raise their own pigs as a source of fertilizer. Most systems for distributing goods were abandoned, but the communal kitchens were retained and split up for economic reasons. Work norms were lowered. Communes everywhere were reduced in size, which resulted in tripling their number. The fact that they were smaller made it easier for rural cadres, who were more familiar with management in rural areas, to be promoted. The policy of "walking on two legs" was maintained, but the less profitable units were abandoned. Others continued to function. In 1960 the Daqing oilfield was opened and promised to have an important political future. Also in 1960, Mao drew up the "Anshan Iron and Steel Charter" which emphasized that the workers' initiative, even in very large units, was more important than technology-oriented and centralized management, which existed at Magnitogorsk, for example.

The urban communes were abandoned as political structures. But they were encouraged to spread as settings within which housewives could develop their own ideas, to serve as small neighborhood workshops and provide collective services. In the summer of 1960 they contained 79 percent of the urban population, according to Li Fu-chun.

1961–1962: general readjustment

In 1960 natural calamities combined with the effects of the Sino-Soviet break and the difficulties of the Great Leap Forward to cause a very serious economic crisis. A readjustment became indispensable, and in 1961 this firmly fixed the antagonistic positions of the left and right. The latter felt it was essential to move on to a different policy. The left had to resign itself to retreating, without giving up the future completely (which was the meaning of the Anshan Charter).

The moderate intellectual circles came to the fore again in 1961,

[5] See document 5.

supported by factions hostile to the Great Leap Forward. The left was not strong enough to prevent a return to cultural liberalism (the "Small Hundred Flowers"). Numerous rightists from 1957 were rehabilitated and reinstated; they urged the abandonment of the scholastic innovations of the Great Leap Forward in order to relieve the intellectuals of manual labor and return to traditional, elitist methods of teaching and hiring teachers. They were scornful of efforts to help workers acquire technical knowledge and include them in cultural production. They preferred the academic "meetings of the immortals" of the vice-mayor of Peking, Wu Han. They produced a very classical, stylized literature appreciated only by the initiates; it caricatured and attacked the Great Leap Forward and even Mao: there were poems with subtle allusions, stylized epigrams in the newspapers (the "evening talks at Yanshan"), and plays containing very clear historical symbolism. Wu Han's play *The Dismissal of Hai Rui*, performed in Peking in February 1961, was an undisguised argument in favor of rehabilitating Peng De-huai, victim of "imperial arbitrariness"; this situation was represented by the case of a functionary in the Ming dynasty removed from office despite his honesty.

The "readjustment" (*tiaozheng*) began to take shape. The Ninth Plenum in January 1961 and the second Lushan conference in the summer gave the official sanction for the rural areas to revert to their former situation. Peasants who felt they had been wronged were encouraged to bring charges against the cadres, which had the effect of challenging collectivization itself. Through the system of *san zi yi bao* (three liberties and one guarantee), the free private plot of land was reintroduced and soon exceeded the anticipated 5 percent of arable land. The free market came into existence again. Collective support was withdrawn from small enterprises, which were left free to the detriment of the less profitable among them. Profit norms were guaranteed on a family basis, which meant that women who had been mobilized by the Great Leap Forward had to return to their homes. The militia resumed its role as an auxiliary force. For profit motives, work teams in the factories lost their initiative to middle cadres and specialists. Hourly salaries and piece-work were reintroduced in 1961.

The crisis in the party no doubt culminated at the beginning of 1962, even though the economic situation had improved again. The left had not been able to interfere with the rightist faction, openly led by Liu Shao-qi, who in January 1962 attacked the Great Leap Forward in front of 7,000 cadres (at the enlarged conference of the Central Committee), and in February before the state conference. He proposed measures to reduce the scope of agriculture and industry. The Program of Readjustment in Ten Points, worked out by Zhou En-lai in April, maintained the "general line" of 1958, but specifically organized the retreat from the overambitious goals of the Great Leap. He defined the order of priorities for planning and the balance of sectors: agriculture, then light industry, then heavy industry. He urged that the peasants who had come to the city during the Great Leap Forward be sent back to their villages; he demanded that "the amount of construction at the base must be limited."

The gains and the future of the Great Leap Forward

Was the improvement in the economic situation in 1962 mainly the result of the readjustment, the partial return to the policy of before 1958? To believe this would perhaps be to misunderstand the true implication of this movement backward. The most important gains made during the Great Leap Forward had not been lost by 1962, and they made economic recovery easier. Nineteen fifty-eight had really been the beginning of a fundamental turning point, and in the context of this change the break between the Soviet Union and China took on its true meaning.

Arousing exceptional collective enthusiasm, the Great Leap Forward was a policy without precedent in any socialist country. It was an "attempt," as E. Collotti-Pischel wrote, "to break the grip of destitution and death," and in some sense "a desperate struggle," and it endeavored to give a decisive answer to the problems of backwardness in all areas. Contributing to the definition of revisionism, its practice led to a challenging of the party itself. Its ability to confront things was evident, but so were its faults, its distance from the masses, and its internal contradictions. In the end, the middle and lower cadres had to bear the whole burden of the mistakes of 1958, in spite of Mao Tsetung's spectacular self-criticism (an exemplary, if isolated, case). For many, it resulted in passivity and a wait-and-see attitude. But most of the criticisms had come from the right: it was not until 1966 that a leftist criticism was expressed by the masses.

ADDITIONAL BIBLIOGRAPHY

Rewi Alley, *China's Hinterland in the Leap Forward* (Peking, 1961).

J. Baby, *La grande controverse sino-soviétique* (Paris, 1966).

Mario Bettati, *Le conflit sino-soviétique* (Paris, 1971), 2 vols.

C. S. Chen and C. P. Ridley, *Rural People's Communes in Lien-chiang* (Stanford, 1969).

David Crook and Isabel Crook, *The First Years of the Yang Yi Commune* (London, 1966).

Kenneth Walker, *Planning in Chinese Agriculture: Socialisation and the Private Sector, 1956–1962* (London, 1962).

DOCUMENTS

1. MILITARY AND HEROIC LANGUAGE OF THE GREAT LEAP FORWARD

Source: T. A. Hsia, *Metaphor, Myth, Ritual and the People's Commune* (Berkeley, Calif., Center for Chinese Studies, 1961), p. 1–2, 16–17.

> *Si-hua* (four transfigurations or "-izations": organization militarized, work martialized, life collectivized, and management democratized);
> Largely for production purpose, warlike discipline and spirit invoked to transform individuals into collective bodies, where "democratic centralism" exercises strict control from above.
>
> *Zhan-tou* (to fight a battle);
> To exert for production.
>
> *Zhan-shi* (a fighter);
> A production worker.
>
> *Zhan-xian* (a battle-line);
> Areas where effort at mass-production is made.
>
> *Da-zhun* (a large army);
> A large body of persons drafted and organized to serve a definite function in socialist revolution and reconstruction.
>
> *Dui-tian xuan-zhan* (to declare war against heaven);
> To overcome natural handicaps in production.
>
> *Zhang-wo di-qing* (to get hold of information about the enemy);
> To understand, through chemical analysis or otherwise, the difficulty faced in production.

Jin-qun (to stage a march);
To advance toward a certain goal.

Tu-ji (to storm attack);
Concentrated effort in a production project.

Da zhan-yi (a major battle);
A production project that requires thousands of laborers and several
months to complete.

Xiao-xing yun-dong-zhan (mobile warfare on a small scale);
Subsidiary work which can be done in spare time and requires only a
fraction of the body of laborers engaged in a major project.

Qie-mi-zhan (a battle of annihilation);
A production project which, because of careful planning and the employment of an overwhelming number of laborers, is assured of complete success.

Dan-jiang pi-ma (to go to battle with a single spear on a single horse);
An example of individual heroism.

Qian-jun wan-ma (great host of mounted and foot soldiers);
A great number of people engaged in production.

Bao-gang (to defend or protect the steel);
To improve transportation and supply of raw materials, fuel, and power
so that work in the steel plants may not be retarded.

Gua-shuai (to wear the commander-in-chief's seal);
To take command; or to enjoy priority in production.

2. WORKER POETS OF THE GREAT LEAP FORWARD

Source: *Poètes du peuple chinois*, an anthology edited by Michelle Loi
(Paris, P.-J. Oswald, 1969), pp. 16, 18–19.

Chimneys

> High, high by the white clouds
> They spout their black smoke.
> What tree will ever be as tall,
> What wild bamboo could ever have their charm?
> They are arms of iron
> Pointing to Heaven's watchword;
> They are enormous brushes
> Painting the homeland's beautiful spring.

The Other Side of the World

Standing at the bottom of the well,
I think of my brothers on the other side.
We dig for happiness,
But they dig for their misery.
No! They are digging the grave of Wall Street!
In America the wells are horrible jails!
Sweat and blood dampen the ditches.
They are burying someone in the alley
At the mouth of the well, and the cries of women
Are the only witness.
The voice of menace growls,
sobs rise from the alleys,
How many mothers no longer have children,
How many children are without fathers?
Blood flows in the gutters,
Wagons cart off the dead felled by injustice.
. . . No, it is not a well they are digging,
It is a blood debt, it is hate.

When the well has gone on and on,
It will catch fire more quickly.
In the bowels of the earth
A terrible wind will howl
As bombs burst wildly
Like the fire of the stars!

3. Using the inspiration of the old legends to face the enemies
and dangers threatening China

Source: *Do Not Be Afraid of Ghosts*, a collection of ancient stories (Peking,
Academy of Sciences, 1961), preface.

The ghosts and spirits of the legends and stories do not exist, but there
are many phenomena that resemble them. On a greater scale, here are a few
examples: international imperialism and its stooges in various countries,
contemporary revisionism incarnated by Tito's clique in Yugoslavia,* natural
cataclysms, certain poorly reeducated elements from the landowner class
and bourgeoisie who have seized leadership positions in some base organizations and have made attempts at restoration. Even though of lesser importance, the difficulties and failures one meets with in daily life sometimes
recall phantasmagoric phenomena.
    . . . In the story *How Zhen Bengnian Revived a Hanged Woman by Blow-
ing on Her* taken from the collection *What Confucius Did Not Say*, the hero,
who brought the hanged woman back to life by blowing on her, was acting
in a very ominous situation. The hanged woman, stiff and immobile, blew a
breath from her twisted mouth on the living man that was so cold that it

---

* At this time (1961) Soviet revisionism had still not been directly attacked.

went through him to the bone, made his teeth chatter, set his hair on end, and almost put out the blue flame in his lantern. But what happened next is significant. Because the ghost could breathe, Zhen said to himself, why can't I do the same? And then he filled his lungs and blew such a powerful breath that the ghost finally dissolved like a wisp of smoke.

. . . Doesn't this tell us of the right attitude we should have when we are faced with reactionary forces both within and without, with natural and artificial disasters, with all the things we see that do not correspond to reality?

. . . This little collection includes many other stories and tales. What they all have in common is that they illustrate the following truth: ghosts are not frightening. They can be defeated and vanquished by man. But if he is facing a particular monster, as in the case of a concrete struggle, the man must be prudent and clever to achieve the final victory. There is a profound meaning in this. Even though ghosts do not exist, their evil nature, which was recognized long ago by legend and superstition, nevertheless made our ancient authors resolve to base their stories on the accumulated experience of men in their real life and in their struggle against all that is wicked.

4. Mao's self-criticism regarding the Great Leap Forward

Source: Stuart Schram, *Chairman Mao Talks to the People* (New York, Pantheon, 1975), pp. 142–145.

. . . Before August of last year my main energies were concentrated on revolution. I am a complete outsider when it comes to economic construction, and I understand nothing about industrial planning. At the West Tower I said: "Don't write about [my] wise leadership, I do not control a thing so how can you talk about wisdom?" But comrades, in 1958 and 1959 the main responsibility was mine, and you should take me to task. In the past the responsibility was other people's—En-lai, XX—but now you should blame me because there are heaps of things I didn't attend to. Shall the person who invented burial puppets be deprived of descendants? . . . Who was responsible for the idea of the mass smelting of steel? Ke Qing-shih or me? I say it was me. I had a talk with Ke Qing-shih and spoke of six million tons. Afterwards I sought out people to talk about it: XXX also said it was possible. In June I talked about 10,700,000 tons. Then we went ahead and did it. It was published in the Peitaiho communiqué; XX put forward some ideas and believed that it would be all right. With this, we rushed into a great catastrophe, and ninety million people went into battle. As I said, the person who invented burial puppets should have neither sons nor grandsons.

. . . Next I was referring to the people's communes. I do not claim to have invented the people's communes, only to have proposed them. The Peitaiho Resolution was drafted according to my suggestion. At that time, it was as though I had found a treasure in the regulations of the Cha-ya-shan [Commune]. When I was in Shantung a reporter asked me: "Are the people's communes good?" I said: "They are good," and he published it in a newspaper. There was a spot of petit-bourgeois fanaticism there, too. In future reporters should keep away.

I have committed two crimes, one of which is calling for 10,700,000 tons of steel and the mass smelting of steel. If you agreed with this, you should share some of the blame. But since I was the inventor of burial puppets, I cannot pass on the blame: the main responsibility is mine. As for the people's communes, the whole world opposed them; the Soviet Union opposed them. There is also the General Line. Whether it has any substance or not, you can share some of the responsibility for this. The proof is to be seen in its implementation in industry and agriculture. As for the other big guns, other people should also take some of the responsibility. Boss Tan, you have fired a lot of big shots, but your shooting was inaccurate, you had a rush of blood to the head and did not take enough care. You communized too quickly. It was talked about first in Honan, then accounts of it spread rapidly in Kiangsu and Chekiang. If you are careless in your speech, you will not keep control of things. You must be more cautious. Your strength is that you are energetic and willing to take responsibility; much better than those who are sad and dismal. But when you fire big guns on important questions, you should take care. . . .

Chapter Five

The Struggle Between the Two Lines: *1962–1965*

In 1962, China's direction became more clearly defined. In foreign relations the ideological contours of the Sino-Soviet conflict were more distinct; and domestically the Great Leap Forward had raised questions that had either been evaded or had remained unanswered up till then. It had come to a temporary pause—which was something of a compromise—with Zhou En-lai's Program of Readjustment (April 1962). The measures he had advocated as being necessary were accepted by the left, which had to catch its breath. But for the supporters of the classical position, these measures seemed to open the way to a "return to normal," as it was called by the leadership in Peking in 1962–1963. This was undoubtedly the kind of completely equivocal situation Mao had in mind when he called the year 1962 "a turning toward the right" in the personal *dazibao* he posted on the door of the Central Committee in May 1966.

During the period 1962–1965 there was a resurgence of the political and ideological struggle between the two lines. Progress toward the Cultural Revolution was very much affected by the rural socialist education movement, whose course proved to be erratic, irregular, and discontinuous. For within the movement a confused battle was being fought, and the conservative element in the Communist Party was powerful enough to deflect the movement from

113

its initial objectives—education and mobilization against the "spontaneous capitalist tendencies" in the countrysides.

In areas such as teaching, culture, and health, elitism and conservatism were rife, which widened the gap between leaders and led, intellectuals and masses, and theory and practice. In the other camp, the left reacted by launching ideological counteroffensives: this was how the plan for an attack against the general staff gradually took shape.

1962, a Year of Taking Stock

The Sino-Soviet conflict

After two years in which there was little public discussion of the Sino-Soviet conflict, this conflict again became an issue at the end of 1962. When Mao Tsetung made his famous appeal in September —"Never forget class struggle!"—he was addressing not only people who were ignoring this principle in China, but people outside of China as well.

In April and May 1962 there were border incidents around the Ili River in the northeastern part of Xinjiang province (the Soviets were deporting Chinese) and again in September 1963 in Naouchki, between Soviet customs officers and Chinese railwaymen. But these border conflicts, the legacy of the "old tsars," were only manifestations of the profound differences between the USSR and China over questions of principle.

The deepening of the ideological disagreement threw new light on the contradictions that existed within China itself. A struggle was being waged against both "external revisionism" and "Chinese revisionism"; moreover, in China the debate was public: *Renmin Ribao* regularly published attacks by the "brother parties" against the CCP, as for example Jacques Duclos's speech in spring 1963. Between 1963 and 1964 China published the *Nine Articles*, accusing the Communist Party of the Soviet Union of having betrayed the principles of the October Revolution, of "restoring capitalism" and of being "in collusion with American imperialism." At the end of the ninth article, "On Khrushchev's Phony Communism and Its Historical Lessons for the World," Mao Tsetung presented fifteen points that explicitly related the current Sino-Soviet conflict to China's current political needs: drawing attention to the bond between intellectual and manual workers, to the participation of the cadres in production work, to democracy in the army and the take-over of public security duties by the people, these fifteen points not only enumerated the conditions that would allow the country "not to change color," but also set forth a preliminary program for the Cultural Revolution that was soon to come.

The Sino-Soviet conflict, as well as Khrushchev's "capitulation" in the Cuba affair and his attitude toward China's differences with India at the end of 1962, led the Chinese to a swifter and clearer realization of what the restoration of capitalism in their own country might mean; yet it was also felt that these events could contribute to disguising certain domestic contradictions. "We spent the whole of 1961 arguing with Khrushchev," Mao later said.

Lastly, a conciliatory tendency in Chinese foreign policy surfaced at that time, and it was criticized by Zhou En-lai in his government report at the Third National Assembly (December 1964): he called it the policy "of the three appeasements and one reduction" (*sanhe yishao*)—appeasement of imperialism, revisionism, and reactionary tendencies, along with the reduction of aid to the Third World. One target of this criticism, for example, was Chen Yi, the minister of foreign affairs, who had signed the agreements of the second Geneva Conference and the Laotian compromise (1962).

Spontaneous capitalist tendencies in rural areas

The difficulties and setbacks of 1960 and 1961 had caused the cadres to become demoralized and ideologically lax. "Spontaneous capitalist tendencies" reappeared in the villages, even though they had been the traditional zone of leftist influence, especially as represented by the system of "three liberties and one guarantee" (see above, Chapter 4). It was at about this time than Deng Xiao-ping, secretary-general of the party, declared: "As long as we increase production, we can even revert to individual enterprise; it hardly matters whether a good cat is black or white—as long as it catches mice, it is a good cat."

Other initiatives were taken locally: for example, during the summer of 1962, Chen Bo-da, a member of the Politburo, sent "investigation groups" to the Xinlong brigade of the July First People's Commune near Shanghai before going there himself, and proposed that all the pigs in the brigade be given back to the families, thus doing away with collective pig raising. "The contribution to the state can only be greater," he said.

A large number of people's communes put "work points in a leading position," according a more important role to industrial crops than to grains and setting up a complete system of bonuses when production quotas were exceeded and penalties when they were not met.

In addition to these rightist practices in the rural areas and the wave of economic liberalism, the exodus from rural areas was a serious blow to the collective economy: peasants went to the cities to hire themselves out as temporary workers. The rural cadres, whose morale was very low and whose duties were particularly onerous, engaged in corrupt practices, including the illegal appropriation of collective funds, the extortion of money or grain from peasants, etc. A general tendency to ignore the political implications of the wave of liberalism paved the way for the reappearance of various feudal practices, from witchcraft and superstition to marriages arranged by go-betweens and involving dowries. In certain sections of the country, it was later said in China, "power had changed hands"; here and there, old landowners felt strong enough to demand that the peasants pay back debts contracted before the Liberation. At the same time, this general situation crystallized in a severe struggle within the party.

The analysis of the Great Leap Forward and the Tenth Plenum

Each of the two camps made a different assessment of the Great Leap Forward and had a different idea of what path should be taken afterwards. The conservative line felt that above all the Great Leap Forward had been an economic movement that had failed drastically; it was actually opposed to the very premises of the "three red flags" of 1958, which it denounced as "petit bourgeois fever" and "peasant utopianism," echoing Khrushchev, who spoke of the "Trotskyism of the communes." These economic concepts were based on a fairly widespread tendency to deny class contradictions in the rural areas: "In this production team," people would say, "there are no old landlords and no old rich peasants . . . ; the landowners no longer own land today, so what class struggle could there still be?"

As for the left, it saw the Great Leap Forward as a new mode of development which could strike a decisive blow against the "three differences' (mental-manual, worker-peasant, city-country), even though this was a long-term objective: at first one would have to operate at a loss as far as actual returns went. Above all, it felt that the present difficulties were mainly a result of the liberal concessions that followed from the readjustment policy after the Great Leap Forward. Thus, where women's work was concerned, capitalist tendencies were strengthened by the fixing of production quotas on the basis of each home (see Chapter 4).

This was the context in which Mao made his famous appeal to the Tenth Plenum of the Central Committee in September 1962: "Never forget class struggle!" This appeal was at once a cry of alarm against Socialism's ideological and economic setbacks (the "turning toward the right" which he later denounced), and a signal for the start of a counteroffensive against the people who had spoken out in *Renmin Ribao* a few weeks before against "hastiness," the people who recommended moving forward "deliberately," who demanded that everyone "concentrate on economic modernization" (*Renmin Ribao*, January 5, 1963) and who, politically, asked for the "revision of verdicts"—in other words the rehabilitation of Marshal Peng De-huai, who had been removed from office because of his opposition to the Great Leap Forward.

As the economic situation continued to improve toward the end of 1962, the Tenth Plenum officially recorded the reversal of priorities in favor of agriculture; this was the greatest market heavy industry could have. From now on the theme was "take agriculture as the base and industry as the dominant factor." It also confirmed the fact that the production team was the basic unit in the people's communes. The Tenth Plenum made no mention of readjustment and was actually anxious to revive the spirit of the Great Leap Forward. It decided to start a Movement for Socialist Education whose aim was clearly defined: "To break the encirclement of the spontaneous tendencies toward capitalism."

The Struggle Between the Two Lines in the Rural Areas in 1963 and 1964

Even though the Tenth Plenum had responded categorically to the current problems—by launching a mass movement based on the theme of continuing the revolution—the Socialist Education

Movement up to December 1964 was plagued by difficulties and setbacks. Originally conceived as a national movement, it hardly affected the cities at all: the left stuck to its strategic principles and chose to concentrate its attacks on this one main front. Most importantly, the fact was that the "headquarters of the bourgeoisie" were most securely established in the cities and bureaucratic unwieldiness was more cumbersome there than anywhere else.

The line taken by the movement for Socialist Education, and its political stakes

The movement was first tried out in a "laboratory situation" in certain regions of Hunan and Hubei from the end of 1962 to the summer of 1963; elsewhere, at the beginning of 1963, a movement "toward the base" (*xiafang*) was begun; upper-echelon cadres (from the level of the province or the *xian*) went to the country and there practiced the "four *with*s" among the peasants and rural cadres: eating with, living with, working with, and discussing with. The first official text that made the Movement for Socialist Education into a national movement was the result of twenty local investigations: this was the "Draft of a Resolution by the Central Committee of the CCP Concerning Certain Problems in the Current Work in the Countrysides" (May 20, 1963), also called the "First Ten Points." Written under Mao's personal direction, the text is concise and fairly general, leaving plenty of room to maneuver around the central concern, the class struggle. The movement had to be conducted according to the method defined by Mao Tsetung and called the "fine rain and gentle breeze" method; it had many objectives, including the following:

1. Ideological education through the denunciation of both capitalist tendencies and the neglect of the class struggle.

2. Strengthening of the collective economy by giving the land and the agricultural tools that had been granted to individual families under the policy of "three liberties and one guarantee" back to the people's communes.

3. Defining of the role of mass associations in relation to the party and, in the present movement, the role of peasant associations in relation to the work teams.

4. The "four clean-ups" (*siqing*), an experiment originally tried out in the Baoding district of Hebei province whose aim

was to clear up accounts, inventory grain stocks, use public goods, and record work points.

The "First Ten Points" stated that it was necessary to make a frontal attack on the subversive activities of the "four elements" (corrupt elements, speculators, thieves, and degenerates); on the other hand, it expressly stipulated that mistakes made by the rural cadres—illegal acquisition of goods, waste, etc.—should be considered "contradictions within the people" and dealt with through discussion and persuasion: "The masses say: 'the cadres work all year long for the commune members. If their mistakes are corrected, it is all right.' " (Point VIII of the "First Ten Points"). In order to combat corruption, especially common among the base cadres, the total number of annual subsidiary work points of teams and brigades was reduced—since these went to pay the administrative part of the work done by local cadres in the countrysides. At the same time, a system was called for that would involve the cadres in production work, sometimes with a minimum quota of workdays per year. At the beginning of the movement, the system was worked out as follows: *xian* cadres—60 days; commune cadres—120 days; brigade cadres—180 days. Later it underwent a slight change so that the first two categories were assigned more than 100 days and the third from 150 to 200 days. In the spirit of the "First Ten Points," the aim of these measures was the "transformation of our conception of the world" and the resolution of the leader-follower contradiction.

Faced with the important political task of "reconstructing the basic organs of the party" (Point X) and with the principle that the movement should "be based on the poor and middle peasants of the lower class," the formulators of the May 1963 decision found it necessary to pose an essential question: what place and how much power to give the mass associations, in this case the peasant associations, who now became known as the "associations of poor and middle-poor peasants." No precise answer was given: if they fell under the authority of the party, they would then be required to take a more active part in the politics of rural life. This timid challenge to the omnipotence of the party's hierarchical apparatus would later gain ground, but in the meantime it was enough to provoke a hostile reaction from the conservatives, and this point, like the entire initial basis of the Movement for Socialist Education, was to be later distorted in various ways.

The narrowing of the movement

The wide margin for initiative that was at first given to the movement was greatly reduced by a rigid administrative codification contained in a new text. This text, which appeared in September 1963, was entitled "Several Specific Political Formulations by the Central Committee of the CCP on the Movement for Socialist Education in the Country" and known as the "Second Ten Points." Attributed to an upper-echelon party official who "always acted in league with the Chinese Khrushchev" (*Renmin Ribao*, November 23, 1967)—this was probably Deng Xiao-ping—these directives played a part in changing the movement by reducing it to the "four clean-ups"; at the same time, they reflected the distrust of certain highly placed cadres who later formed work teams and took leading roles in the movement, thus attempting to control the challenge from the base. Even though the May directives insisted on the need to make investigations and listen to the peasant associations, now the work-team formula, which had already been used during earlier mass movements, was adopted again and its function systematized. "Parachuted" into a people's commune, the team consisted of several hundred provincial or *xian* cadres who had to be politically "pure"; the team would engage in an extended action in a "chosen point."

Another task that the "Second Ten Points" set out to accomplish was to draw up a new, precise analysis of rural classes and to examine the social origin of members of the party, the Women's Association, the Youth League. As it carried out this examination, with a view to strengthening the "leadership core," the Socialist Education Movement abandoned some of its tasks and took on certain new ones, like the rectification movement within the party. The ideological aspects of the movement was still extremely vague: the "Second Ten Points" was now hardly more than a practical guide for carrying out sociological studies. First of all, it was necessary to "rely on the poor and middle peasants": this category now had to be dissected and purified, separating the good elements from the bad. Furthermore, an understanding attitude was necessary in dealing with the children of landowners and rich peasants. Another act of indulgence, which would later be regarded as suspect by the Cultural Revolution, was that in certain places the "hats"—defamatory labels applied to the four bad elements—were indiscriminately removed.

Although the "Second Ten Points" still retained some vestige of the initial "fine rain and gentle breeze" method, between the autumn of 1963 and the summer of 1964 what mainly characterized both the text and the practice of the movement was that people "pulled the burning sticks out from under the cauldron," as subsequent articles said, using a popular expression: the movement lost its substance and the mass line was muted; it was more a matter of purifying than of educating. To begin with, the rightists in the party had reduced the scope of the Movement for Socialist Education; later they would become much more aggressive.

The "Taoyuan experiment"

The "Taoyuan experiment" was to become the basis for a concept of the movement that was not simply authoritarian but almost terrorist. This experiment came to be performed because Liu Shao-qi, President of the Republic, wanted to apply his own concept of the movement; he also found the method of investigation proposed by Mao Tsetung "outmoded" and "inefficient."

From November 1963 to April 1964, Wang Guang-mei, Liu Shao-qi's wife, went to live with the rich brigade of Taoyuan in Hebei and led a work team there. According to what was later revealed during the Cultural Revolution by the newspapers of the Red Guards, she organized the construction of a road, the "Road of the Great Lady," and a hydraulic power station at state expense; when she left, she bestowed a large sum of money on the commune. Soon the Taoyuan experiment was praised in documents studied all over the country as the model experiment of the Socialist Education Movement. Taoyuan promoted a type of secret work: according to Liu Shao-qi, "As soon as the work team enters a village, it should begin doing secret work"; movement policy should no longer be "left to the masses" (Mao), but handled from above. "The masses must look to the *gugan* (the framework), the *gugan* must look to the nucleus [of leaders], the nucleus must look to the work teams, and the work teams must look to the leaders": this was Wang Guang-mei's formula. The Red Guards would later compare Liu Shao-qi's concept of the movement to "a film script whose director was the work team, the pure and impure cadres being the actors and the masses the audience."

The struggle between the two lines at the leadership level became more serious as it became clearer; having returned from his investigations in the countryside, in June 1964 Mao Tsetung stated what he believed were the six criteria for determining whether or not the Socialist Education Movement was working: (1) Had the poor and middle peasants really been mobilized? (2) Had the problem of the "four clean-ups" among the cadres been solved? (3) Had the cadres taken part in manual labor? (4) Had a good nucleus of leaders been established? (5) When bad elements which had engaged in dishonest activities were found out, did the masses really mobilize to criticize them, or was this left up to higher authorities? (6) Had production increased or decreased?

Yet in spite of this reminder of the mass line, it was the Taoyuan experiment that was to leave its mark on the rest of the movement; according to its supporters, the job of the work teams that came in from outside was to wage a campaign against corruption, to award good marks to the good cadres and assure them protection and promotion, and to punish the rebellious. This paternalistic attitude, along with the growing contradictions between the local cadres and peasants on the one hand and the work teams on the other prepared the way for the sudden dramatic events of the movement at the end of 1964.

The party machinery's counterattack

In the last months of 1964 a line was imposed that was later called "leftist in appearance, rightist in essence" and which was expressed by a text Liu Shao-qi published in September 1964, commonly known as the "Revision of the Second Ten Points." His analysis, principles, and proposed methods differed radically from those put forward in May 1963.

The work teams were made considerably more powerful and the peasant associations were reduced to a rigid vertical system under their strict control. "The entire movement must be directed by the work teams," said the text; they would decide when the local political leadership had been usurped, and when this happened they would take over the leadership themselves. The principal danger in the way the movement was conducted was no longer excessive severity but too great indulgence (one example being the change in provisions for children of landed proprietors and rich peasants). Earlier injunctions against fighting the upper middle peasants too vigorously and against ousting local cadres were suppressed; Point 6 went so far as to say that certain base cadres "have even degenerated into agents and protectors of class enemies." Cases of corruption and petty theft, formerly considered to be contradictions within the people, now became "by nature antisocial."

The target of the movement was enlarged to include numerous cadres and peasants, and this was later known as "attacking the majority to protect a handful": at the end of 1964 there was an intense wave of repression which took the form of recalling or transfering many rural cadres—between 70 and 80 percent were dismissed from the base. At the same time there was an effort to recruit new militants into the party.

In his speech on October 1, 1964, Peng Zhen, the mayor of Peking, painted a black picture of the movement; as for the official press, which until then had been almost completely silent concerning the movement as such, it abruptly changed the tone of its news about the campaign. But the lively and complex struggle that had been going on for two years between the two camps had sharpened and clarified the contradictions, and by the end of 1964 it already bore within it the seeds of an antibureautic and antirevisionist break.

Preparations for an Antibureaucratic and Antirevisionist Break

Although the campaign was the main front of the struggle at that time, differences of opinion that were just as profound also existed in more suppressed forms in other areas like education and culture —areas dominated by what was later called the "bourgeois dictatorship." The aim of the left would be to thrust its way in and try to break up these large domains which were "still governed by the dead" (Mao Tsetung).

The "Kingdom of the Dead"

There was a liberal side and a repressive side to the domination of a number of areas of the superstructure by conservatives. High mandarins associated with Zhou Yang—the vice minister of culture and president of the Union of Chinese Writers—and protected by Peng Zhen, the mayor of Peking, criticized the Great Leap Forward and called for a literature that was more neutral, less stereotyped. At that time, Chinese movie theaters were showing documentaries that glorified the "honest functionaries" (quing-guan) of the feudal era and minimized the importance of the rebellious peasants; they also showed films like *The Lin Family's Shop*, which was based on a novel by Mao Dun, minister of culture until 1964, and described the internal conflicts of a "dishonest" shopkeeper who was "anxious to remain honest." Many operas, plays, and films tried to appeal to Confucian values—integrity, filial piety—to help surmount contradictions and reconcile functionaries and peasants, capitalists and workers, former members of the Guomindang and the Communist Party.

Prominent people like Jian Bozan and Wu Han supported this tendency. Jian Bozan, a historian, was criticized on the eve of the Cultural Revolution for his "historicism": according to him, the only way to analyze a historical figure was to return to the past, to situate oneself in the period being studied, at a distance from current politics, which could only distort history. Jian Bozan also defended the theory of the "concession policy," according to which perceptive leaders of the feudal class made concessions to the rebelling peasants and reestablished order, so that the two classes could benefit from this policy and history could continue to advance. As for Wu Han, author of the play *The Dismissal of Hai Rui*, he quoted the phrase "assimilate the past critically" in support of the idea that Confucian values should continue to be venerated. In *The Communist Concept of Life*, the philosopher Feng Ding told what his concept of happiness was: "peace, not war, good food and beautiful clothes, a house that is spacious and light, love and harmony between husband and wife and between parents and children."

Symposiums were held from time to time in which small groups of intellectuals took part; for example, a symposium on Confucius organized by Zhou Yang was held from November 6 to November 12, 1962, in Shandong. The "Old Master" also had a prominent place in Liu Shao-qi's work, entitled *How to Be a Good Communist* (the "*Xiuyang*"). This book, which dated from the Yanan period, was republished in August 1962 during a wave of liberalism and attempts to rehabilitate Peng De-huai. Sixty million copies were printed. The notion of "purity"—the same notion that was applied to work teams in the Socialist Education Movement—is discussed in the book in a particularly significant way.

There was also a repressive side to the domination by the prominent academics. The same Zhou Yang and Peng Zhen who supported a liberal trend in the cultural world exercised severe censorship over young amateur writers; they encouraged the writing of pamphlets and satires directed against the left and the Great Leap Forward; they also opposed the Hundred Flowers insofar as it meant that there would be political debates in the schools and universities. Here, the students, most of whom came from the families of cadres, old capitalists, or old landowners, were burdened by a very heavy course load, sometimes as much as thirty-five hours per week; they lived in fear of exams and were taught in a more or less apolitical way; some of them were later directed into research that was cut off from all practical application. In 1964 Mao Tsetung said that this manner of teaching "is destroying the young people."

The public health services—Mao called them the "ministry of the health of the great lords of the towns"—chose to follow the Soviet model; so far, the emphasis had been on training specialists, and medical research was not directed toward finding cures for existing diseases. Between 1962 and 1965 medical practice, which had been to some degree decentralized after the creation of the people's communes, was concentrated in the towns again; during this period the countryside around Shanghai had only 300 doctors, as opposed to 3,900 in 1960.

The Socialist Education Movement, which was originally supposed to extend throughout the country, did not begin to affect the factories to the same degree as it did the people's communes. It took the form of the movement of the "five againsts" (wujan): against corruption among the cadres, against lying, against nepotism, against bureaucracy, and against a lack of connection with the masses. Very few people were mobilized. There were other campaigns during this period, like the one calling for an increase in production and the saving of raw materials. Another movement which, unlike the Movement for Socialist Education, was backed by the Renmin Ribao, clearly indicated how ambiguous the political situation in the towns was: its aim was to "compete [with the advanced], imitate it, overtake it, and help [the backward units (bixueganbang)]"; it was a movement of emulation which praised communist qualities in productive work. Yet at the same time as it dissociated itself from the "championing" (jinbiaozhuyi) and the "individual heroism" of the Soviet model, it did not eliminate either the timidity of the cadres—who were not willing to interfere with the economic development which had begun in 1963—or the economy-oriented concepts widespread among the unions, which were controlled by the "technocrat" right wing of the party.

Because of its experience with the Socialist Education Movement, the reaction of the left when faced with the unwieldy "Kingdom of the Dead" was to decide that the masses had to be mobilized quickly, even if it meant dispensing with orthodox methods of organization. A poem of Mao Tsetung's published in 1964 said:

> So many deeds
> Cry out to be done,
> And always urgently;
> Time presses.
> Ten thousand years are too long,
> Seize the day, seize the hour!

Leftist offensives: culture

What the left did was to choose certain advanced experiments as examples to sustain the rebellion against the other camp and to revive the spirit of the Tenth Plenum and the Socialist Education Movement in the face of the danger of bureaucracy and revisionism.

In a directive dated June 27, 1964, that was not made public, Mao Tsetung—who had again and again indicated how displeased he was with the prominent figures of the cultural world—talked about these people, who in the last fifteen years "have behaved like bureaucrats and great lords, refusing to associate with workers, peasants and soldiers" and "who during *the last few years* have slipped to the very brink of revisionism." The ideological offensive whose aim was to liberate history, philosophy, and art would be conducted on two levels:

1. Between 1964 and 1965 the press published fairly scholarly academic articles criticizing mainly high-ranking intellectuals like the philosophers Feng Ding and Feng You-lan and the historians Jian Bozan, Hou Wai-lu and Zhou Gu-cheng; the latter was attacked by a young Shanghai journalist, Yao Wen-yuan, for his theory that "the spirit of an era" is simply the harmonious combination of the opposing views of the different social classes. The political value of these polemics was not always very clear. Zhou Yang started the campaign of criticism with his speech to the Academy of Sciences on October 26, 1963; Peng Zhen was made director of this "Cultural Revolution"; and in 1964 Lu Ding-yi, a member of the Politburo, was in total control of the propaganda and culture services. The fact that all three of these men were opposed to the very movement they were directing did not help clarify the situation.

2. The fight was also conducted on another level, where
harder for the cultural authorities to control it since it took ra
new forms. The workers and peasants began to "write the..
history"; there was a collective reevaluation of the past—individual,
family, local, and national—through the "five histories" (*wushi*):
the individual history of the workers and of the poor peasants, and
the history of the factories, the people's communes, and the villages.
Stories and memories of the past helped to clarify the present contradictions; this movement was following the principles of the Socialist
Education Movement as they were defined during the Tenth
Plenum, but it was also challenging current methods of teaching:
"A study of history without any connection to the present is impossible; if you study the history of modern times without bothering
with the history of the villages and families, it is not worth a tinker's
damn; nor can ancient history be studied except in connection with
the present reality. . . . A person who buries himself under piles of
books learns less and less the more he studies" (Mao Tsetung,
1964).[1]

In 1964 and especially in 1965, the revolution in teaching was
revived with a project begun during the Great Leap Forward in
1958 and stopped by its opponents in 1959: this was the "half work,
half study" (*bangong banxue*) system: under this system, experiments were made locally to reduce the difference between intellectual work and manual labor[2]—small factories were built in the
universities—and between cities and rural areas: schoolchildren
left the cities to help with the harvests; scientific researchers and
especially young people who had finished secondary school went
"into the mountains and the plains"; schools and even "half work,
half study" universities were established in rural areas, where education improved appreciably. The left was also worried by the fact
that the cadres were getting older and that the students, more
preoccupied by their exams and by obtaining a good position than
by "transforming their concept of the world," were not very aware
politically, and it began urging that students be trained to carry on
the revolution.

Philosophy should be "freed from the conference room and
philosophy books" and "transformed into a sharp weapon in the
hands of the masses" (see Point 10 of the First Ten Points of May

[1] See document 1 at the end of the chapter.
[2] See document 4.

1963). In May 1963 Mao's philosophical piece "Where Do Correct Ideas Come From?" (taken from the introduction to the "First Ten Points") cut short the philosophical polemic born of the Great Leap Forward; it criticized the mechanistic Marxism of "certain comrades" who rejected action in favor of spirit over matter. The scope of the battle now widened to include the dialectical principle of "one divides into two," and starting in the summer of 1964 this battle suddenly took on a radically different tone from previous philosophical battles: through Yang Xian-zhen, philosopher and head of the Party College, and his formula "two fuse into one," the theory of strategic compromise was attacked. In *Renmin Ribao* of December 9, 1964, Wang Jin-xi, a well-known worker in the Daqing oilfields, said, "This is a fundamental problem. It doesn't matter who is behind it, we must criticize it!" It was the first time this kind of debate had gone far beyond the academic sphere. This time Yang Xian-zhen was reproached not only for his "metaphysical theories" but for his belief that philosophy was something mysterious that only a few specialists could make use of. During the debate, "one divides into two" already seemed to be the philosophical foundation of the approaching Cultural Revolution: the time for compromises was over.

Organized by Jiang Qing, Mao's wife, and Ke Qing-shi, the mayor of Shanghai, the reform of the opera was first greeted with strong hostility and then went ahead in 1964; various festivals were held, including one by the Peking Opera on contemporary themes in autumn 1964, and they provoked widespread discussions about who should be served by art. This reform represented a step forward for the left in that it dominated the scene with productions of new operas and ballets which "put politics in a position of command"—works such as the *Red Lantern* and the *Red Detachment of Women.*

Leftist offensives: the army and production

Following the line of the Tenth Plenum, a movement was started to study and apply the thought of Mao Tsetung, and the army, now led by Lin Biao, was the backbone of this movement. The People's Liberation Army, which was still made up of peasants and workers, started campaigns to study exemplary individuals and experiments for their fight against becoming bourgeois; the campaigns were first confined to the army itself and then extended to the whole country.

On February 5, 1963, *Renmin Ribao* published Mao's injunction, "Learn from Lei Feng." Lei Feng, born to a family of poor peasants, was a simple soldier who was killed in an accident. People were urged to study his qualities as a hero, his qualities as an anonymous individual entirely devoted to the collectivity. In his *Journal,* he had defined his ideal: "To be a screw that does not rust. A screw does not attract attention, but a machine that has no screws will not work." Far from being a sermonizing cult, the study of Lei Feng's example was a response—in 1963 as in later periods—to immediate political needs. In the beginning of 1964, the whole country was urged to "Learn from the PLA." The People's Liberation Army sent propaganda teams for the thought of Mao Tsetung throughout the country, and this was when the "Little Red Book" first became widely known. These teams were supposed to teach the work style of the PLA to the administrative and economic organizations, and also to coordinate and oversee administrative activities by popularizing the phrase "put politics in command." In May 1965, in response to a proposal by the State Council, distinctions of rank and uniform were eliminated from the army. In this way, the PLA allowed the left to circumvent the bureaucratic obstacles put in its way by the right wing of the party and to inspire people with the spirit of the Socialist Education Movement wherever it had been misrepresented. Now mass organizations were stirred up ideologically through the intermediary of the militia, which was becoming active again after the lull of the 1962 readjustment and was inspired by the texts of Lei Feng.

Two other examples—in industry, the oilfield of Daqing (in Heilongjiang) and in agriculture, the production brigade of Dazhai (in Shanxi)—were presented to the people as "advanced models" in the movement to break away from bureaucracy and revisionism, a movement that had apparently stopped in 1964. During this period, agriculture was urged to "follow the examples of Dazhai," the brigade led by Chen Yong-gui which had transformed a whole countryside by "self-reliance," emphasizing the ideological "revolutionizing" of the peasants and fighting against authoritarianism and bureaucracy. Dazhai was going in the opposite direction from Taoyuan, the "model brigade" of the conservatives. Individual plots of land were eliminated after the great flood of 1963, at the demand of the peasants of Dazhai. But the national campaign to study Dazhai was not begun until much later, because from the very beginning it had to contend with hostility from advocates of "modernization above all" and the slackening off of collectivization in the rural areas. As for the Daqing workers, they were fighting against the "three differences" by developing a "Yanan spirit": they had to make sure their standard of living was not superior to that of the local peasants; they had to use simple local equipment to build scattered living quarters; and they had to participate in agricultural activities.

The pioneers of Daqing were also in the forefront of the mass movement to study philosophy. It was thanks to Daqing, a legacy of the Great Leap Forward, that beginning in 1963 China could essentially fill its own oil needs.

These new and limited experiments would later form a point of reference for the reevaluation of the Socialist Education Movement in the first days of 1965, in answer to Liu Shao-qi's directives of September 1964 and the wave of terror in the countryside.

The "Twenty-three Points"

At the end of December 1964, Zhou En-lai announced the redefining of the movement: the "four clean-ups" were thenceforth broadened in the political, economic, "organizational," and ideological domains. Soon afterward, a national work conference convened by the Politburo adopted a very short document drawn up under Mao Tsetung's personal direction and called the "Twenty-three Points." This text, composed in January 1965, outlined in rather general terms how the movement would be continued; but what was more, it marked the beginning of what was really the eve of battle before the Cultural Revolution.[3] Point 2 plainly designated the target: "people in positions of authority in the party who are going the capitalist road." Besides this declaration of war there was a severe theoretical criticism of Liu Shao-qi's last theses, published at the end of 1964, according to which the basic characteristics of the movement were "the contradiction between being correct and not being correct in four different areas (politics, economics, 'organization,' and ideology)," "the overlapping of contradictions within the party and contradictions outside the party," and "the overlapping of antagonistic contradictions and contradictions among the people"; what was criticized about these theses was that they could be applied to any society at any period.

[3] See document 2.

The work teams, of whom all that was demanded was that they be "politically and ideologically pure," played a much smaller part now. On the other hand, the peasant associations had greater power and autonomy: the "Twenty-three Points" proposed that these organizations "seize power" temporarily when the local administration was usurped. The local cadres were no longer the target of the movement; a certain control would be exercised over them, but control "from below" was more important than control by higher bodies.

Between October 1965 and March 1966 a movement was started to "instill the revolution" in party committees in the *xian*; a debate was begun about the positions taken by *xian* cadres who, seeking stability, believed that "if production is going well, then the policy is good."[4]

The Cultural Revolution was to begin at a time when some rural areas were hardly or not yet affected by the Socialist Education Movement. The mobilization of the Red Guards would challenge an official policy that in the beginning tended to isolate the two movements, thus causing the Socialist Education Movement to burn itself out and be reborn in the Cultural Revolution.

The political balance between 1962 and 1965

During the sharp tensions of these four years, the leftists were slowly developing the idea of a "rebellion" at the base to settle the debate once and for all. The formula already existed, though in a discreet form, in the ninth of the "Twenty-three Points" of January 1965. In 1967 Mao would say that during the Socialist Education Movement he had unsuccessfully sought a formula and a method for mobilizing the masses on a large scale.

But between 1962 and 1965 the left was not only impeded by its own inexperience; it was in severe conflict with the official political machinery, which was solidly in the hands of its adversaries. For example, there was the party's principal daily newspaper, *Renmin Ribao*, which was at that time so quick to print pieces by the conservative faction and so much more reluctant to print pieces by the radicals: it had reported a good deal about the Taoyuan brigade and very little about the Dazhai brigade. There was also the leadership of the CCP, which Liu Shao-qi and Deng Xiao-ping were

[4] See document 1.

systematically making stronger and more unwieldy. Since 1961 the provincial committees of the party had been governed by regional secretariats (six for the whole of China), which widened the barrier between the base and the center. The heads of these super-provincial secretariats, real viceroys, were later among the first "general staff" to be bombarded in 1966–1967. There were also the Communist youth organizations; they were hardly active any more and had very little influence. To give a new impetus to their stagnant recruitment they suddenly tried to swell their numbers by massive formal admissions: they gained eight and a half million new members in 1964–1965. In this way the youth had lost contact with the nation's political life; the Red Guards were to restore it brutally. In fact, the youth was a critical sector, all the more so since the repercussions of the Great Leap Forward had caused unemployment to go up, particularly among young people.

The Central Committee of the CCP did not meet once between 1962 and 1966, between the Tenth and Eleventh Plenums. This was a sign of a shaky political balance, which the Cultural Revolution was to topple quite abruptly.

ADDITIONAL BIBLIOGRAPHY

Richard Baum and Frederick C. Teiwes, *Ssu-Ch'ing: The Socialist Education Movement of 1962–1966* (Berkeley, 1968).

Y. Viltard, *Le système politique chinois dans le Mouvement d'Education Socialiste 1962–1966* (Paris, 1975).

P. Tissier, *Deux modèles d'avant-garde: Taking pour l'industrie, Tachai pour l'agriculture* (Paris, 1975).

DOCUMENTS

1. CHAIRMAN MAO'S CONVERSATION WITH HIS NIECE (1964)

Source: Mao Tsetung, Joint Publications Research Service (JPRS), U.S. Department of Commerce, 52029 (December 21, 1970).

Hai-rong: But there is the son of a cadre who doesn't do well. In class he doesn't listen attentively to the teacher's lecture and after class, he doesn't do homework. He likes to read fiction. Sometimes he dozes off in the dormitory and sometimes he doesn't attend the Saturday afternoon meeting. On Sunday he doesn't return to school on time. Sometimes on Sunday when our class and section hold a meeting, he doesn't show up. All of us have a bad impression of him.

Chairman: Do your teachers allow the students to take a nap or read fiction in class?

We should let the students read fiction and take a nap in class, and we should look after their health. Teachers should lecture less and make the students read more. I believe the student you referred to will be very capable in the future since he had the courage to be absent from the Saturday meeting and not to return to school on time on Sunday. When you return to school, you may tell him that it is too early to return to school even at eight or nine in the evening; he may delay it until eleven or twelve. Whose fault is it that you should hold a meeting Sunday night? . . .

Hai-rong: But now our school spends the whole Sunday night holding meetings—class meetings, branch headquarters committee meetings or meetings of study groups for party lessons. According to my calculation, from the beginning of the current semester to date, there has not been one Sunday or Sunday night without any meetings.

Chairman: When you return to school, you should take the lead to rebel. Don't return to school on Sunday and don't attend any meeting on that day.

Hai-rong: But I don't dare. This is the school system. All students are required to return to school on time. If I don't, people will say that I violate the school system.

Chairman: Don't care about the system. Just don't return to school. Just say you want to violate the school system.

Hai-rong: I cannot do that. If I do, I will be criticized.

Chairman: I don't think you will be very capable in the future. You are afraid of being accused of violating the school system, of criticism, of a bad record, of being expelled from school, of failing to get party membership. Why should you be afraid of so many things? The worst that can come to you is expulsion from school. The school should allow the students to rebel. Rebel when you return to school.

2. Some problems arising in the course of the rural Socialist Education Movement

Source: Richard Baum and Frederick C. Teiwes, *Ssu-Ch'ing: The Socialist Education Movement of 1962–1966* (Berkeley, University of California Press, 1968), pp. 121, 126.

V. *Work Methods*

1) Within the movement as a whole, provincial, special district, and hsien level party committees and work teams, relying on the great majority of the masses and cadres (including cadres who have cast aside their misgivings and doubts), must gradually carry out the "3 unifications" with respect to the masses, cadres, and work teams.

2) Once the movement has begun, we must immediately explain its meaning to the cadres and masses, and we must inform them of our policies. We must clearly declare that, no matter what commune or brigade, and no matter whether during or after the movement, the use of pretexts for opposing the masses of commune members will not be permitted.

3) The work teams must, during the movement and during the process of struggle, arouse the poor and lower-middle peasants, organize class ranks,

discover activist elements and train them to form a leadership nucleus, and work together with them. We must not be quiet; we must not be mysterious; and we must not confine our activities to a small minority of the people.

4) In the course of the movement, from start to finish we must grasp production. At the same time, we must pay attention to grasping each year's distribution (the question of livelihood). If we do not grasp the questions of production and distribution, we will become divorced from the masses and will bring grievous harm to our cause.

5) We must proceed on the basis of local conditions. Reality demands this. Whatever problems the masses require to be solved must be solved. Whatever imbalances occur in our work must be rectified.

6) In the movement, we must boldly unleash the masses; we must not be like women with bound feet—we must not bind our hands and feet. At the same time, we must make a deep and fine penetration, and must not make a big fuss over nothing. We must set the facts in order, explain principles, eliminate simple, crude work methods, severely prohibit beating people and other forms of physical punishment, and prevent forced confessions.

7) To sum up: in the course of the movement as a whole, we must make use of contradictions to win over the majority, oppose the minority, and attack and defeat all who persist in taking the capitalist road—always a very small minority. Some people have committed mistakes which can still be rectified. With regard to those people who are the target of the Four Cleans movement, we must be good at discriminating among them and treating them differentially, taking the worst people and isolating them or narrowly confining them.

XX. *Four Great Democracies*

All communes and brigades must learn from the People's Liberation Army and carry out political democracy, democracy in production, democracy in financial affairs, and military democracy.

XXII. *Methods of Thought*

We must strive to avoid one-sidedness and partialness. Everything must be analyzed, no matter what it is.

To view everything as absolute, motionless, isolated and unchanging is metaphysical. To spend one's time cataloguing great piles of superficial phenomena, or compiling great quantities of rules and regulations is scholasticism, which renders people unable to receive the necessary leadership. We must be proponents of dialectical materialism; we must oppose metaphysics and scholasticism.

3. SELF-CRITICISM OF A XIAN CADRE ON THE EVE OF THE CULTURAL REVOLUTION

Source: *Renmin Ribao*, October 18, 1965.

The key points that determine the success or failure of leadership work are that the leadership cadres of the *xian* give up their grand airs, that they leave behind stereotypes, and that all their actions and words have the greatest interests of the masses at heart.

In the past few years the improvement work in the *xian* has been fairly successful: fields that almost always used to be dry are now fields of high and steady yield; our *xian* used to lack cereals and now we have a surplus; schistosomiasis,* which had affected people's health for thousands of years, was wiped out. The party policies have spread throughout the countrysides and the party's prestige among the masses continues to grow.

Because of this good situation, some of us have gotten swelled heads, have become vain, and have begun to consider ourselves the embodiment of the truth. The manifestations of this phenomenon are preferring praise to criticism, liking to hear the same opinions as one's own but not conflicting opinions. A work style cut off from the masses is now in evidence. On the ideological level all sorts of stereotypes have appeared, such as tasks being handed down by superiors, the notion of experience, and the notion of experience coming from the outside. . . . As soon as tasks come from the higher echelons because they have thought them up, the work is first of all divided up; second, there is a great rush to finish it; and third, there is criticism. Meetings, telephone calls, documents—everything is sent to the base. But a real penetration of the masses, listening to the opinions of the masses and the local cadres, understanding concrete situations—these things are not seen very often. . . . And as soon as we meet with some obstacle, we do not look for the cause among the top-ranking leaders, trying to be firm in implementing directives and maintaining a strong conception of organization; on the contrary, we blame the local cadres. Many comrades among us go to the countrysides to conduct investigations. But from the very beginning they have stereotyped ideas; if they conduct an investigation, it is only to find the things they themselves need and to verify their own ideas. . . .

Wen Xiushan,
Committee Secretary of the Fuqing *xian*
in Fujian

4. PRE-TEEN DELINQUENTS AND SOCIALIST EDUCATION

Source: Edgar Snow, *The Other Side of the River* (New York, Random House, 1962), pp. 276–279.

I spent an afternoon in the "Children's Study-Work School" where 185 children between ten and fifteen were being reformed by gentler methods of thought remolding. Peking had one other reform school, with about 100 juvenile delinquents aged fifteen to eighteen, which I did not see. The Children's Study-Work School had some notable features worth reporting. Its roomy compound was in a good residential neighborhood not far from the Winter Palace. There were no guards except one elderly gateman and no

---

* An infection caused by a worm; its most common variety is bilharziasis.

special precautions to prevent escapes. "Usually they come back voluntarily," I was told by Mme Wang Si-yan, the principal. She was a diminutive woman dressed in a white blouse and dark skirt, her black hair bobbed and caught in curls behind her ears. Her energy and enthusiasm for her job, in contrast with her stature, reminded me of my own spirited grade school principal.

"The methods we follow here," said Mme Wang, "are in accordance with the principles laid down by Mao for all primary school teachers. We must love our students like parents, combine affection with strict justice, respect them as much as adults, understand each one as a distinct individual, and inculcate in them socialist ideals of service and unselfishness. The cause of delinquency in children nearly always lies with their parents. All our teachers here realize that the most important thing is to set an example. We participate down to sharing the dirtiest chores such as cleaning floors and toilets. All the work in the school is done by the children and teachers."

Mme Wang considered that her charges were all reflections of the failure of the "old society" and "hangovers of capitalism," but "class background" figures she gave me did not seem conclusive evidence. According to her, 40 percent of the little delinquents came from working-class families; 20 percent were orphans or from broken homes or had lived with old people too disabled to work or look after them; 25 percent were the children of *ganbu*; and 15 percent were from homes of "former capitalists or policemen." I expressed interest in the quarter from families of cadres. Forty-six in a city of more than seven million was not many, but the relative percentage was high. Weren't cadres themselves supposed to be models of deportment?

"They may work for socialism but still be bad parents," she said. "Remember that they also come from the old society and may backslide in their domestic life. When parents are too busy to look after their children, when they neglect to give them love, the result is always the same; the children become willful, spoiled, aggressive, and do things to win attention. They begin to lie and steal and get into trouble."

"The majority of our children are unusually bright, not stupid." Mme Wang spoke of their "unusual pride" and "vanity" and how readily they responded when given recognition and responsibility. One "bad" boy had refused to study or work for two months. "I can stand sitting through just one class," he said. "Then I have to hit someone." One day he contrived to tie his teacher's feet to his desk so that when he tried to stand up he was thrown to the floor. The boy expected to be beaten but the teacher dismissed class to talk to him. . . .

It was not easy for a stranger to question these children about their past errors—for which they were far from fully responsible—without embarrassing them, and I soon desisted. They seemed to work well together and were cheerful and looked healthy. "Disturbed children" and "incorrigibles"? No, said Mme Wang, they had no special methods for handling them, except plenty of love and "to follow a cool line" with them. They responded to the reward system as the others did. Teachers (three male and four female) were all qualified normal school graduates who had been given special training in a party school before coming here, but they were not using any foreign or Russian system of child psychology. The worst form of disapproval was the threat of expulsion from the pupils' association—loss of "membership," ostracism and disgrace. Mme Wang said that in three years she had never had to expel a child from the school itself. That was fortunate, she added; she would have to turn him back to the courts and she was not clear herself about what would then happen.

On further reflection the principal said that yes, there was one particular difficult case of a "disturbed" girl. She was seventeen now and the oldest child there; she had failed in her studies and had had to repeat. She was not really stupid but incredibly shy and reticent; her real reason for failing seemed to be fear of returning to "the outside." She had had a completely loveless childhood, full of beatings and abuse, had been raped when a small girl, had never known a home before she came here, and now dared not face the world. She was pointed out to me at one of the sewing tables. She held her head down and I watched her embroider for a moment; her work was exquisite, far more skillful than the others'.

"What will you do with her?" I asked when we moved on.

"I don't know yet. We are trying to decide." Mme Wang obviously took a more than casual interest in this young woman. I wondered what kind of childhood she herself had had but I never found out. "If Lin-ling were a little brighter," she went on, "we might find some kind of assistant's job for her here, but maybe that would be begging the question. However, we'll find a solution."

Thought remolding has its limitations no less than "the couch."

Chapter Six

The Cultural
Revolution:
1965–1969

The "Great Proletarian Cultural Revolution" (*wuchanjieji wenhua-dageming*) was a phenomenon without precedent or equivalent in the history of Chinese communism or any other communist movement in the world. For several years the country was torn apart and thrown into confusion as much at the leadership level as at the base. The speed with which the crisis developed and the forms it took were very different according to the different social milieus and regions, and kept changing as time passed. Because of this diversity, it could not be mechanically controlled by the center, and yet the center never lost overall control of it.

What was at stake in the crisis, during which all the country's political structures were challenged, were the original options of Chinese communism outlined at Yanan and again during the Great Leap Forward: the mass line, the rejection of a society of order and conservatism—which could only fall into capitalism and revisionism—the conviction that the class struggle therefore would continue during the period of transition toward socialism and that the new bourgeoisie could be just as deadly as the old bourgeoisie, and also the conviction that the institutions of socialism meant nothing without an ideological revolution in political consciousness.

138

From Academic Debate to Fighting in the Factories: *November 1965–January 1967*

Even before the actual Cultural Revolution began, the advocates of the two lines were involved in a number of cultural disputes; for example the disputes over the Peking Opera, over historical method, and over the philosophical principle of "one and two" (see Chapter 5). But the attack in November 1965 on the play *The Dismissal of Hai Rui* set off a whole chain reaction politically, involving the university, the state structures, and the CCP itself within just a few months. The crisis, which had been growing for years, was suddenly rousing the whole country.

Fighting around the municipality of Peking (November 1965–May 1966)

Official texts which appeared later fixed the date of the beginning of the Cultural Revolution as November 10, 1965, when the Shanghai *Wenhuibao* published a severe criticism of the play *Hai Rui* written by a young Shanghai journalist named Yao Wen-yuan, allegedly at the suggestion of Mao. The play dated from 1961 and had at that time expressed the reservations of people who were upset by the bold actions of the Great Leap Forward (see Chapter 4).

After some controversy, the author of the play, Wu Han, published a self-criticism in February 1966 and the Peking press was satisfied. Wu Han was the deputy mayor of Peking and the municipal authorities seemed anxious not to let the affair go very far. Peng Zhen, mayor of Peking, was one of the most prominent figures of the regime and had been a close associate of Liu Shao-qi since the civil war against the Guomindang. It might seem surprising that he was allowed to handle the controversy, but perhaps Mao was only trying to embarrass him. The fact was that Peng Zhen kept the discussion brief, working with Lu Ding-yi, head of the party's propaganda services. The Peking press only published articles hostile to Wu Han after a delay and at irregular intervals. In the beginning of 1966 Peng Zhen was head of the "group of five" officially in charge of starting the "Cultural Revolution"—the phrase was already in use. Right away it was clear that there were two very different approaches to the controversy, and they took shape around two texts published in February. The "report of the group of five" kept the controversy academic. On the other hand, a report on a work seminar held in Shanghai in which Mao, Lin Biao, and Jiang Qing took part related the discussion of Wu Han's play to a larger dispute; it insisted on the need for a campaign against bourgeois ideology and the *sijiu* (the "four olds": old habits, old ideas, old customs, and the old culture). At the same time the *Jiefangjunbao*, the official army newspaper, printed a series of articles which took the same position. Thus the army very quickly assumed the role of doing political work, which it would continue to do throughout the Cultural Revolution.

This, then, was the beginning of a political turning point. In March Mao spoke of "overthrowing the King of Hell in order to free the little devils." He was clearly calling on the cadres to criticize their superiors. At the same time he persuaded the Central Committee to form a new work group in charge of the Cultural Revolution which would answer directly to the Politburo. The "group of five" was ousted, and in June Peng Zhen and Lu Ding-yi were relieved of their offices, as was Zhou Yang, officer in charge of cultural affairs in the Central Committee. Had the balance of forces suddenly changed? Or had the party machinery tried to cut its losses by getting rid of certain leaders whose reputations had been compromised? In support of this hypothesis was the meteoric rise of Tao Zhu, a Cantonese leader who replaced Lu Ding-yi in June in the key position of officer of propaganda and became fourth in the party hierarchy.

The political stakes of the crisis were outlined in the "May Sixteenth Circular," in which the Central Committee identified the enemy: "The representatives of the bourgeoisie who have infiltrated the party, the government, and the army are a bunch of counter-revolutionary revisionists. . . . Among us there are certain individuals of Khrushchev's type who have been trained to succeed us." They clearly had Liu Shao-qi in mind. The May Sixteenth Circular, then, which was reserved for the internal party apparatus, changed the target of the movement from the cultural sphere to the sphere of political power, and from the municipality of Peking to the whole country. In Mao's eyes, the movement should go beyond the state and party apparatuses, should start from the base, and should thoroughly criticize certain leading cadres. The students were the first to respond.

Red Guards and work teams in the universities

Public opinion was aroused. Everywhere people began to criticize revisionist influences and the cadres responsible for the "black line," mostly using the *dazibao* method (large-character posters). This method was commonly used in China to express individual or collective discontent—sometimes it was spontaneous, sometimes organized as part of a nationwide campaign. The first *dazibao* in Peking University (*Beida*) was posted on May 25 and signed by seven people, including Nie Yuan-zi, a young woman who was a philosophy assistant. It had enormous reverberations, and on the advice of Mao it was taken up by newspapers and radio as a "Marxist-Leninist and revolutionary" character poster. In its contentious style it charged three leaders of *Beida*—including the rector, one of Peng Zhen's close associates—of obstructing the current criticism movement and confining it to an academic setting. The authors of the poster called for a broad mobilization of the people against them. In response, the students began to cover the university walls with open letters in which they argued in favor of a proletarian system of teaching, something the authorities resisted. The students, the first to be affected by the Cultural Revolution, were posing the question of instruction methods. They demanded that the university be less cut off from society, that it open its doors more to workers and peasants and stop letting the sons of cadres in the back door. They demanded that "red" training replace the training of "expert" technocrats, the future elite of a revisionist society; in order to do this, it was necessary to "put politics in command."

At the base, people became increasingly discontented, and "Red Guards" (*Hongweibing*) were formed among university and high school students—and soon among young workers in Peking, large towns, and rural areas. As for the party apparatus, it tried to defend the established order with its "work teams" (*gongzuozu*) supervised from above since they had been created on Liu Shao-qi's initiative. The period in which these work teams were most active coincided with the fifty days when Mao was absent from Peking. Some people in the West thought that Mao had actually been defeated in June–July in the leading bodies of the party and had had to leave Peking. Others thought that Mao had planned this strategic withdrawal himself, preferring to reestablish contact with the base so that he could counterattack more effectively later. In any case, this was the time when his adversaries temporarily seized power again.

In June 1966 Liu Shao-qi and Deng Xiao-ping, secretary-general of the party, tried to put obstacles in the path of the Cultural Revolution by positioning work teams. Groups of several dozen experienced cadres were sent into the factories, the countrysides, and especially the universities; often they were only continuing to do what they had done at the end of the Socialist Education Movement (see Chapter 5) to control it and limit it. Wang Guang-mei, Liu's wife, went to the Qinghua University in Peking in person. At first the students thought she could help them criticize the authorities; but she and her work team became tougher and tougher as the political accusations piled up and as the radicalism of certain students became more and more obvious. The general tendency of the work teams, in effect, was to establish themselves in the "hot points," where they would supervise and restrain the criticism movement. They denounced the activities of the Red Guard as counterrevolutionary. The students rebelled against the work teams' tendency to control everything from above, against what they called a "white terror"; they rejected the very formal sessions during which cadres were supposed to perform self-criticisms. At Qinghua, the student Kuai Da-fu, future leftist leader, composed a *dazibao* directed at the rector, entitled, "What is this comedy, comrade Ye Lin?" Following his example, other people demanded explanations for the fact that the work teams tended to block the initiatives of the base and the masses; they stated that they had no confidence in these work teams, which in the end did not make it clear "who our friends are and who our enemies are," who supported the privileges of certain cadres (whose dining rooms and dormitories were separate from those of the students, for example), and who worst of all kept the right wing in power. Faced with the rebels, who were mobilizing around Kuai, the party committees encouraged the moderates, who were prepared to defend the order with directives from above. The movement continued to develop, and by the beginning of August detachments of Red Guards had been organized in numerous schools and universities in the capital.

It might seem paradoxical that the "advocates of the bourgeois line" within the party branded their adversaries with the insulting epithet "counterrevolutionaries," thus using Maoist ideology to criticize revolutionaries who claimed to adhere to the same philosophy. The fact was that during the Cultural Revolution, reference to Mao and his thought, as crystallized in the "Little Red Book," was the only political reference, even for those who were "waving the red flag in order to fight the red flag"; the difference between the people who were supporting the movement and those who were hostile to it could only emerge in their concrete activities.

The Sixteen Points (August 1966)

In the middle of July Mao returned from his trip or retreat, which he had spent in the South of China, mainly in Shanghai. He was to take a stand openly against the work teams, thus officially supporting the movement of the Red Guards, which had begun spontaneously and was henceforth integrated into the strategic play of political forces.

Mao swimming the Yangzi at this time was a clear symbol to everyone of the need to become totally committed to the movement. He returned to the political scene and publicly posted his own *dazibao* on the door of the Central Committee in Peking: "Bombard the headquarters!" (*paoda silingbu*); he contrasted the spontaneity of the Red Guards, who were the first of the masses to mobilize and to understand that everyone should "talk, discuss, criticize," and the conservatism of the cadres who advocated the bourgeois line. Shortly after Mao returned to Peking a meeting of the Eleventh Plenum of the Central Committee was held, lasting from August 1 to 12. It published a communiqué assessing the preceding period, condemning the work teams and their bureaucratic activity, which was against the mass line, and called for a consolidation of the dictatorship of the proletariat to prevent revisionist attempts to take over leadership of the party. The communiqué also emphasized the creative contribution of "Mao Tsetung's thought" (*Mao Sixiang*) to Marxism-Leninism. The plenum adopted a "Declaration in Sixteen Points," a veritable charter for the Cultural Revolution, whose goals and methods it defined.

Point 1 identified the targets of the Cultural Revolution: the elements "committed to the capitalist road" (*zouzipai*) who had infiltrated the party and held leadership posts in it, and also the prominent academic figures who were spreading bourgeois ideology. Point 2 urged support for the revolutionaries, whose general orientation, with the exception of various errors, had always been correct. In order to combat resistance to the Cultural Revolution, the quality of the party's work should be measured by its capacity to lead the masses, who should liberate themselves "by themselves" through taking action; "in no case can we act for them" (Points

3 and 4). Furthermore, within the party it was necessary to "rely on the left and strengthen it, win over the center, and isolate the right, which means rallying 95 percent of the cadres and masses" (Point 5). Point 8 distinguished four types of cadres: those who were good, those who were comparatively good, those who had made serious mistakes without being anti-party, antisocialist rightists, and finally a small number of anti-party, antisocialist rightists.

Point 6 reaffirmed the need to identify the contradictions among the people—"nonantagonistic" contradictions—and those between the people and its enemies. It went on to say that people in the minority should be persuaded through reasoning (*wendou*) rather than coercion or force (*wudou*) because they might be right—as in the case of the minority of students opposing Liu's line. Point 7 went farther and clearly condemned the activities of the work teams who "organized counterattacks against those members of the masses who had composed criticisms through *dazibao*." Point 9 referred to the system of elections set up by the Paris Commune, in which there had been democracy at the base and direct control of the state administrative apparatus.

The main points, then, defined the targets of the Cultural Revolution—the cultural and educational institutions and the party bodies where the battle between the two lines was taking place. The statement reaffirmed the principle of mobilizing the masses and urged that this mobilization be stimulated—which reversed the tendency of the preceding period. On the basis of this text, which had wide reverberations in China, the movement of the Red Guards became more solidly structured and eventually the struggle expanded to include the factory workers.

The campaign of the Red Guards (Autumn 1966)

Echoing the press, which insisted on the need for the participation of the masses, the student agitation was also expressing a specific rebellion against the academic authorities. The young people in the Red Guards received their political education during the time they spent in the provinces, where their intention was to take part in the "affairs of state." During this whole period, China underwent an enormous upheaval. The students, backed financially by the state and with its political support—particularly in the press—traveled free all over the country. "Exchanges of experience" (*chuanlian*) put young people from Peking in contact with provincial

people, and others left on "Long Marches" (*changzheng*) covering
several thousand kilometers. This atmosphere of a politicized country
fair culminated with a huge gathering on August 18 when Mao
passed one million Red Guards in review and was presented with
their arm band. At the end of August, a "General Red Guards
Liaison Department" was created.

But in the last months of 1966 divisions were already apparent.
Some of the Red Guards were inclined to "criticize everything," to
"distrust all the cadres." Others, mobilized and supervised by the
local and provincial party apparatuses, were anxious to "protect the
party committees." There were already clashes between the two
tendencies.

The Shanghai Commune

The young people and the Red Guards, which had now been
entrusted with the mission of giving impetus to the struggle, could
only be relied upon temporarily. It became necessary to give over
the management of the criticism campaign to a more stable structure, since the classical party and state apparatus had virtually
ceased to function. What was more, the students, who were so
quick to mobilize and respond, formed too limited and too unstable
a social base for the movement. It was necessary to appeal to the
workers, especially those working in the large industries in the
towns. These two needs were met by the formation of the short-
lived Shanghai Commune and the more permanent commune of
the Triple Union Revolutionary Committees in the beginning of
1967. For a time, Shanghai, the largest industrial city in China,
replaced Peking—the student center as well as center of the official
apparatus—as the main focus of the Cultural Revolution.

This extension of the movement was greeted with ill will by all
the higher cadres who, led by Tao Zhu, had only regarded the May
Sixteenth Circular as a makeshift document; they had abandoned
Liu Shao-qi, but only in order to preserve the power of the existing
structures. This compromise, symbolized by the sudden rise of
Tao Zhu, was upset by the revival of the movement, and in Decem-
ber Tao Zhu suddenly fell from power. He was replaced by Wang
Li, a radical militant from Peking.

As it reached the factories in Shanghai and other industrial
centers, the Cultural Revolution came into conflict with moderate
administrative cadres, the CCP apparatus, and the more favored

sections of the working class, who were the cadres' main support. In Shanghai, the mayor, Cao Di-qiu, and the CCP officer, Chen Pei-xian, had been impeding contacts between Red Guards and workers for some time. Nevertheless, by the end of 1966 the radical workers had organized themselves into a "Rebel Workers' H.Q." At that point the conservatives tried to slow down the protest movement in the factories by granting a number of salary increases and easier hours, which led to a sort of disguised strike. In January, the left, made up of local cadres of the CCP like Zhang Qun-qiao, intellectuals like the journalist Yao Wen-yuan, and radical workers like Wang Hong-wen, moved to counterattack. It denounced the "economism" offensive and called for an end to the strike. It took control of the local organs of the press. On January 6, during a meeting attended by one million people, Zhang Qun-qiao announced that Cao and the other conservative leaders of Shanghai had been ousted. An "urgent appeal" was made on January 9 to "take power" (*duoquam*) in the city; the center supported this move from Peking. On February 3 Zhang proclaimed the accession of a new political power, the Shanghai Commune, a name that echoed both the Paris Commune, to which the "Sixteen Points" had explicitly referred, and the urban communes of the Great Leap Forward. On February 24, however, Zhang, back from Peking, announced that the name had to be changed to "Revolutionary Committee of Shanghai": the city could not isolate itself by adopting political forms that were too advanced for the rest of the country.[1] This formal concession did not affect the success of the "Shanghai Revolution" and of the radical leaders of Shanghai: this was to be the beginning of their national political rise during the following period.

The Turbulent Restoration of Order: *February 1967–April 1969*

Once the Cultural Revolution was established in the largest city in China, a long period of instability began. For more than two years, attempts to restore order were thwarted again and again by agitation on the part of the left and the right which the Ninth Congress of the CCP only appeared to quell. The leaders of the

---

[1] See document 1 at the end of the chapter.

center were faced with very complex dilemmas: how far could the criticism of the cadres be allowed to go without disrupting even the minimal functioning of the state apparatus in both domestic and foreign affairs? What kind of balance should be established between criticism of rightist revisionism and criticism of the extreme left with its anarchist-tending factionalism? What place should the army have in the Cultural Revolution, when its ability to intervene and its very unity might be affected by its active participation in the movement with its periods of agitation?

The February countercurrent and the local takeovers

In February one indication of the tendency to restore order was the appeal to the young people to break off their "Long Marches" and return to their universities and factories. The same tendency was behind an editorial in *Hongqi* encouraging people to treat the cadres correctly, putting into practice the policy of a wide-open "Grand Alliance" which would exclude only a small minority. During this first attempt to reintegrate the criticized cadres, the rightist leadership felt this was the moment to come to the fore-front again; what was more, it was outraged by the Red Guards' riotous activities, indiscreet investigations, and intransigent criti-cisms, especially in the central ministries. Its main spokesmen were the minister of agriculture, Tan Zhen-lin, and undoubtedly also the minister of foreign affairs, Chen Yi. To frustrate this "February countercurrent," the center defended the protesters: their excesses were less important than the gains their movement had made. At the same time the army was urged to help stabilize the Cultural Revolution—it was asked to help the leftist forces, and not to re-press them. In April it was specifically stated that the army should not make arrests, nor use armed force, nor dissolve groups of Red Guards or other mass organizations which had sprung up spon-taneously, but only to use persuasion in cases where excesses had been committed or during overt crises, thus playing the role of arbitrator. Were these recommendations (the "Ten Points") always followed? Probably not, judging from incidents involving the army, such as the Wuhan incident in July 1967 (see below).

Wherever the Cultural Revolution was solidly enough estab-lished, the restoration of order took the form of "revolutionary committees." These new local power bodies were based on the "Triple Alliance" (*sanjiehe*): the revolutionary rebels, the army, and the cadres who supported the movement. At Shanxi, for example, of the 245 members of the new provincial committee, 110 represented the rebels and other mass groups, 59 the former cadres, and 68 the military. But by the end of the winter of 1967, these new revolutionary committees had only been set up in a small minority of the provinces and districts—Shandong and Shanxi, old areas of peasant radicalism ever since the war against Japan, the outlying provinces of Heilongjiang and Guizhou, and the cities of Shanghai (here, the former "commune") and Peking.

The push toward the left: spring and summer

The failure of the February countercurrent and the new political balance brought about by the Triple Alliance (even if it had only received formal sanction in a few provinces and in two urban districts) created favorable conditions for a push toward the left. In February and March, a congress of Red Guards and conferences of militant workers—and later peasants—were held in Peking. In the spring, very restless, aggressive protest groups sprang up all over China and relentlessly bombarded the administrative and political headquarters, in the universities as well as in the factories and offices. Among these were the group called *Jinggangshan* (named after the oldest Maoist red base, which dated from 1928) at Qinghua University in Peking, the group called *Lian Si* ("Fourth Liaison Headquarters") at the diesel factory in Shanghai, and other groups of the same kind in Sichuan, Canton, and the Northeast. Quite often these groups were torn apart by factional quarrels, by "mountain topism" (as Mao described it that autumn), and by an irresponsible form of anarchy. In spring 1967 they abandoned the ideological struggle (*wendou*) and engaged in bloody brawls (*wudou*). Was the rise of these centrifugal and extremist tendencies mainly the fault of a central headquarters, the "May Sixteenth Group" (or Group 516), which was effectively active in Peking and in the autumn was accused of having organized the disturbances that took place all over China? Certainly there was contact between extremist groups from different cities. But the sociological factors should also be taken into consideration, the convergence of certain types of behavior which appeared in various places in the country arising from specific social bases—young inexperienced workers, recent immigrants to the cities, students; in the fall even the underworld was attacked, which threw a different light on the theory of a well-organized central conspiracy.

In the spring, the leftist tendency attacked Liu Shao-qi directly. It criticized his treatise on the "self-perfecting" (*xiuyang*) of the Communists, reprinted in 1962 (see Chapter 5). In July, the Red Guards staged an enormous sit-in, noisily surrounding his home and remaining there day and night: these were "Liu's crickets." But the protesters' attacks against the highest officers were now openly affecting Chen Yi and through him—less and less discreetly—Zhou En-lai. The sector of foreign policy provided a favorable terrain for the rebels' radical criticism. By its very nature, foreign affairs was an area covered by state secrecy; it was "foreign" to the experience and control of the masses (unlike the institutions of economic management, for example). In July the extreme left took over the ministry of foreign affairs, seized dossiers, recalled diplomats, and goaded Chinese living abroad into radical activities in Burma, Cambodia, Indonesia, and Hong Kong, which provoked a brutal repression by local authorities. Yao Deng-shan, a diplomat who had returned from Indonesia after anti-Chinese riots broke out, was made temporary director of the ministry. He organized the attack on and burning of the British mission in Peking in August, or at least allowed it to happen.

During the same period, brawls between leftist factions became more frequent and more violent. They took place, for example, in Shanghai in the large factories; in Sichuan, where hundreds were killed at the Number 1 Chengdu textile factory; in August in Canton, where there were bloody incidents involving supporters and opponents of a "Revolutionary Alliance" in conflict with the military commander of the city; and at Shenyang among three enemy factions. It was a time of real troubles and insecurity which culminated in the serious incidents at Wuhan in July. Two envoys from the center—Wang Li, one of the leaders of the university leftists, and Xie Fu-zhi, minister of security—were arrested on the initiative of one of the rebel organizations of the city, the "Million Heros," with the support of certain units of the army; the fighting spread through the region and left many dead; only Mao's active personal intervention was able to stop it. Not only were these riots serious in themselves, but they were also resulting in something that the center had systematically refused to embark upon: the questioning of the army, the beginning of political protest within the military units. After the Wuhan and Canton incidents, the heads of the extreme left, Wang Li, Qi Ben-yu, and Nie Yuan-zi, specifically urged that revisionism be eliminated from the army.

The autumn turning point and the lull

In August, Mao, who had just returned from a tour of inspection in Central China, and the other leaders of the center decided to put a stop to what was happening—to slow down the gradual slide into extreme leftism and to dissociate the Cultural Revolution from it. Posters everywhere criticized and denounced "Group 516." Jiang Qing, who in July had still been declaring that it was necessary to "attack with words but defend oneself with arms," said in September that this resolution had "only applied to the given circumstances" and that "we have no need of an armed struggle": this amounted to a discreet form of self-criticism. Jiang Qing, then, ceased to support the extreme left in Peking (these statements were made during her arbitration between the rival armed factions of Anhui). Wang Li was removed from the Central Group of the Cultural Revolution, and Mao said of him that "Wang Li made more mistakes in forty days than Chen Yi made in forty years." It had therefore been made clear that the movement should not continue to challenge the "higher civil servants" like Chen Yi and Li Zian-nian, nor Zhou En-lai who was behind them. Again the universities were urged to reopen and the students to resume their studies.

A series of decisions and directives—the clearest of which circulated in Peking under the name of "Text of Two Thousand Words" without ever having been officially published—distinctly formulated the resolutions of this "great turning point" of September 1967: to promote a very broad grand alliance, to push for the resumption of production, to let almost all the cadres return to their duties, to clear the air of the attitude of distrust toward them, and to free as many of them as possible from the sessions of severe criticism—in short, to reach a political reconciliation. These September and October directives denounced the extreme left as such both for its destructive strategy and for its unmethodical and irresponsible style of work; it was accused of conspiracy (the "516") and collusion with the underworld; the army was henceforth entitled to seize the arms stockpiled by "little generals" who had been deprived of power. The October 17 directive said specifically that the army should intervene to support "the left, not the factions"; the military should take an active part in raising agricultural and industrial production, ensure military training domestically, and safeguard the national territory. In the following months, the military effectively took over the management of academic institutions, which had resumed their functions.

At the time of the October 1 festival, leaders of the university leftists like Wang Li and Qi Ben-yu were still in the reviewing stand, but Chen Yi had reappeared beside them: the balance between the political trends had been reversed. Now a period of calm and stability set in. University life went through a state of détente, and the student movement ran out of steam. The Red Guards' posters were now allowed only on the campuses, and the urban landscape changed color. The reintegrated cadres, the militants of the Revolutionary Committees, and the teachers were given courses of instruction along the lines of "eliminating egotism and criticizing revisionism" (*dousipixiu*), in accordance with "Mao Tsetung's thought". After the upheavals of the spring and the turbulence of the summer, the tendency was toward a methodical resumption of work and of production in the factories and communes.

A second countercurrent in February and the last periods of agitation

In February 1968 the trend toward stability was suddenly upset; the occasion for this was an obscure crisis involving Xie Fu-zhi, minister of security, Nie Yuan-zi, the last representative of the extreme left of Peking in the center, and three pro-leftist military leaders, including interim Chief of Staff Yang Cheng-wu. There was talk of a conspiracy. The three leftist military leaders were deprived of office and arrested. This affair, which remained mysterious, was attributed at the time to a "right-wing countercurrent" like that of February 1967. But it clearly indicated that there was a crisis brewing in the army. Looking back on it, a better explanation may be that it was provoked by the plans of Lin Biao, who was anxious to oust certain adversaries from leading positions in the army. The regional military command went through as many profound changes now as it had after the crisis.

The spring of 1968 was also marked by one last outburst of student factionalism. For example, week after week, at Qinghua University in Peking there was fighting between the "Earth Faction" (from the Geology Institute) and the "Sky Faction" (from the Aeronautics Institute). To put a stop to the riots, thousands of unarmed workers occupied the university in July, in a sort of non-violent invasion, without returning the fire or hand-grenade attacks of the students, who were convinced that they had to defend themselves against these misled revisionists; Mao, in the midst of his own crisis, met with the "little generals" of the students one last time to persuade them to give up their factional rivalry. In Canton and Nanning (in Guangxi), other bloody fights were still taking place at that time.

The stabilization of 1968

Liu Shao-qi, who had become the symbol of everything the Cultural Revolution was attacking, and who remained its principal target, was attacked again in the spring. He was denounced as an agent of the Guomindang, which occasioned a redefinition of the Cultural Revolution: it was to be a continuation of the old struggles of the CCP against the Guomindang rather than a new struggle based on new values and contradictions peculiar to a socialist society seeking its fundamental options. In October, the Twelfth Plenum of the Central Committee removed Liu from office permanently and expelled him from the Communist Party.

Between January and May 1968 the "power takeovers," in other words the establishment of revolutionary committees as temporary organs of local power, extended to almost all the provinces. The list was complete at the end of the summer when revolutionary committees were formed in Yunnan, Fujian, Guangxi, Tibet, and Xinjiang—regions whose political balance was doubly shaky because of their complex ethnic composition and strategic geopolitical location. In September a plenary meeting of the revolutionary committees of all the provinces was held.

Within the stable situation that existed at this time there was also a great deal of political and social intermingling. Starting in June, huge numbers of students were sent into the countrysides; for example, at Qinghua the student body was reduced by four-fifths. In October the first "May Seventh Schools" were opened.[2] Their purpose was to rally the cadres and reeducate them through

[2] On May 7, 1966, Mao had urged the cadres to reeducate themselves through manual labor and study.

manual labor within special institutions. Starting in 1968, this movement affected 100,000 cadres in the province of Guangdong.

But the policy of stabilization proved to be difficult to carry out. Many of the cadres who had been criticized were unhappy and not very eager to cooperate actively. The crisis in the army had not been resolved, and its extent was not evident until 1972, at the time Lin Biao was ousted. The return of the cadres to their duties went more slowly than had been anticipated. The provincial revolutionary committees were unstable, fragile, and in many provinces they were sustained only by the military element which dominated them. This was true of those that had taken the longest and the most trouble to form, whereas the first ones, which had appeared in the beginning of 1967 in the most radical regions, were dominated by militant "rebels." The congress of the CCP announced in 1967 for 1968 had had to be postponed several times. In the fall, Mao called for a "transfusion of proletarian blood in the party," which was a discreet way of pointing out that the CCP apparatus did not even begin to represent the most animated forces in the nation, particularly the proletariat whose leading role "in all domains" Yao Wen-yuan, one of the leaders of the Shanghai left, had affirmed in an article that appeared in August. But Yao's warning was undoubtedly addressed to the army rather than the right-wing elements nostalgic for the "revisionist-bourgeois" way.

The Cultural Revolution: *An Attempt at a General Analysis*

As is often the case in the writing of history, our analysis is full of hindsight observations ("running the film backward" as Marc Bloch has said); it is necessarily based in part on later developments, and as time passes, it therefore becomes fuller.

The Lin Biao crisis in 1972, for example, posed a number of questions about the role of the army in the Cultural Revolution and also about the degree of unity in the center during the movement.

The targets and the stakes

The Cultural Revolution was an expression of the tensions and conflicts surrounding *the fundamental choice of a type of society*:

ch kind of socialism would China have? Its aim was to con-
date and pursue the options of the Yanan period and the Great
ap Forward—the mass line, the priority of political consciousness
and collective determination ("politics in command"); it therefore
put less emphasis upon technical imperatives, material incentives,
and more generally the role of the "forces of production" in social
evolution. These *political options*, according to the Chinese Communists, had to be consolidated at the very level of the collective
consciousness ("the superstructure"); it was in this way that the
revolution was *cultural* in the broadest sense of the term—it involved not only arts and letters, but the whole ideology and concept
of the world.

The Cultural Revolution, then, attempted to block tendencies
to restore capitalism, tendencies which the Chinese Communists
believed naturally existed in any socialist society. They saw these
dangers materialize in the Soviet Union, whose evolution became
a veritable nightmare for the Chinese leaders: they saw the de-
generation of socialism, the appearance of revisionism, and the
return to a society based on money, technology, and a powerful
privileged class (even if it did not privately own the means of
production). The creators of the Cultural Revolution were therefore
convinced that in a socialist society still in a transitional stage, the
natural play of economic forces would tend toward this restoration
of capitalism. Time was therefore against them, and they could not
afford to delay. They were particularly alarmed at the beginning of
1965 by the plan for economic development prepared by the management faction and presented by Zhou En-lai; this plan proposed
that the effort at modernization be concentrated on a small number
of centers which were already favored, like Shanghai: in these
places it would be easier to establish an organic connection between
advanced industry and agriculture (involving tractors or chemical
fertilizers, for example). These options, by encouraging a selective
and technologically oriented development through various centers,
posed a direct threat to the gains of the Socialist Education Movement and the whole mass line based on the priority of politics.

These theoretical issues were expressed concretely by the fact
that the older generations would constantly be replaced by the
younger generations. In 1966, eighteen years after the Liberation,
a generation reached adulthood which had known only socialism
and tended to consider it a regime automatically conferred by
history, something that could be comfortably taken for granted.

How could one make sure the young people would carry on the revolution? How should they, who had never known the oppression and the struggles of earlier times, be involved? Some kind of shock treatment was necessary—particularly since many young people were sons and daughters of cadres who were already ensconced in their privileges. Year after year, starting in 1950, a larger and larger proportion of the students in the University of Peking were sons of privileged people. This slow and insidious change had to be stopped immediately.

The Cultural Revolution, then, depended on the young people, at least on the majority of them. This was the meaning of the appeal to the Red Guards. The old militants from the period of armed struggle had appealed to the young people, bypassing the group of cadres established since 1949 in bureaucratic administration because of an irrevocable socialist mandate. There was a good deal of antibureaucratic feeling in the Cultural Revolution. This struggle against the rigidity, authoritarianism, and excessive machinery in the state, the party, the schools, and the economic management was an extension of earlier antibureaucratic campaigns—the 1942 zhengfeng,[3] the "three antis" of 1951, and the Hundred Flowers of 1956–1957. The intricate machinery of the state and the party had to be simplified and made to involve the masses; it also had to be rejuvenated (the average age of the cadres was forty in 1965).

All these issues concerned human beings, living people. In this sense, the Cultural Revolution was also a struggle for power. The balance within the Central Committee had been shaky since the beginning of the sixties. Mao was not clearly supported by the majority. He was confronted with a group of high administrators who often were comfortably ensconced in their privileges and who had taken advantage of the uncertainties after the Great Leap Forward to consolidate their positions and their policy of "restoration"; for example, Liu Shao-qi and Deng Xiao-ping were powerful individual targets but they were also political symbols. The purpose of the long campaign against them was not only to get rid of them (which could have been accomplished quickly) but also to show people why this was politically necessary.

In order to realize the fundamental objectives of the movement, an abrupt change was necessary, a fundamental upheaval that would disrupt the continuity of the "socialist construction." This break in

[3] See Volume 2, Chapter 11.

the rhythm, unprecedented in the evolution of other communist countries, occurred eighteen years after the taking of power and affected the whole country; it really was a revolution—a ruthless challenge to the privileged class and an attack against a certain social balance. This challenge came from below, through the mass movement, and also from above, under the direction of the center and specifically Mao, who declared that he had always led the movement and controlled it.[4] In the final analysis, then, what was the moving force behind the Cultural Revolution? How did the aspirations of the base to "bombard the headquarters" tie in with the decision of the nucleus of Maoists to give free rein to these aspirations within certain limits and to rely on them to reverse the course of Chinese socialism?

"Bombard the headquarters . . ."

The breakup was ruthless: hierarchies and rules that had been acepted since 1949 were overthrown. "The lid on the class struggle has been blown off," said Mao in July 1967. "It is right to rebel" was the Red Guards' favorite slogan. The agitation, the struggle against privileged people—advocates of the black line—had reached the factories, the offices, and the campuses. It was a combination of joyous festival and severe confrontation. The cadres were rudely shaken. An indication of how unpopular they were was the fact that the center, which did not want to go too far, kept insisting that they were "95 percent good." The storm had overwhelmed them, even though undoubtedly the initiators of the movement had only meant to submit them to the control of the base. They found themselves paraded through the streets wearing defamatory hats, subjected to long sessions of collective criticism alternating with manual labor—all the while receiving their normal salaries.

The creative vitality of the movement was also indicated by the quantity and quality of the news. Besides the official organs like *Hongqi* and *Renmin Ribao*—containing general directives that required the skill of a specialist to decipher—there was a rich proliferation of *dazibao*, posters, tracts, and small newspapers.

The fact that the Cultural Revolution progressed at different speeds according to the different provinces, levels of hierarchy, and

[4] See document 2.

social structures (office or factory, campus or village), was also a very clear sign that it was a popular movement. The center planned and controlled only the overall values and general limits of the movement (except in the case of particularly serious incidents, like the Wuhan incident in July 1967). The implementation of the movement, whether fast or slow, was left up to the base as a function of the specific relations between political forces.

Suddenly Chinese political life had accelerated. Under this pressure, structures were shaken, the machinery creaked, the transmission belt jumped. Particularly affected were the "secondary apparatuses" that had been copied from Soviet models during the fifties, and which were as unwieldy as the party machine without having its responsibilities; these included such instruments as the Federation of Women, the Federation of Unions, the Federation of Communist Youth, and the Writers' Union. All of them quietly disappeared in 1966. Numerous prominent figures associated with the black line were dismissed from office after having been rudely criticized: among them were the ideologists Lu Ding-yi, Zhou Yang, and Hou Wai-lu; the military men Luo Rui-qing and He Long; the trade unionist Liu Ning-yi; and the financier Bo Yi-bo. Their habit of holding a large number of semihonorary offices[5] made them particularly vulnerable to being criticized from all sides at once by the base. Mao was thinking of them when he stigmatized "those comrades who lag behind on the road like old women with bound feet" (September 1967).

But this sudden explosion of creativity brought in its train disorder, anarchist-type factionalism, the settling of scores, and all kinds of excesses, including suicides that were more or less provoked and bloody fights. In Sichuan alone, Han Suyin was told, 90,000 died. In the months of April and May 1967 there were 133 armed battles, leaving 63,000 victims, according to K. S. Karol. The phenomenon of the extreme left was the most spectacular of these negative tendencies. It would be too easy to attribute this to the effects of conspiracy (the "516") and the uncontrolled elements of the underworld, uprooted by the economic consequences of the Great Leap Forward. Long after the Liberation, the socialist society

---

[5] See Chapter 3. Liu Ning-yi occupied several leadership positions in union affairs, in international relations, and in the party secretariat. Bo Yi-bo also headed a number of banking, industrial, and economic enterprises (especially having to do with short- and long-term planning); he also belonged to the Politburo and the State Council (with limited administrative powers).

in China still included vast middle classes which were not directly integrated into production and whose average age was quite low because of the population explosion and the relative rigidity of the labor market. These young members of the middle class, who were at once enthusiastic and disoriented by the movement, and were prepared to commit any excesses, formed readily available troops for the "little generals." In summer 1967 the confusion reached its height, sterile conflicts dragging on and on among the crowd of "headless dragons." Throughout the movement, the extreme left had shown that it had real tactical dynamism; but it had never been able to use its social base to guarantee strategic leadership of the movement and counter the center with a coherent plan.

. . . but only up to a certain point

Throughout the Cultural Revolution, the "right to rebel" had operated within a political field defined by a whole system of unwritten but very powerful rules. Mao was already playing a considerable part personally. He had taken the initiative of letting loose the forces of disorder, at the same time prescribing definite limits to them. His position was strengthened by the "cult" later attributed to Lin Biao and which he accepted for tactical reasons, in order to use it against his adversaries: there were badges, slogans, statues, the "Little Red Book," and bombastic epithets ("Great Helmsman," *weida duoshou*). His prestige was so great that rival factions outdid one another trying to share it; this was the phenomenon known as "waving the red flag against the red flag," a source of confusion for the masses as well as for foreign observers.

But Mao was not isolated. During the entire movement he had the support of a center (*zhongyang*) which did not necessarily have a majority in the statutory proceedings of the CCP. This center consisted of the members of the Politburo who supported the movement, with the addition of active elements like Jiang Qing. The makeup of the center therefore varied according to the changes that individuals underwent (see the cases of Tao Zhu and Wang Li). The center acted through two ad hoc bodies—the Ceneral Group of the Cultural Revolution and the Military Commission.

On the other hand the party, as a vast collective structure, had virtually ceased to function. Only some of its members were active in the temporary bodies they belonged to in the center or locally. The party's privileged political mandate was therefore being challenged, but only as a concrete organization, defined by its leaders, its practice, and its work style. As a principle, its superior legitimacy remained intact, in spite of the efforts of the ultra-left. Liu was attacked as "the highest of those who, *even though they belong to the party*, are committed to the capitalist road." In 1968 the party gradually began to function again with the help of the army, re-affirming the principle that the proletariat was the leading force in the nation.

The Cultural Revolution had thus been sustained without being allowed to extend into certain "sanctuaries." One was advanced scientific research: China's first hydrogen bomb exploded in the midst of a national crisis in August 1967. Diplomacy was another: the attacks of the ultra-left against Chen Yi and his ministry brought about his downfall, but this was only a momentary aberration. It was during the Cultural Revolution that relations between China and Canada were normalized, which was the first step toward the admission of China to the UN. Another sanctuary was the higher echelons of the administration: it was agreed that the "rebels" could remove subordinate and middle level cadres, but only the center could remove the heads of large ministries. The effect of this was to leave Zhou En-lai out of range of the protest; and Zhou En-lai represented the "weight of things." Lastly there was the army, which was a very active agent of the movement but not an area of protest. It had to operate politically too, by *wendou* and not *wudou*. And was the army Lin Biao? At the time, there was hardly any difference between Lin's policy and that of the Maoist center. Mao's reservations about his "dauphin," expressed in July 1966 in a letter to his wife, were still secret.

The fact that the Cultural Revolution was limited and temporary affected its institutions too. The Triple Alliance and the revolution-ary committees were temporary organizations. The movement stopped before these institutions could be radically changed to in-corporate Paris-type democracy from the base; even though certain texts in 1966 referring to the Paris Commune suggested that such changes had been made. In the same way, the May Seventh Schools aimed at transforming the cadres, tying them in with the masses, not at challenging the cadres-masses duality ("the water and the fish"). On all these points the extreme left was at odds with the center.

Every time one of these limits, one of these sanctuaries, one of these unwritten rules was violated, the center vigorously redirected the movement. This happened in Shanghai in February 1967, when the commune threatened to cause changes in the organization of a succession of political structures. It happened again in Wuhan in July 1967 when the extreme left tried to extend the movement into the army. And in Peking in August 1967, when Zhou En-lai, Chen Yi's ally, risked being attacked.

A revolution involving the youth

The training of "revolutionary successors" among the younger generations was one of the main goals of the movement at the very time when the Youth League was more or less dormant—and had been especially since the Great Leap Forward. It was not just the students who were very active in the rebel groups; all the youth— young workers and office employees included—threw themselves passionately into the Cultural Revolution: there were the "Long Marches" of 1966, the free use of transportation, the exchanges of experience (*chuanlian*) with workers throughout the country (whereas chances to discover the country on long journeys had been rare until then), mass demonstrations, and raids on the houses of the rich and privileged. There was also sexual freedom, something uncommon in socialist China, which was usually so reserved.

The style of the young people left a deep mark on the Cultural Revolution. It was a creative, coded style, with an extraordinary profusion of organizations with picturesque names, caricatures, and imaginative slogans. The vocabulary was very rich, freighted with connivance and implications. Noninitiates, whether Chinese or foreign, could not begin to understand it. This great collective festival was really only open to people who mastered its language.

The young people seemed to be particularly preoccupied by their relationship with the past, their place in history. With passion and anguish they tried to assess the positive and negative aspects of the first seventeen years of Chinese socialism—the span of their own lifetimes. For them, the past was only valuable as a way of better defining the future, which belonged to them. They were therefore wary of the pitfalls of history as collective and repressive memory, what they called the "black materials" (*heiliao*)—that is, the reports and dossiers about their activities, which they suspected the criticized cadres of accumulating to be used against them later. They demanded the destruction of the *heiliao*. The fact that in their movement they were profoundly conscious of history is evident also from the names chosen by the rebel groups, names that evoked the high points and the strong periods of the Chinese revolution: Jinggangshan and the Long March, Beifa in 1927, and the Northeast (Liao Shen) Campaign in 1948.

During the Cultural Revolution, however, the limits of the young people's political capacities had become clear: they were able to put life into the movement, make it colorful, and contribute to its dynamism, but they were not able to lead it. Left on their own, they had been at the mercy of the "headless dragons" (*wudoulong*), their factional fighting, their sudden reversals of policy, and their excesses.

A revolution in culture and education?

The Cultural Revolution had overthrown the traditional institutions of cultural production—such as they existed in this socialist country—the Writers' Union, the art centers, the publishing houses, the newspapers, and the museums. Here, as in other areas, there was very vigorous criticism of the black line. The movement had forced intellectuals to examine themselves, to reassess their privileges, and to define suitable activities for "serving the people." For example, it launched a radical criticism of the old Peking Opera and also of professional and elitist sporting events. But in the short time it existed it had been too chaotic, too rich for truly large-scale intellectual and artistic creation to take place. Rather, the Cultural Revolution itself was conducted from one day to the next in a cultural way, with its spirited *dazibao*, its slogans, and its open-air debates, which became so many spectacles in which everyone participated intensely.

Where education was concerned, the effect of the breakup had been just as clear; it had opened the way to the profound reorganization that would gradually occur during the seventies on the theme of *kaimen banxue* (open-door teaching). On the campuses in 1966 and 1967 there was very vigorous criticism of university teaching for being bookish and authoritarian. The young students had met workers in the course of the "Long Marches," and again, while the universities were being taken over by the authorities in 1968, they had come into contact with workers and soldiers—sometimes very brutal contact; so that these young people—many of whom were the sons and daughters of cadres—were forced to emerge from the confined world of their studies.

Economic goals in the cities and rural areas

Not only did a minimum level of production have to be ensured
(Point 14 of August 1966: "Promote revolution and ensure production"), but the working relation between economic priorities and
political priorities had to be reevaluated: what was in question was
economist thinking. There had to be concrete goals, not theoretical
controversies. Advocates of the black line refused to allow political
protest to be organized where production was taking place, especially in the factories. At the end of 1966 in Shanghai, for example,
local leaders hostile to the movement tried to distract the workers'
attention with complicated problems involving profit bonuses, wage
scales, and technical division of work. One caricature showed Liu
Shao-qi and Deng Xiao-ping trying to derail the train of the Cultural
Revolution by putting bundles of money on the tracks. At the
beginning of 1967 the Cultural Revolution extended to factories
and the working class everywhere: this was an important stage.

The movement itself completely disrupted production, especially
in 1967: transports were disorganized, there was fighting in the
factories, and there were protests in the planning services. Yet even
though no statistics exist to prove it, official and unofficial accounts
agree that during these troubled years industrial and agricultural
production was generally satisfactory. Essential economic needs
were fulfilled.

From the very beginning the movement had been defined as
mainly urban (Point 14 in 1966). It only affected the rural areas
some time later and in an attenuated form, and the villages were
not shaken by mass meetings, tensions, and violent crises, as the
cities were. Was this because the campaign for a socialist education
in 1964, whose target was the rural cadres, had already prepared
the way? More than anything else, it seems that in the villages the
Cultural Revolution took the form of a campaign for making the
economic and social structures and the organized bodies more
flexible, and also for freeing the energies of the people.[6] For
example, there was the movement of the "barefoot doctors";[7] there
was the reform of rural schools, which stopped forcing the pupils
to follow a program copied from the level of the cities and began
giving priority to the real needs of young rural children; and there

[6] See document 4.
[7] See document 5.

was the reform of the system of work points and compensation to simplify it.

The international situation

In the context of the international situation, the Cultural Revolution oscillated between two opposite poles. In the mid-sixties it belonged in the context of the increasing numbers of radical struggles both in the Third World and in the West. But it also had to confront the growing importance of the two superpowers and was forced to determine its defense position in relation to them.

Throughout the Cultural Revolution, the Chinese authorities and especially the Red Guards made many gestures of solidarity toward the Vietnamese resistance, the struggles of the Portuguese colonies and the American blacks, the Naxalite guerrillas in India, and "May 1968" in France. This attitude of militant solidarity made it much easier for the "516" to take over the ministry of foreign affairs in the summer of 1967. For the first time, the People's Republic began breaking a number of traditional rules of diplomacy, especially the principle of Chinese citizens abroad not taking part in local politics. Chinese living in Southeast Asia were encouraged to revolt, Chinese students in Paris demonstrated against the Soviet Embassy, and Chinese sailors staged aggressive parades in Genoa and Colombo. When the "516" fell, these tendencies disappeared.

Then there was the threat of the superpowers. The Cultural Revolution was taking place in the midst of the American war in Vietnam, which was being waged on China's very doorstep. The situation was very dangerous. In 1966, students were digging trenches on the Peking campuses. The Cultural Revolution's atmosphere of decentralized militarization was not only caused by factional fighting and internal disorder but also by the desire to resist aggression by "counting on our own forces." The fear of Soviet pressure was just as vivid. In 1968, while the Red Army was entering Prague, Kosygin was in Delhi and Suslov in Tokyo; tension mounted in March 1969 with the incidents involving the border islands in the Amur. These worries may have increased the tendency to restore order in 1969, the tendency to end the movement.

An unfinished revolution?

"In seven or eight years, we will have to start another cultural revolution to eliminate other demons . . . and we will have to repeat this many times," Mao declared in the middle of the Cultural Revolution. What were the other demons?

At the leadership level, the Cultural Revolution initially bene-fited the radicals, but at the cost of a compromise with certain military groups associated with Lin Biao, certain "higher manage-ment clerks." The crises of 1972 and 1976, which resulted in the elimination of Lin Biao and Deng Xiao-ping, showed how fragile this balance was, and it was upset again after Mao's death.

What was more, certain aspects of the bureaucracy that had been attacked in 1966–1969 tended to reappear. The fact that they had been attacked so vigorously during that period was no guarantee for the future—except that a precedent was established for setting up political mechanisms for attacking them again.

The Cultural Revolution had affected different areas of society to very different extents. It had affected teaching, culture, industrial production, and base political administration much more than rela-tions between cities and rural areas, for example, or relations be-tween men and women.

More generally, although the Cultural Revolution had allowed the left to take the advantage again, it had not resulted in a defini-tive commitment to one of the two lines of development that China had been hesitating over since 1949—one emphasizing the political mobilization of the masses and initiative from below, and one favoring selective projects and the economic criteria of management from above (see Chapter 8).

By suspending, even if temporarily, the working legitimacy of the party and state machinery and their irrevocable mandate, and by affirming the need for other attacks of the same sort in the future, the Cultural Revolution may possibly have represented an original and specific contribution by Chinese communism to the old Marxist vision of the withering away of the state.

ADDITIONAL BIBLIOGRAPHY

Jean Daubier, *A History of the Cultural Revolution* (New York, 1974).
Jean Esmein, *La Révolution culturelle* (Paris, 1970).
William Hinton, *The Hundred Days War: The Cultural Revolution at Tsinghua University* (New York, 1972).
A. Jelokhovtsev, *La révolution culturelle vue par un soviétique* (Paris, 1968).
K. S. Karol, *The Second Chinese Revolution* (New York, 1974).
Alberto Moravia, *La Révolution culturelle de Mao* (Paris, 1967).

Klaus Mehnert, *Pékin et la nouvelle gauche* (Paris, 1971).

Victor Nee, *Revolution and Bureaucracy: Shanghai in the Cultural Revolution* (in the anthology *China's Uninterrupted Revolution*, edited by Victor Nee and James Peck, New York, 1975, pp. 322–414).

Joan Robinson, *The Cultural Revolution in China* (London, 1969).

Union Research Institute, *Documents of the Great Proletarian Cultural Revolution* (Hong Kong, 1968).

G. Mury, *De la Révolution culturelle au Xe Congrès* (Textes choisis, Paris, 1973, 2 vol.).

DOCUMENTS

1. ONE OF THE LEADERS OF THE SHANGHAI COMMUNE ASKS THE PEOPLE NOT TO BE TOO "ADVANCED" FOR THE REST OF THE COUNTRY

Source: Neale Hunter, *Shanghai Journal* (New York, Praeger, 1969), pp. 260–262.

. . . We are left with the impression that Zhang Chun-qiao's return marked the end of an era. From February 23, the city was his. The apparent ease with which he resumed control can no doubt be explained by whatever he brought back from his 12-day stay in Peking. . . .

He must have had some success in arranging a compromise, for the next day he spoke to a capacity crowd in Culture Square, and the meeting was televised all over the city. I watched this telecast in our hotel lounge and found it a fascinating spectacle. The Chinese with me evidently thought so too. They had put up with months of uncertainty and reams of exaggerated, contradictory, and stereotyped descriptions of plots and counterplots, sieges, and skirmishes. Like the rest of the city, they had often been bewildered. Now, all of a sudden, here was the man who held the key to the mystery.

It was the man himself who impressed, not because he was impressive but simply because he was a *person*. Shanghai had been a battle ground of shadows for so long. Now, at last, the people had someone to focus on. It was as if an immortal had left his kingdom of clouds and was sitting in your living room dropping ashes on the carpet.

He was startlingly casual, with a long, furrowed face more like that of a peasant than a bureaucrat. He was also a born wisecracker, with the gift of deadpan, and often had his audience laughing heartily. Underneath, there was a toughness; although he drawled his words and spoke the idiom of the people, one sensed he was used to being obeyed. He inspired confidence by addressing his listeners directly, informally, without notes, and without undue political jargon. He also had the amusing and relaxing habit of fishing single cigarettes from a pocket of his rather scruffy military-style jacket and bending away in mid-sentence to light up. This was a far cry from the usual stiff atmosphere of official speech-making in China.

He spoke for about 2 hours but bored no one. The gist of his message was that, yes, he had seen Chairman Mao in Peking. Three times, to be precise. In the Chairman's opinion, it was too early to set up a Shanghai

Commune, the main reason being that Shanghai was further advanced in the Cultural Revolution than the rest of the country, and if it declared itself a Commune, then other cities would want to do the same. This could short-circuit the movement by clamping a premature formula on a process that should reach its own conclusion through free and open debate between divergent opinions.

What worried Chairman Mao, he went on, was a tendency among some Rebel groups to demand the overthrow of *all* people in authority, whether revolutionary or reactionary. This had resulted in attacks on as high a body as the Central Cultural Revolution Group. The line had to be drawn somewhere, the Chairman had said, and, for the purposes of this movement, it had been drawn at the Central Cultural Revolution Group, whose members had been chosen by Mao himself and were therefore sancrosanct. (Zhang Chun-qiao did not have to remind his listeners that he and Yao Wen-yuan were members of this group.)

Having dealt with his enemies, he went on to discuss the local situation. Shanghai, he said, was China's most complex industrial metropolis. It could not be governed by students or workers alone. As everyone knew, he laughed, he and the Rebels had been somewhat out of their depth trying to keep Shanghai going. To ensure that the city functioned efficiently under its new administration, two allies were essential: the high army officers, who could keep counterrevolutionary forces under control, and the top-flight cadres, who knew from long experience how to get the best from the system.

This last feature provided the element of compromise. He put the number of top administrators at 6,000. They could, he said, be replaced, but only with great difficulty and over a long period of time. But there was no need to replace them, because most were "good or comparatively good," and even those who had "made mistakes during the movement" could be rehabilitated and welcomed to the Rebel ranks.

2. MAO TSETUNG ACCEPTS THE RESPONSIBILITY FOR THE DISORDERS IN THE CULTURAL REVOLUTION AND ASKS THE LEADING CADRES TO ADAPT THEM-SELVES TO THEM

Source: Jerome Chen, *Mao Papers* (London, Oxford University Press, 1970), pp. 42–45.

TALK AT THE WORK CONFERENCE OF THE CENTRE 25.10.1966

Second, the great Cultural Revolution raised havoc—I mean [my] comment on Nie Yuan-zi's big-character poster, [my] letter to the Tsinghua Middle School, and my own big-character poster. It was done in a short period of time—June, July, August, September, and October—less than five months. It is not surprising that many comrades have not yet grasped its meaning. It covered a short space of time but it had tremendous momentum —in both exceeding my expectations. Once the Peking University big-character poster was broadcast, the whole nation rose up. Before the letter to them was made public, the Red Guards of the whole country began to move. The tidal waves strike you with all their might. Since I am responsible for this havoc, I can hardly blame you if you grumble. . . .

The democratic revolution went on for twenty-eight years, from 1921 to 1924 [*sic.* 1949?]. At the beginning, no one knew how to go about it. The path was found by path-finders who in the twenty-eight years had [periodically] summed up [their] experience. It was impossible to ask comrades to understand [what they were doing]. . . . But big-character posters and the Red Guards attacked and they succeeded in attracting attention. It is impossible to ignore them. The revolution has come to your doorstep and you must quickly sum up your experience. . . .

. . . Seven or eight secretaries [of the party] out of ten began to receive [the Red Guards]. They were thrown into a panic by the Red Guards. . . . They lost the initiative when they were taken aback by some of the questions. But the lost initiative can be recovered. That is why my confidence in this conference has increased.

. . . I ignited the great Cultural Revolution of the past five months. [But] it is only five months, a short time, compared with the twenty-eight years of the democratic revolution and seventeen years of the socialist revolution. It is understandable that there should still be ignorance and inconsistencies after less than six months. In the past, you worked on industries, agriculture, and communications, but not on a great cultural revolution. Similar situations existed in the Ministry of Foreign Affairs and the Military Commission. What you did not expect has now come. Let it come, I think it is a good thing to have this tidal wave. Brains which have not thought for many years may think again under its impact. At the worst, it is just a mistake. . . .

. . . I would feel sorry if you could not pass this test. I am just as anxious as you are. It has not been a very long time yet and I do not blame you, Comrades. . . .

3. THE COLLECTIVE CELEBRATION IN THE STREETS OF PEKING

Source: Jean Daubier, *A History of the Chinese Cultural Revolution* (New York, Vintage, 1974), pp. 135–137.

In February 1967 the Chinese streets offered an extraordinary spectacle: the walls, the shop windows, even the sidewalks were covered with posters, big-character slogans, and caricatures. The last-named, which were usually done in a series and were remarkable for their subtlety and humor, depicted various episodes of the battle being fought. The most common targets were Liu Shao-qi, his wife Wang Guang-mei, Deng Xiao-ping and Tao Zhu, but other high functionaries were also sometimes singled out. By their number, their bright colors, and the satirical talents of their authors, they made the city streets of China look as though they had suddenly been transformed into so many pages out of some enlarged picture magazine. One series of caricatures showed Liu Shao-qi being given an X-ray examination which revealed his "black" heart—black in China symbolizing every evil under the sun, including revisionism, which is the worst sin of all. In another one

Tao Zhu was shown opening an insurance office specializing in protecting revisionists; in still another He Long was portrayed in the costume and with the characteristics which in the old Peking opera had indicated a militarist of feudal China. . . .

Peking, like all of China, seemed in a state of high excitement. All day long processions wound their way through the streets. Students and workers, on foot or in trucks, came and went in a welter of meetings, and everywhere they went they bore a sea of unfurled banners and flags and portraits of Mao, and wore distinguishing armbands. At the main intersections, along the main thoroughfares and in the immense Tien-an-Men Square, knots of people formed and re-formed; crowds gathered, made contact, exchanged information, and went on their way or joined another crowd. Never had so many handbills been given out; never had so many worker-organization and Red Guard newspapers been sold. In Peking some 200 such papers were sold regularly, by students and workers, who hawked them at every major intersection. . . .

The GCCR had set up a reception center near Tien-an-Men which was a focal point for all visiting organizations from the capital or the provinces. It was here they left and picked up messages, reports, questionnaires, and it was to this center they came for information. Loudspeakers blared constantly, not only from the tops of trucks that were parked at busy intersections, but also in schools and offices, factories and work sites: the latest news was given, any new declarations made were passed on, and the speakers were not above indulging in a diatribe now and then, all of which produced a tremendous cacophony.

It was fairly common to see people parading through the streets to the sound of gongs and drums, carrying two-sided posters with the double sign of happiness on one side and a flower-framed portrait of Mao on the other, to celebrate publicly the transfer of power they had just effected where they worked. In such cases the students or workers affixed on both sides of the door to their school, university, or place of work red wood panels with gilded lettering announcing the formation of a revolutionary committee there. They also adorned the façade with a wide strip of pleated red cloth covered with many-colored flowers, and then hung purple paper lanterns—which are symbols of festive occasions—in their entranceways. And far into the night, one could hear the constant noise of firecrackers exploding—another traditional merrymaking method.

4. THE CULTURAL REVOLUTION IN DAZHAI

Source: K. S. Karol, *The Second Chinese Revolution* (New York, Hill & Wang, 1974), pp. 171–172.

Chen now came to his actions during the Cultural Revolution. "Between February and April 1967, having taken power in the district, we too formed rank-and-file teams that went into all the communes to carry out investigations and spread the directives of Chairman Mao. We helped the cadres to understand their mistakes and accept the criticisms of the masses, their ideology could be changed and they could make a good fres' a revolutionary spirit. We also examined the problems of each brig understand their difficulties better and give them some help, not to punish this or that person. We started 'flying teams,' which helped the backward places; we put fields under cultivation even on waste land, to produce selected crops as a common effort, thus encouraging the understanding of the masses. This hard work was not in vain; in the Xiyang district the 1967 harvest was 40 percent up on 1966. As you've seen for yourself, most of the brigades are now catching up with Tachai. . . .

Before coming to my questions, Chen mentioned a few personal problems. Here again, he sought to bring out a general contradiction from his own example. He admitted frankly that the many honors showered upon him were becoming a weight on his shoulders. He was afraid lest the numerous duties he had been obliged to take on should divert him from his work on the spot. As a member of the Central Committee, vice-chairman of the Provincial Revolutionary Committee, assigned to speak for Dazhai in the provinces, in Peking, and even abroad—he had already been to Albania— he was afraid of becoming like one of those cadres in the work teams who, after giving good service to the people, had got out of touch. "I have decided to work with my brigade in the fields for at least two hundred days a year, and I must carry out this aim at any cost. I often say to myself, 'You were born in a family of workers and you must not forget how to work with your hands, or you'll forget your class origin.' " . . .

5. A SPECIALIST IN INTERNAL MEDICINE GOES TO THE COUNTRYSIDE TO LEARN FROM THE POOR PEASANTS

Source: Maria Antonietta Macciocchi, *Daily Life in Revolutionary China* (New York, Monthly Review, 172), pp. 273–274.

"I am a specialist in internal medicine. In the fall of 1968 I went into the countryside to learn from the poor peasants. Once our team stopped in a village where there was a woman who was considered incurable. The family was already preparing for the funeral. I decided I had to pay a call on this woman too. I examined her closely and I realized that she had a generalized arthritis; she had not been treated in time and she had swelled up. I asked her family, 'Why didn't you ever take her to a doctor?' Her husband told me angrily that they had taken the sick woman on a stretcher to a city hospital four years before, that this had cost them much money, but that the hospital had told them she was *incurable*. Back in her village, the woman took the medicine prescribed for her but the sickness worsened steadily. I learned from her husband that the doctor in question belonged to the same hospital as I did. When I returned, I looked through the files and found that the doctor who had made the incorrect diagnosis was me." Here he lowered his head like a guilty man. "I was tremendously upset and full of self-contempt. . . . I returned to the countryside and again took up my work with the barefoot doctors; I had, at all costs, to cure this woman. The treatments I gave her were for me the beginning of a struggle to see the world differently. Each day I went to her house, I devoted all my attention to her, I observed her unceasingly; I adopted different treatments and mixed Chinese and Western medicine. After two months, the sick woman's health improved, she was able to get up, to take her first steps, and at length she could do a few light tasks."

The professor's lips are trembling. He is tense. His eyes are fixed on the table, as if he were at confession before us.

"After I changed my ideology, I cured twenty patients who had been considered 'incurable.' In truth, I believe it was the poor peasants who cured me of my ideological sickness, and not I who cured the peasants. If intellectuals do not pay attention to their own conceptions of the world, and seek to change them, they may possess a very high scientific level, but they are not in a position to serve the people."

Chapter Seven

After the Cultural Revolution: *1969–1976*

A period of reconstruction followed the destruction that had marked the Cultural Revolution. Leadership structures and institutions were reestablished—drawing on the principles and new ideas that had emerged from the Cultural Revolution—and political life was debureaucratized through increased participation of the masses. The struggle between the two lines became a daily phenomenon, almost open and commonplace. Contradictions were coming to a head, and in the space of six years Lin Biao disappeared and Deng Xiao-ping again became a center of controversy.

From the Ninth Party Congress to the Fall of Lin Biao

The Ninth Congress marked the start of the rebuilding of the country's institutions, beginning with the reconstruction of the party organizations. This took place slowly because of the ideological turmoil of the preceding period and the violent internal conflicts that led to the fall of Lin Biao.

The Ninth Congress of the Communist Party

The Ninth Congress, prepared for throughout early 1968 by means of extensive internal debates, was held for twenty-three days in March and April 1968; a total of 1,512 delegates attended. Almost nothing is known about these sessions, which took place behind closed doors. The congress listened to a general political report from Lin Biao, adopted new statutes, and elected new leaders. These moves tended both to integrate the gains of the Cultural Revolution and to consolidate party unity, if only in appearance, but the congress also established, at least in public, the personal rise of Lin Biao. The new statutes opened the party to workers, poor peasants, and soldiers—the "new blood" of the proletariat. Article 5 established the right to disagreement without fear of sanctions. The new Politburo included many active participants in the Cultural Revolution: Jiang Qing, certain soldiers, and leaders of the former Shanghai Commune such as Yao Wen-yuan and Wang Hong-wen.

The report indicated that "struggle-criticism-reform must be waged conscientiously," which was explained by Mao in the following terms: "To found a Triple Alliance revolutionary committee, to wage large-scale criticism, to cleanse our class ranks, to consolidate the party organizations, to simplify administrative structures, to reform all irrational rules and send administrative and technical personnel to work at the base. In general, these are the stages of struggle-criticism-reform."

A congress of unity, at least on the surface, the Ninth Congress called for the unity of the people, particularly concerning intellectuals of the old school and cadres who had committed errors. The great majority of the intellectuals "were able to or wanted to integrate themselves with the workers, peasants, and soldiers." They had to be reeducated by them. As for the cadres, "those who had committed errors as leaders engaged in the capitalist way but who were nevertheless good elements," they had to be "liberated" at the proper time and given "appropriate work as soon as they had raised their political consciousness and gained the comprehension of the masses."

The party had to be rebuilt, and, as the new statutes emphasized, "the organs of state power of the dictatorship of the proletariat, the People's Liberation Army, the Communist Youth League, the organizations for workers, poor and middle-poor peasants, the Red Guards and other mass revolutionary organizations must without exception accept the leadership of the party." The primacy of the party in society was thus reaffirmed.

Lin Biao seemed to dominate the congress. His role as Mao's official successor was stipulated in the very statutes of the party. Later it became known that the first version of the general report, which had been drafted by Lin Biao and Chen Bo-da, had undergone substantial revisions after collective discussions. Zhou En-lai later said that in fact Lin Biao knew that he was already in decline. But the general report appeared to be his. Whatever Lin Biao's personal ambitions, his rise can be understood only in a double context: international tension (Prague, Vietnam, and border disputes with the Russians over the islands in the Ussuri River) and the army's continuing influence in the political life of the country. The rebuilding of the party had advanced very slowly; in many cases it had been the army that had organized, if not controlled, the work preparatory to the congress and therefore the selection of the delegates. At the Ninth Congress there was a fragile balance among what would later be recognized as Lin Biao's military faction, the old cadres symbolized by Zhou En-lai, and the new activists.

The army

The army was the only organization in the country to remain intact after the party and the administration had ceased to fulfill their traditional leadership roles. Along with the cadres and the "revolutionary rebels," the soldiers were one of the fundamental elements of the Triple Alliance which formed the base of the local and provincial revolutionary committees. They acquired a dominant position on the Central Committee and Politburo created by the Ninth Congress. The new Central Committee was made up of 279 members (permanent members and alternates), of whom 123 came from the army (or 44.1 percent), 75 from the cadres (26.9 percent), and 81 from the masses (29 percent). In the Politburo the military was even more heavily represented: of the 21 members 11 were soldiers (55 percent), 5 were from the cadres (25 percent), and 4 from the masses (20 percent).

The events that followed, however, were not due to a direct antagonism between civilians and the military: the struggle between the two lines was not divided up in this way, even though the Lin Biao affair mainly involved top-ranking military men.

The rebuilding of the party

The reconstruction of the party remained a difficult process until all the provinces had a party committee. Starting in 1969 certain leaders of revolutionary committees were criticized for their work styles, which were characterized by arrogance, negligence, and severity.

In certain cases the soldiers on the revolutionary committees were accused of not considering points of view expressed by the two other elements of the Triple Alliance (cadres and representatives from the masses) and of diverging from the mass line by using constraint and administrative decrees instead of persuasion and explanation. In a speech given at the First Plenum of the Ninth Central Committee on April 28, 1969, Mao went even further when he said that in a great number of cases "the leadership is not in the hands of true Marxists or in the hands of the masses and workers." And even, "in some places there were too many people arrested." And finally, in the same speech, addressing himself to the military: "There is nothing from either your previous or present lives to make you mortal enemies . . . You simply clashed, had some differences of opinion, somebody did something like criticizing you or opposing you. You counterattacked and as a result a contradiction arose. . . ."[1]

The reconstruction of the party depended on the rebalancing of the Triple Alliance in the revolutionary committees—which were the basis of the new party committees.

Increasing the representation of the cadres in the revolutionary committees meant rehabilitating those who had been criticized and had gone through self-criticism and a period of manual work in the May Seventh Schools. This did not happen without difficulties; it offended the numerous rebels of the Cultural Revolution as well as certain military men who feared a return to the past. The critics of arrogance, who were supported by certain new leaders and the statement that "too many people were arrested," worked in favor of the rehabilitation of the cadres criticized during the Cultural Revolution.

One of the major factors in the delay of party reconstruction was the application of the so-called open-door principle, which meant consulting the masses and recruiting—in the party organs that were

---

[1] *Chairman Mao Talks to the People*, p. 287.

undergoing reorganization—Red Guards and revolutionary rebels; the press denounced extremist tendencies, and occasionally there were violent incidents. The left and right currents confronted each other in the process. For some, the reconstruction of the party was an internal matter that had nothing to do with the masses. Those who considered themselves the most revolutionary and advanced, those who had joined the rebel cause at the very beginning of the Cultural Revolution, felt that they should be given the task of re-building the party. These errors were also committed by certain groups that had been formed in the preceding period and who claimed to be above the party: they wanted to consign the party to the role of a mass organization. These tendencies were accused of "anarchism" and "theories of polycentrism."

The reconstruction of the party began at the base, at the level of the production units, and then slowly spread to the district level. In October 1970 only sixty of them (out of 2,000 in the country) had rebuilt a party committee. The pace suddenly accelerated, and between December 1970 and July 1971 each province formed a new party organization.

The origins of the Lin Biao affair

The political report drawn up by Chen Bo-da and Lin Biao for the Ninth Congress had been rejected by the Central Committee. The minister of defense had to write a new one "under the personal direction of Mao Tsetung." With the Ninth Congress—and even before—began the "tenth major struggle" within the CCP.

To simplify matters, what was called "Lin Biao's antiparty clique" was made up of elements who had a common interest in opposing the line established by the Ninth Congress; these included Lin Biao, who knew that he was no longer Mao Tsetung's official successor even though the official documents designated him as such, Chen Bo-da and the others who saw the end of the Cultural Revolution's ultra-left radicalism coming, and some regional military leaders who had had de facto political power since the Cultural Revolution and saw this power coming to an end with the reconstruction of the party.

The divergences between these groups and the line defended by Mao crystallized around three major questions:

1. The reconstruction of the party and the state with the participation of those who had been criticized in 1966–1969. This

provoked the opposition of the ultra-left connected with Chen Bo-da and the fears of some military leaders who had acquired a taste for power.

2. Differences on foreign policy, especially concerning the Soviet Union, the normalization of relations with the United States, and perhaps also Vietnam.

3. The problem of economic development. Lin Biao would later be accused of both trying to continue Liu Shao-qi's revisionist theories (according to Zhou En-lai at the Tenth Congress) concerning the priority of production and wanting to bring communism to China too soon. These accusations perhaps only appeared to be contradictory (see below); Lin Biao's group seemed to have a tendency to prefer a rather hasty and technologically oriented economic development imposed from above without the political support of the base. More generally, Lin Biao's personality and political line were profoundly contradictory: the more he demagogically pushed for extreme solutions, the more he tended toward authoritarian practices. That is why after his fall he could be denounced first as a leftist and then as a rightist.

The "tenth major struggle": the plot

The reconstruction of the party according to the guidelines of the Ninth Congress met with resistance that was overcome only little by little. At the end of 1969 the group in charge of the Cultural Revolution, the principle base of leftism, was dissolved—a sign that Chen Bo-da had fallen from political favor. At the same time an investigation was made into the activities of the May Sixteenth Group, an organization of Red Guards, a symbol of extremism and violence during the Cultural Revolution, which had been accused of wanting to attain communism immediately and of persecuting the veteran cadres of the party.

The first open confrontation between Lin Biao and his group and Mao took place at the Second Plenum of the Central Committee at Lushan at the end of August and beginning of September 1970. The only thing from this meeting that is available to us is the "Résumé of Talks Between Chairman Mao and Various Comrades During His Inspection Tour":

> During the Lushan Conference in 1970 they [Lin Biao and his group] engaged in a surprise attack and in secret activities. Why didn't they dare to act in the open? Clearly, they had

something to hide. So they first dissembled and then made a surprise attack. They hid their plan from three of the five members of the standing committee of the Politburo as well as from the great majority of the comrades on the Politburo. Only a few "big generals" were let in on the secret: Huang Young-sheng, Wu Fi-xian, Ye Qun, Li Zuo-peng, Qiu Hui-zuo, Li Xue-feng, Zheng Wei-shan . . . . In my opinion, their surprise attack and intrigues masked intentions, an organization, and a program that were well defined. Their program was to appoint a state chairman, and to extol "genius"; in other words, to oppose the line of the Ninth Congress and to defeat the three-point agenda of the Second Plenum. A certain person was anxious to become state chairman, to split the party, and to seize power. . . .[2]

In fact, the chief point for Lin Biao and his group at Lushan was the problem of state chairman. In the plan for the new constitution that had been discussed all over China following the spring of 1970, this position no longer existed and had been replaced by a collective leadership. The prime minister (Zhou En-lai) became the most important figure. But Lin wanted to reintroduce the position of state chairman. Insisting on Mao Tsetung's "genius," Lin's partisans wanted Mao to assume this position. They figured that Mao would refuse and that Lin Biao would then be given the position of head of state. This maneuver failed.

After the Lushan session Mao had to act cautiously in order to undermine Lin's positions; Lin had powerful support, notably among the provincial and central military authorities. Mao took three measures to undermine Lin Biao's group. He unleashed an ideological campaign aimed at the higher cadres of the party, which marked a definitive break with Chen Bo-da, his former secretary, who had been so close to him during the Cultural Revolution; an emphasis was placed on dialectical materialism and historical materialism as opposed to idealism and metaphysics. This was what Mao called "throwing stones." Secondly, the Military Commission of the Central Committee controlled by Lin Biao was reshaped, as expressed in Mao's imagistic language: "Earth which is too hard is closed off to the air; if it is mixed with sand the air can enter it. The Military Commission needed the addition of several new elements. This is what I call adding sand." The third measure at-

---

[2] *Chairman Mao Talks to the People*, pp. 290–299.

tempted "to undermine the foundations of the wall" by reorganizing the Peking military region.

More and more isolated, according to the official version, Lin
Biao devised a plan for a coup d'état, which was named the "project
of 571 works," [3] with the help of his wife Ye Qun and his son
Lin Li-guo. The plot, which included the assassination of Mao
Tsetung, according to this version, was put into operation but
quickly failed. It was then that Lin is claimed to have fled for the
Soviet Union in a plane that crashed in the People's Republic of
Mongolia on the night of September 12–13, 1971.

Lin Biao, Confucius, and the Bourgeois Right: The New Targets (1972–1976)

With the party organizations being rebuilt and Lin Biao and
his group eliminated, 1972–1973 were years devoted to the criticism
of Lin, to the reestablishment of the party's authority, to the readjustment of the army's role, and to rebuilding state and mass
organizations. Former high-ranking leaders reappear (Tan Zhen-lin,
Li Jin-quan, etc., and most importantly Deng Xiao-ping). The
ideological campaigns criticizing Lin Biao were a serious attempt
to deal with the problems of the transition toward communism.
Far from slackening off, the struggle of the two lines remained
very intense.

Normalizing political life

At the end of 1971 the military problems had still not been
settled. There were soldiers at the head of most provincial revolutionary committees who were at the same time in charge of the
newly created party committees. There was a vast campaign aimed
at these soldiers, which proclaimed that "the army must study the
people" (even though the people had been held up as a model all
during the Cultural Revolution) and that "the party controls the
gun."

The army gradually disappeared from the leadership bodies and
confined itself to tasks more specifically its own, while at the same

[3] Or "project of armed uprising." The pronunciation of the ideograms of the figures
5–7–1 (wu, qi, yi) also means "armed uprising." See document 1 at the end of the
chapter.

time there was an increase in the importance of the cadres who had been reinstated as well as the youngest cadres who had emerged from the Cultural Revolution. In leadership organizations the soldiers were now responsible only for strictly military matters; the slogan "prepare for the coming of war" remained an important watchword.

At the end of 1973 the regional military leaders were stripped of their political functions in the revolutionary and party committees. At the same time there were changes made in the regional command. The meaning of the Triple Alliance was expanded. To the alliance among cadres, the masses, and the military was added the alliance among youth, the middle-aged, and the old.

Lin Biao accused of being a leftist . . .

After his fall Lin Biao was first accused of being a leftist, and through him certain tendencies of the Cultural Revolution were argued to have been excessive, particularly in the area of economic management. Among the tendencies that were condemned, the label "material incentive" was given to certain methods of reward that varied according to the amount an individual produced, and efforts to improve technical knowledge were labeled "technicalist" and "apolitical." Also condemned was the tendency to refuse all rules and regulations on the pretext that some of them were irrational, as well as the call to divide up resources more broadly at the expense of socialist accumulation. Also questioned was the tendency to shift the accounting units from the production teams to the brigades. This leftism also led to a criticism of individual allotments of land and complementary economic activities, which were the source of "spontaneous capitalist tendencies among the peasants."

. . . and then a rightist

In early 1973 the criticism of Lin Biao abruptly changed direction: he was now denounced as a rightist and a disciple of Confucius. The shifts in these accusations were part of the jolts that continued to rock China following the upheavals of 1966–1969. To compensate for the frequently overharsh sanctions against the cadres during the Cultural Revolution, there was a tendency to carry their rehabilitation too far and thus to exaggerate the errors and dangers of ultra-leftism: this was later called the movement of restoration. On the other hand, against this movement of restoration there was a tendency to emphasize the continuing peril from the right, which therefore weakened somewhat the scope of the accusations against leftism as the chief danger. These two opposing movements were indissociable from one another both before and after the fall of Lin Biao; they went together though first one, then the other, was emphasized in public propaganda.

By implication, the *pi Lin pi Kong* movement linked traditional Confucian conservatism with a new conservatism. This was less the conservatism of Lin Biao himself than the conservatism of the organization men who stood to profit from his fall and regain the upper hand. This development corresponded to a relative rehabilitation of radicalism, which for a certain period had been negatively associated with Lin Biao. It was emphasized that to direct all criticism against ultra-leftism would be to miss the target. What was denounced in Lin Biao was his two-faced character, the intriguer and plotter in him.

In insisting on the "new gains" (*xin cheng wu*) bequeathed by the Cultural Revolution, such as the May Seventh Schools, the systematic participation of the cadres in manual work, the departure of young students for the countrysides, the revolution in teaching, and the development of rural medicine and the "barefoot doctors," there was an implication that Lin would have been opposed to these things. In fact, the arrival of young people in the countrysides was compared in "Project 571" to reeducation work camps; administrative simplification and the departure of cadres for May Seventh Schools were described as a kind of hidden unemployment. But this defense of the Cultural Revolution was no longer undertaken against the eliminated Lin Biao. In exalting the "new gains" the left was taking aim at the moderate administrators, who were becoming more and more influential.

The Tenth Congress of the CCP

The Tenth Congress of the CCP took place in September 1973. It confirmed the line established by the Ninth Congress and formalized the changes in the leadership personnel following the Lin Biao affair as well as the weakening of the role of the military in the political life of the country. It reintroduced the ideological movement with the *pi Lin pi Kong* campaign—against Confucius and Lin Biao. But these two targets were not equal. Even though Lin

Biao was presented as a disciple of Confucius, the brunt of the criticism was directed against Confucianism itself and the right-wing current that had developed during the anti-leftist campaign launched after the fall of Lin Biao.

The historical debate over Confucius

This debate dealt with a very ancient period; it concerned the respective roles of two political schools—the "Confucian" scholars and the "legalists"—when the Emperor Qin Shin-huang was unifying China in 221 B.C. The leaders of the *pi Lin pi Kong* campaign saw this period as the beginning of the feudal era, the successor to slave society. The legalists were presented as the defenders of the rising feudal class, who gained power by creating a centralized state. They were depicted as adopting materialistic views (man will defeat heaven) which opposed the idealist belief in "submission to heaven's will"; the progressiveness of their political and economic reforms for the period was emphasized. They advocated "rule by law" instead of rule by "rites": the laws should be known by everyone and be applicable to everyone. The Confucianists, drawing on tradition, were seen as opposed to the most advanced class of the time and as trying to maintain the old order of things, the slave system. Although the Confucianists attempted several reforms, it was only to defend themselves against the legalists, an attempt to adapt tradition in order to save it.

After the creation of the centralized state, the new ruling class of landowners continued to apply legalist theories as long as the old aristocracy and the Confucians threatened its domination. It stopped doing so each time the oppressed peasants revolted; it preferred to invoke Confucianism, which defended tradition and the social hierarchy. This conflict between legalist thought and Confucianism, the *pi Lin pi Kong* campaign proclaimed, had continued throughout the history of China as a struggle between progress and backwardness, between reform and the maintenance of the status quo.

This conception of history was thus enriched by a new idea— that Chinese society had not evolved only through the contradiction between the peasantry and the landowners, but also through the Confucianism-legalist contradiction, the contradiction between the old and the new. This contradiction still existed at the present time, but the role of legalism had been taken by socialist ideology. The limited reign of the Chinese bourgeoisie before 1949 as the class that controlled the means of production, in spite of its economic weakness, rendered it incapable of creating its own ideological system to replace Confucianism. That is why the progressive element of the national bourgeoisie had no choice but to follow the ideas of the New Democracy elaborated by the CCP, the only political force capable of saving China; the reactionary element had to lean on Confucianism to defend its power ideologically.

The importance given to the legalism-Confucianism contradiction in their view of their past is a result of what many leftists had learned from the Cultural Revolution; this fact underlines the particular attention given after 1966 to problems of ideology and superstructure in the evolution of society and the emphasis placed on the permanent dangers of restoration and regression.

Criticism of Confucian morality

The notion of the a priori was denounced—the type of thinking that dominates science and leads to such ideas as natural gifts (*cai*) and inborn genius; these are ideas that make one assume that the world is divided into intelligent people and fools and that the one group was meant to lead the other. This aspect of Confucianism was a direct reference to Lin Biao, for whom only heroes and geniuses made history, while "the people are preoccupied only with earning money and trying to make a fortune." Confucius's elitist principles were more widely attacked so that each person would be led to question certain social attitudes that were still shared by everyone. For example, the superiority of mental work over manual labor, or the belief that the world is divided into intelligent people and fools (the majority); or the idea of benevolence (*ren*), the theory of the golden mean, and virtue, which were all abstract moral principles. All this, it was said, inevitably led to passivity, submission, and a follower's mentality, and everyone should act against it. During one of the more intense periods of the *pi Lin pi Kong* movement the low status of women was attacked, for women had been relegated to an inferior rank by Confucius, whereas now total equality with men was sought.[4]

This movement was not simply a consideration of China's past in scholarly articles. Criticism was collective, and it was conducted

[4] See document 2.

in work places, in factories, in schools, and in countrysides, where "theory groups" were created for the systematic study of Marxist classics and the analysis of the conflicts between the legalists and the Confucianists. Confucian principles were also denounced in terms of the individual experience of each man and woman. The study of philosophy and history became a daily activity of the masses.

The criticism of revisionism renewed

The *pi Lin pi Kong* campaign was tied to the criticism of new rightist tendencies. These had surfaced even before the fall of Lin Biao at the time of the rehabilitation of the cadres who had been criticized during the Cultural Revolution. Supported by the anti-leftist criticism brought against Lin after 1972, they tended to question the gains of the Cultural Revolution in several areas:

—Material rewards reappeared: bonuses and days off. Profit was once again the principle criterion of growth, and there was a reliance on the cadres and experts. Special status was given to the most economically advanced agricultural regions and to the importing of foreign technology.

—Certain cadres were reluctant to participate in manual work and showed little enthusiasm for the ideological movement in progress.

—Sons of cadres who were students at the university had entered "through the back door" (which was a reference to the "services" performed by the cadres for each other); there was a reluctance to admit students from the working class and peasantry into the university;[5] too much importance was given to book learning and theoretical knowledge at the expense of practice and contact with society.

—In the realm of literature a certain number of productions were criticized, notably an opera performed in Shanxi, *Climbing the Peach Tree Mountain Three Times*, which was seen as an attempt to "change the verdict" on Liu Shao-qi.

All these phenomena of the restoration were attacked by the radicals, who pointed to the gains of the Cultural Revolution; this included the right and the duty "to stand against the tide," a 1974 slogan that reflected a balance of forces unfavorable to the left.

[5] See documents 3 and 4.

Criticism of the "bourgeois right"; dictatorship of the proletariat

This new campaign was based on the fact that new property relations had been established in China since 1949: socialist ownership by the whole people (86 percent of industrial production and 92 percent of commerce) and collective ownership (90 percent of farm land) predominated, while private property had survived only locally. But everywhere there were still economic structures inherited from the old society: unequal salaries and money exchanges, unequal distribution according to work, in short, everything brought into question by the term "bourgeois right" (*zichanjieji faquan*). This discussion campaign did not try to attack a specific target such as Confucianism, but rather to provoke reflection on the basic problems of Chinese socialism; it was the occasion for reaffirming the "dictatorship of the proletariat," which was the only counterbalance to the natural bourgeois tendencies of the economy.

If the principle "he who does not work does not eat" was a guarantee against the return of capitalism, it nevertheless perpetuated a certain inequality because of the differences in physical capabilities, level of instruction, and technical knowledge among workers. The persistence of such a system would therefore consolidate "bourgeois" tendencies such as the competition for degrees (the level of technical knowledge was one of the criteria for differences in salary) or the phenomenon of working more to earn more (the competition for bonuses or work points). These tendencies, due to the very existence of the principle of distribution according to work, could only weaken gradually, to the extent that the communist consciousness of each person was raised. For this reason great importance was placed on the slogan "put proletarian policy in command."

The system of exchange through money, even though it was strictly regulated by the socialist state, also contained seeds of revisionist tendencies that could be monopolized by the old or new bourgeoisie. It begins with people "who break their backs to succeed in a 'juicy' affair and who hardly work at all for a small affair, and who balk at a job that will not bring any profit. From this has arisen the disparity and imbalance between supply and demand for certain goods and the contradiction between social production and social needs."[6] This could lead back to a profit economy, at first on a small scale, which would then lead to a real restoration of capitalism.

In confronting these phenomena, it was said in China, several contradictory attitudes surfaced: a rightist attitude, which wanted to let things take their course, or simply not do anything to limit them; and the ultra-leftist attitude, which wanted to abolish the bourgeois right immediately. The correct attitude for those leading this ideological campaign was to restrain them within the proper limits, which corresponded to the economic and ideological development of society through the dictatorship of the proletariat. The dictatorship of the proletariat did not consist only of repressing counterrevolutionaries; it had to allow the innovations of the Cultural Revolution to develop and it had to consolidate its gains.

Political equilibrium (1972–1976)

With the Tenth Congress of the CCP, the criticism of Confucius, and the debate over the bourgeois right, the balance seemed to tip once again in favor of the radical current, symbolized by the "Shanghai group," which had come to the forefront during the Cultural Revolution; Yao Wen-yuan, Wang Hong-wen, and Zhang Qun-qiao were the principal leaders of these campaigns. But what was their real support from the base at this time?

The "restoration" tendencies that appeared in 1970 remained very strong under the guise of the "imperatives" of order and management. These tendencies were strengthened following the fall of Lin Biao because of the ultra-leftist accusations against Lin, which favored the gradual return of Deng Xiao-ping to important positions in the party and state. In 1966–1968 he had been harshly criticized as the right-hand man of Liu Shao-qi and the head of the black line; in 1974–1975 he rose to the status of prime minister without title, working side by side with Zhou En-lai, who was already immobilized by illness and who no doubt gave his approval to this move. In spring 1974, for example, Deng appeared at the United Nations in New York. But Zhou's death in 1976 put an abrupt,

---

[6] *Hongqi*, no. 4, 1975: "An Ideological Weapon for Restraining the Bourgeois Right."

though temporary, end to his brief return to the leadership of the country. In 1977, Deng was officially rehabilitated and began to play a highly prominent role in the government.

The instability of the Chinese political balance in 1972–1976 no doubt reflected an incessant and subtle vacillation between a rejection of the ultra-left, which favored the return of organization men, and a rejection of conservative and management tendencies, which reinforced a radical but not ultra-leftist current. In 1975, for example, the radicals took the offensive with the campaign against the bourgeois right at the very time of Deng Xiao-ping's trips to the West. In 1975, as the last historical leaders of Chinese communism began to leave the scene, the fundamental debate between the two lines remained open.

China at the United Nations

Years of unofficial contacts, the tour of American Ping-Pong players in Peking, and Nixon's spectacular China visit in 1972 prepared the way for Washington's turnaround: it would accept the entrance of the People's Republic of China into the United Nations—a proposal that had been defeated every year since 1950—and the exclusion of Taiwan.

During this period Chinese diplomacy was double-edged: thwart the influence of the two superpowers (the United States and the Soviet Union) and answer the Soviet threat, which was considered more important. This was what led China on the diplomatic and economic levels to approach the "intermediary" capitalist powers of Western Europe, to rely on right-wing Western political forces (Strauss, Heath, Nixon), and to support authoritarian regimes in the Third World such as Iran, Ethiopia, and Pakistan. This led to a decrease—at least superficially—in the aid Peking had given in the sixties to revolutionary movements, such as to Dhofar and Eritrea in the Middle East. For better or for worse, China had entered the game of international state-to-state politics.

China's entrance into the United Nations also facilitated economic and technical contacts with the West, the purchase of factories and patents, and the development of exchanges, particularly in the "advanced sectors." All this strengthened the economist and revisionist tendency (Deng Xiao-ping) and the tendency to give special treatment to economic progress on the international level.

The Influence of the Cultural Revolution on China

The mark of the Cultural Revolution was seen in the desire to reduce the "three great differences"—between workers and peasants, cities and countrysides, and manual and intellectual work;[7] it was also present in the newly raised ideological level of the masses and their increased control in leadership and management, which caused the relationship between "leaders" and "led" to be reexamined. But to what extent remained to be seen.

The countrysides

The gap between city and country remained very wide, but it had been somewhat reduced by a better standard of living in rural areas. The increase in agricultural production is an example of this improvement: grain production reached 275 million tons in 1974 (compared to 220 million in 1965). The general increase in the value of agricultural production for 1974 was 51 percent as compared to 1964. This resulted from an enormous effort to improve the irrigation system—electrifying irrigation, drainage, and pumpage—the intensive development of chemical fertilizers (fertilizer production jumped from 7 million tons in 1964 to 30 million tons in 1974), the selection of plants, the diversification of crops and the increase in the number of yearly harvests, as well as the harnessing and regulation of major rivers (notably the Huai and the Hai). North China no longer had to rely on the South for grains and suffered no major shortages during the great drought of 1971 because of reserves built up by each production team. But this was also the result of industrializing the rural areas (90 percent of the districts had one or more factories for manufacturing or distributing agricultural products) as well as the lowering of sales prices of certain products (a 15.7 percent drop in the price of diesel motors, harvesters, trucks, and pumps) and a general increase in the production of tractors (there were six times as many tractors as in 1965 and 32 times as many cultivators); the surface area plowed by tractors had doubled since 1965.

[7] See document 5.

The development of rural medicine was characterized by the appearance of "barefoot doctors" (one million in 1974)—peasants who had been quickly trained to meet local needs and who were capable of treating the most common illnesses—and of doctors who had come from the cities (from hospitals and medical schools), as well as by a tighter network of medical facilities. All districts and most communes had a simplified hospital, and all brigades had a dispensary. The emphasis was placed on hygiene and prevention. A cooperative system of care was also put into operation (*hezuo yilliao*): medicine was free for a nominal yearly charge of one or two *yuan* per person.

More generally, the concrete experience of the peasants was used consistently in scientific research. Popular knowledge and specialized knowledge came closer together.

Education was another area that set the cities apart from the countrysides. In 1965 thirty million children of school age received no instruction of any kind.[8] Primary and secondary school attendance increased by 30 percent on the national level (50 percent in Tibet) between 1965 and 1973—a year in which 90 percent of school-age children attended school.[9] In fact, these figures primarily dealt with the rural areas and particularly the poorest regions. This improvement was made possible by the adoption of systems that were flexible enough to respond to local conditions: evening classes, part-time study, traveling classrooms in mountainous regions and pasture lands in which the population was spread out, an increase in the number of schools so that they would be located closer to the pupils' homes, the shortage of teachers offset by the participation of workers and students in teaching tasks, etc.

Industry and the cities

The increase in industrial production between 1964 and 1974 was due to new relations established in the factories: workers, cadres, and technicians (another form of the Triple Alliance) worked together in devising new projects, machines, and products, and in improving the quality and quantity of production.

The movement of ideological liberation often brought about unforeseen growth: oil production went from 8.7 million tons in 1964

[8] *Renmin Ribao*, February 10, 1974.
[9] *Renmin Ribao*, May 18, 1975.

to 65 million tons in 1974, even though it was generally conceded that China is not very rich in oil. The same was true for the discovery of new coal deposits near Yunnan. The growing awareness of the fact that the Chinese were just as capable as the advanced industrial countries led to increased naval construction, the manufacture of computers, civil engineering projects, etc.

Education

If primary education was essentially becoming more open and secondary education was on the verge of becoming more open as well—although more slowly—higher education was still available only to a small minority. Even though university graduates came from the working class and peasantry more frequently than was the case before the Cultural Revolution, it was felt that they should not make up an intellectual or social elite but rather should be "cultivated workers with a socialist consciousness." The changes made to attain this goal affected all areas of education: subject matter, which had to be based on concrete problems (which did not exclude research in the universities, institutes, and the Academy of Sciences); shortening the number of years of study both in secondary schools (a cycle of nine or ten years including five primary years and four or five secondary years, divided into upper and lower cycles) and in higher education (generally three years); and a change in methods, with an emphasis placed on the connection between theory and practice, between the school or university and society, and between knowledge from books and its application. The link with manual work was maintained through various systems: organized training programs of pupils and students in industrial and agricultural production units, organizational ties between factories and universities and schools, the setting up of workshops and farms by the schools in which the work was done by the students themselves. Teachers for higher education were recruited directly from production units (factories and people's communes) based on new criteria: a minimum of two or three years work, completion of at least the lower secondary cycle, and the recommendation of the masses.

Secondary school was no longer an automatic stepping-stone to the university. In fact, between 1969 and 1974 some ten million "young students" from the cities (that is, graduates of secondary schools) went to live in the country where they worked on farms or did other jobs that required a certain amount of training (accounting, teaching, barefoot doctors).

This period also saw an important development in special teaching in the countrysides and factories to solve immediate technical problems. In the people's communes crash courses (two weeks to several months) were set up for technicians in agronomy, mechanized farming, and veterinary medicine that responded to concrete needs. The most developed form of this kind of teaching was the workers' universities set up by the factories for training technicians and engineers. Studies were either full-time or part-time and the course lasted for about two years. *Renmin Ribao* of June 6, 1973, reported for example that twenty-four factories from Shenyang had already created their own worker universities, which were attended by 1,200 students who worked in those factories.

Political life

The Cultural Revolution was also an attempt—however imperfect—to bring the leaders and the led closer together, to increase the participation of the lower echelons and the masses in decision making and political affairs, to give ideological education at the base, and to debureaucratize the administration. According to Zhou En-lai, the number of functionaries in the central government was reduced from 60,000 to 10,000. In industrial and commercial enterprises it was common for the administrative personnel to be reduced by two-thirds.

The cadres were brought closer to the masses and everyday reality in several ways. In the factories and people's communes they regularly participated in manual work, either in the workshops or the fields. For the cadres of the various administrations the May Seventh Schools were created: these were farms attached to each organization whose members worked there for different periods of time (several weeks, several months, or even one or two years). The chief activity there was agriculture and political study.

The increased participation of the masses in the workings of power—which did not affect the special status of the party—was accomplished through the revolutionary committees which had been created during the Cultural Revolution and institutionalized in the 1975 constitution adopted by the Fourth National People's Assembly. These committees were set up in each production unit, organization, and school, and included permanent members and workers who were elected by the base and could be ousted if they did not do a satisfactory job. Their makeup had to reflect the double Triple Alliance: masses-cadres-technicians and young people–middle-aged people–old people. In general, the revolutionary committees took care of management and the party committee took care of political work. Revolutionary committee members were not officially allowed to belong to the party so that a "double power" situation would not be created. However, the balance between the two organizations was unstable; as the Cultural Revolution receded, power increasingly returned to the party committees. In time, the revolutionary committees were to be abolished (1978).

Free expression for the masses was also guaranteed by the constitution, notably the "four great democratic measures" (*sida-minzhu*): the free expression of opinions, the broad exposures of points of view, wide-scale debates, and the use of the *dazibao* (article 13), as well as the right to strike (article 28). On the surface there was no major political crisis in China between the fall of Lin Biao (1972) and the fall of Deng Xiao-ping (1976). But latent tensions remained very strong and appeared suddenly after Mao's death. Basic conflicts between the conservative management line and the radical line (see Chapter 8) often entailed personality conflicts. The "Shanghai Four" (Zhang Qun-qiao, head of the political department of the army, Wang Hong-wen, number three man in the party hierarchy, Yao Wen-yuan, in charge of ideological affairs and information, and Jiang Qing, who had inspired the campaigns for proletarian culture), who were the very active promoters of the campaigns against Confucius and the bourgeois right, were also on very bad terms with Zhou En-lai and attacked him in private. Their propaganda was more defensive than offensive, which was probably an expression of their growing isolation. Little by little it seemed that they were reduced to factional intrigues, which was a prelude to their brutal fall in October 1976. Did this isolation reflect a certain organic weakness in the leftist line, a certain weariness after so many shake-ups and ideological campaigns? Or did it mean that the "Four" themselves had been gradually cut off from the mass line that they had been defending with such vehemence since the glory days of the Shanghai Commune? And at what point did Mao, weakened by illness, finally stop supporting them, and even approving of them?

Between 1972 and 1976 these conflicts remained hidden and openly affected only isolated cities or provinces, such as Zhengzhou in 1973 and Hangzhou in 1975; the *dazibao* flourished and the authorities were soundly criticized, but without openly upsetting the balance of power at the central level. The potential seriousness of these conflicts can be measured by the fact that in order to delay them as long as possible many top-ranking leaders did not retire from their jobs in spite of their advanced age. But in the space of less than a year many of them died: Deng Pi-wu (born in 1886), Zhou En-lai (born in 1898), Kang Sheng (born in 1896), Zhu De (born in 1886), and finally Mao Tsetung, who died in September 1976 at the age of 83.

Mao's death

Zhou En-lai's death had already led to a certain amount of upheaval: less than a month after it occurred Deng Xiao-ping was ousted. A very vigorous campaign of critical discussion attacked the economic program prepared by Deng in 1975 ("Several Problems Relating to the Acceleration of Industrial Development"). This text insisted on the importing of advanced techniques, the exporting of mining products, on the individual responsibility of the managers of businesses, on the promotion of the most productive workers and the raising of their salaries. In other words, the struggle between the two lines had started up again concerning the fundamental choices of the Chinese way (see Chapter 8, document 4).

However, this apparent defeat for the management tendency did not give the upper hand to those who had most vigorously denounced this new economic emphasis at the leadership level. Deng was not succeeded by the Shanghai Four, but by an organization man, Hua Guo-feng. Born in 1920, he was of the generation that had come to leadership positions after the Liberation. He had been one of the cadres who had been strongly criticized during the Cultural Revolution. His slow and steady rise during the seventies, at first at the provincial level in Hunan, and then in the public security area, meant that even before Mao's death the party and state apparatus was quite stable, in spite of the upheavals that had shaken it. One wonders if the ideological campaigns (against the bourgeois right, the Peking Opera, and the criticism of Confucius) led so actively by the Shanghai gang, were often merely tolerated by the leadership and considered to be unconnected with it. Only Mao's lingering presence protected them. These campaigns largely failed to arouse the public, which had grown weary of so many initiatives of this nature. In effect, the political isolation of the Shanghai Four, which led them to take refuge in authoritarian practices and resulted in their brutal and easy elimination after Mao's death, had already sealed their fate.

Mao's death marked the end of an era. For many Chinese Mao was the very image—as well as the leading agent and decisive instrument—of all that had been accomplished, transformed, and built in the country over the past half-century and especially since 1949. Mao had always been identified with the leftist line, particularly with the collectivization campaign of 1955, the Great Leap Forward, the Cultural Revolution, and the anti-Confucius campaign. He represented the link between the militant, frugal, and fraternal tradition of Yanan and the demands, as well as the temptations, of the complex organization of an enormous modern country. At the same time he set an example with his highly nonconformist thinking and style, which was at once lucid, sarcastic, and corrosive, and which had been condensed in the texts the Red Guards had collected under the title *Mao Tsetung Sixiang Wansui* (*Long Live the Thought of Mao Tsetung*) and which the organization men had been so reluctant to publish officially.[10] Mao, whose personality cult had attained such outrageous proportions during the Cultural Revolution, gradually withdrew from concrete, everyday responsibilities in the seventies, both to make public affairs less dependent on his presence and to devote himself more to ideology and less to active power. Before his death Mao became obsessed by the uncertainties of the post-Mao period. In his confidential letter to his wife written in 1966 he even envisaged after his death that "the rightists in power might use his words to gain power for a certain time." But his intellectual and political heritage will have a lasting effect on China, whatever might happen concerning his succession.

[10] The four partial collections of these texts published in the West are listed in the general bibliography at the beginning of this book. The most famous of these unofficial texts is a letter from Mao to his wife filled with self-effacing doubts on his own role. Four others are reprinted in this book: "Do Not Fear Difficulties" (1957), the self-criticism of the Great Leap Forward (1959), the advice to his niece (1964), and the evaluation of his responsibilities in the Cultural Revolution (1966).

ADDITIONAL BIBLIOGRAPHY

Marianne Bastid and Jean-Luc Domenach, *De la Révolution culturelle à la Critique de Confucius: 1969–1974, France-Asie*, 1974, no. 3.

DOCUMENTS

1. THE EVALUATION OF CHINESE POLITICAL LIFE BY LIN BIAO ACCORDING TO THE "PROJECT OF 571 WORKS"

Source: *La Nouvelle Chine*, no. 16, March 1974, pp. 18–26.

This document was distributed officially in Peking after the fall of Lin Biao; it is attributed to Lin Biao and is said to have been written by him in the spring of 1971.

. . . The days of B-52's power are numbered.* In the coming years he will quickly have to arrange for his succession.

He is worried about us. Rather than have our hands tied, it is preferable to go into action.

Political domination will follow military domination [illegible words].

Trotskyists of the pen willingly deform Marxism in their own interests. They use all sorts of false revolutionary words to deceive the people. Their theory of uninterrupted revolution is none other than Trotsky's theory of permanent revolution.

The target of their revolution is the Chinese people; the first to be attacked are the army and those who do not think as they do.

Their socialism is in fact a kind of social-fascism. They have turned the state apparatus into a machine in which people devour one another, a machine of reciprocal oppression. The political life of the party and state has become a tyrannical patriarchy.

Of course, we do not deny the role that he [Mao] played in the unification of the country. Because of that we have given him an eminent place in the history of the revolution and have given him our support. But now he has abused the confidence of the people and the position they have given him; he is going backward in history and has become the Qing Shi-huang of modern times.

. . . Raise the banner of B-52 to destroy his power and appease the opinion of the masses. Ally ourselves with all the forces we can; liberate the majority; concentrate the attacks against B-52 and his handful of tyrants; liberate the greatest number, protect the greatest number.

What they [Mao Tsetung and his supporters] call attacking a small handful is merely concentrating the fire on a different group each time in order to defeat them one by one. Today they use one to strike out at another; tomorrow they will use the second to strike out at the first. Today a small

* B-52 refers to Mao Tsetung.

handful, tomorrow another small handful; if one adds it up, many people are included. . . .

. . . They create contradictions and splits in order to rule by dividing. Each one of their destructive acts reinforces their leadership position. . . .

. . . Frankly speaking, all the people ruined by B-52 were scapegoats.

Some of the past propaganda concerning B-52 was justified by the needs of history. Some of it was explained by the concern for national unity, some of it by the need for resistance against the outside adversary. But some of it came from his fascist oppression. . . .

Concerning these comrades, it would be appropriate to proceed to a materialist analysis, to provide them with explanations and give them our support. All those abused and oppressed by B-52 must be freed on the political level. . . .

2. WOMEN FROM THE SHAOXING DISTRICT PARTICIPATE IN THE CRITICISM MOVEMENT OF CONFUCIUS AND LIN BIAO

Source: *Chine 75*, no. 2 (text in *Jiefangjunbao*, March 16, 1974; excerpts translated into French by Michelle Lol).

The Shoaxing district is the district in which the great writer Lu-xun was born

In his story *New Year's Sacrifice*, Lu-xun describes the tragic life of Sister-in-law Lin, showing how in the old society working women suffered exploitation and oppression from the reactionary classes in power and carried the injustices of the Confucian doctrines on their bodies and in their flesh. It is a typical example of the misfortunes suffered here in Huangfu by women workers.

. . . "In the old society," said Du Cai-yun, head of the eastern brigade, "the Confucian morality of the 'three obediences and the four virtues' and the 'three submissions and five rules' destroyed the youth of countless women and ruined the lives of countless unfortunate victims. This happened to my first cousin. It was before the Liberation. Her father had arranged a marriage for her, but as soon as the marriage was set, the husband died! But still she had to go through the ceremony of 'crossing the threshold' because from now on 'as long as you live you are a member of your in-laws' family, and when you are dead you will be a spirit of that family. It is before their altars that you must kneel.' As she obstinately refused to do this, the in-laws sent people over to 'take back what belonged to them' by force. She did not see any way out of her situation, and in her extreme anger she threw herself into the river and drowned."

. . . "In the old society," said Fan Zhu-hua, the vice-president of the Women's Association of the commune, 'why was it that we, the women workers, submitted to these miseries generation after generation? And why don't we submit to them anymore? It was not at all because of Lin Biao's statement quoting Confucian doctrine that 'life and death are destiny,'

'riches and nobility are gifts from heaven,' but because of social injustices."
This led her to speak of her own experience: "Before the Liberation my
father rented two meager *mou* of land from the landowners, which was not
enough to support a family of five. My mother had no choice but to leave
and hire herself out elsewhere. At thirteen I was hired as a servant in a
village landowner's house. The oldest of my younger sisters, who was eleven,
was sold as a 'child-fiancée.' When my father became very sick, he went out
begging on the roads, taking along my youngest sister by the hand. I was
given the same food as the dogs and pigs and led the life of a beast of
burden. The master never had a kind word. He beat me with his fists and
feet. When my parents died, both of them of sickness and misery, my little
sister who was then seven years old went off begging by herself, and we
never knew what became of her. It was only after the Liberation that I was
able to escape from the tiger's jaws. Under the leadership of Chairman Mao
and the Communist Party we struggled against the landowners and divided
up the land. We became united in order to move forward on the great and
solid road of socialism. And little by little life became beautiful and good."

. . . While she was comparing the past with the present, Fan Zhu-hua wept
with great emotion, hardly able to speak. "When old Kong," she said, "wanted
to 'return to the rites,' he was trying to restore the slave system, and when
Lin Biao called for a 'return to the rites,' he was trying to reestablish
capitalism. We've had more than enough of the misery of the old society.
We must be more and more vigorous in our criticism of this 'return to the
rites' of Lin Biao's reactionary program which would restore capitalism. We
must absolutely prevent socialist land from reverting back to the old ways."

3. PROTEST LETTER FROM A STUDENT

Source: *Renmin Ribao*, August 10, 1973 (translated into French by J. F.
Olivier).

*A young student living in the country and a candidate for the university
complains of the persistent traditionalism of the entrance examinations for
higher education. He wrote the following letter on the back of his examination copy.*

Respected leaders,
    The exam period is now over, and I would like to tell you of the troubles
I have had at this time.
    I went to the countryside in 1968 and since then I have devoted all my
time and energy to agricultural work. Eighteen hours a day of exhausting work
which has hardly left me any time for studying [for the university admissions
examinations]. After receiving my exam date—June 27—I was able to read
over the mathematics manual only once right before the exams. In spite of
my efforts, I was unable to answer the questions in geometry, physics, and
chemistry in the exam that was held today. I did not want to answer with
absurdities and thus waste the time of those who would be correcting my

work. That is why, wanting to respect discipline and hold to my principles, I honestly preferred to leave. To tell the truth, I do not want to give in to the dilettantish library rats who have done nothing for years. I even feel resentment toward them. The exams were monopolized by these pedants. At a time when weeding was urgent, I did not want to abandon my work to shut myself up in a little room. That would have been to act too strongly in my own personal interest. . . . What torments me is that a written test that takes only a few hours can rob me of all chance of entering the university. . . .

I took all the preparatory classes according to the new system and the new conditions for recruiting students. The professors are well aware of the fact that I have acquired a certain basic knowledge. The questions in physics and chemistry in the exam today were superficial, and if I had spent two days studying I certainly would have passed.

My political attitude, as well as my family and social relations, is pure. For me, a child who grew up in the city, these past few years spent in the country have been a very good test, and I feel that I have made a true leap in regard to my ideology and my conception of the world. I feel absolutely no shame for not having conformed to what was expected of me and the nature of this exam (no one took into account my basic knowledge or my abilities). You can force yourself to deal with things, to skim through the books to get good grades! But in acting this way I would not be very happy. The only thing that reflects credit on me is that I was able to attend the preparatory classes based on the criteria of the new system for education because of the recommendation and satisfaction of the poor and middle-poor peasants as well as the leadership cadres.

Zhang Tie-sheng
Baita Commune, June 30, 1973

4. A WORKER FROM SHANGHAI WISHES TO OPEN THE DOORS OF SCHOOL AND SOCIETY

Source: *Vent d'Est*, no. 3, 3rd quarter 1976. Texts translated from the Chinese press; Editions du Centenaire.

This dazibao *written by a worker from a factory for machine tools in Shanghai was printed by a magazine from that city*, Xuexi yu pipan (Studies and Criticism), *no. 2, 1976.*

A door: this is supposed to be the definition: "A door is an installation that divides space into two parts." Of course, like "the function of the horse's tail," this definition has become a joke.

But in the hands of the bourgeoisie doors have another very definite function; before the Great Cultural Revolution the situation in the schools and certain areas of the superstructure was roughly this: "even though the door has been installed, it is often closed." Everyone who saw the film *Break* remembers the scene in which Sun Zi-qing, the teacher, closes the door—bam!—in the faces of the young workers and peasants. "The doorman of the bourgeoisie, that's what he is!" shout the outraged poor peasants. A door: thus it is used by the bourgeoisie to keep the young workers and peasants away from school. This shows that the schools are a tenacious stronghold of the bourgeoisie.

But the school, that fortress of the superstructure, is nevertheless different from an army stronghold in time of war: when the attack succeeds, it means victory. On the other hand, after the penetration of workers, peasants, and soldiers in the school, the bourgeoisie still uses the door to help it in its stubborn resistance. Let us return to *Break* and take the example of the student from the agronomy institute, the son of poor peasants: he entered through the front door, didn't he? However, the school did not delay in closing its doors completely around him, to such an extent that three years later he could hardly recognize his own mother. The door keeps the workers out of school or locks them inside it, two phenomena of the same type: the maintenance of the hereditary domain of the bourgeoisie.

Besides visible doors, there are also invisible doors. For those that are visible, one can remember the swinging doors in *Break*: they are rather easy to open. As for the invisible doors, they exist in the minds of men, and opening them is another story altogether.

If the minds of men are not emptied of revisionist poison, once the door of school is open, it will close again; but there will also be the door of the family, the door of institutions, and other doors of all shapes and sizes to oppose the socialist revolution of the proletariat in the superstructure.

There are doors in school, and there are also doors in all the other areas of the superstructure. Let us take the example of science and technology; one hears that because of the supposed specialness of this area there should not only be doors, but walls and sentinels as well! The fortified villages of the bourgeoisie are still legion at the present time. Once one is defeated, another can still rise up. Whether it is a matter of doors, walls, or sentinels set up by the bourgeoisie, the proletariat must knock them all down one by one: this is the only way it can exercise its complete dictatorship over the bourgeoisie.

5. HAORAN: A WRITER WHO WANTS TO LIVE AMONG THE PEASANTS

Source: Haoran, *Ma plume au service du prolétariat* [My Pen in the Service of the Proletariat] (Lausanne, Alfred Eibel Editions, 1976), pp. 48–52.

Talk given in 1975 to foreign students in Peking.

The life and struggles of the people are the sources [of my literary work]. To establish contact with this living reality, I first of all try to throw myself into practice.

For example, by going to the country for a while and working with the peasants to transform the objective world while at the same time changing my subjective world; by studying Marxism-Leninism and artistic technique in practice. In our country the conditions are very favorable for throwing oneself into practice; there are also the great *xiafang** movements on the national level; there have already been two of them: the first was during the Great Leap Forward—I went to the province of Shandong—and the second was during the Great Cultural Revolution at the struggle-criticism-trans-formation phase—I went to a people's commune near Zhoukou Dian, the site of the Peking Man. One can thus "combine two activities." Throwing oneself into practice seems to be the best method to me, for then one is able to embody what one thinks and to understand what the people are feeling. But a simple visit is not enough.

Concerning this method, I would like to add that you cannot go for just a little while to the country and sleep on the "kang" to make yourself one with the ideas and feelings of the peasants! That would be too superficial. But some of our writers do just that. There is a proverb that deals with this: "To sleep in the same bed does not mean you will have the same dream." There is one necessary condition for linking oneself to the masses: one must give up the grand airs of the writer, the intellectual, the famous man. When I was a young district cadre and went to work in the fields, I was like every-one else! I did not have this problem!

I was therefore authorized during the Cultural Revolution to participate in the *xiafang* movement and to go to a commune near Zhoukou Dian; I said to myself that this time I would do a novel closer than ever to country life. Before leaving I said that I would like a quiet place to stay, a small room in a granary loft, and this was given to me; I also participated in manual work, helping to put vines on stakes, as it turned out. In this way I hoped to get rid of my grand airs.

One day the vice-secretary of the production brigade came looking for me. "Comrade Haoran, tomorrow the high school students are going to lend us a hand with the harvest. Would you write the welcome speech?" I was very unhappy, for once again I found myself in the situation of the "great writer" writing for the "little" secretary of a cell! [*laughter*] How was this getting rid of my grand airs?

Another thing: the next day around noon I was working on staking vines; this work is rather easy and pretty amusing [*laughter*], but since I was work-ing in the sun, I was sweating a little. Seeing this, an old peasant woman, who was visibly upset, came up to me and whispered in my ear: "Psst! Go rest for a while. No one will say anything!" Once again I was very angry: this was obviously not forced labor! [*laughter*]

It is quite difficult for one to get rid of his writer's grand airs. It is not enough to make great statements such as "I am coming to reeducate myself among you." You must truly participate in the life of the people. So I just decided to go there very simply—and the whole commune came to see me! From morning to night the members of the commune brought me all sorts of things to write: speeches, critical texts, etc.; I even helped the old peasant women write their letters! [*laughter*] My peaceful room was trans-

* Sending intellectuals into the villages.

formed into a veritable club! [*laughter*] And little by little I understood the meaning of this activity: by writing critical texts I understood how the village had struggled against revisionism; by writing letters, I came to understand the people. And thus I was able to enter the life of this village. In fact, I didn't write anything right away, and it was only later that I started *The Great Radiant Way*. It was a matter of losing my grand airs before I could study and understand the life of the village.

Chapter Eight

The
Chinese Way

During the first twenty-five years after Liberation, Chinese social-ism went through a hectic series of crises and new developments, from the Great Leap Forward to the Cultural Revolution and the tensions of 1973–1976. Even a seemingly calm period like the first Five Year Plan was actually filled with sudden breaks and un-expected shifts. Political development was made up of advances and retreats, periods of acceleration and periods of stability, and the upper hand would pass from one line to the other. This development was based on human initiative, on the priority of the political struggle for mobilizing the masses, and on overcoming the various obstacles that stood in the way of this mobilization. The hetero-geneous and discontinuous nature of Chinese historical change thus differed radically from Soviet historical change—which was marked by the mechanical succession of five-year plans, and an ideology emphasizing continuous growth of the forces of production as the way to build socialism.

The Chinese way, which in the fifties and sixties gradually emerged from the experiments and crises, the aspirations of the base and the conflicts at the top, is deeply national in character. Priority has been given to the abilities of the Chinese people, China's unique historical experience, and the specific conditions of the Chinese economy—and thus to the necessity of adapting Marxist principles to Chinese national reality, as had been done during the twenty-five years that preceded the revolution. However, the con-struction of socialism in China has taken place in the context of a double international reality over which China has had no control:

the reality of the socialist camp, until its disintegration in the sixties, and that of the capitalist world. The international situation has restricted the People's Republic of China in its freedom of movement and in its effort to develop along original lines.

This Chinese way, which can be found both in economic strategies and political ideology, truly represents a new communism that differs radically from the communism developed in the Soviet Union between 1930 and 1950 and which was later enlarged to include the other countries of Eastern Europe, often in more liberal form. Since 1950 the People's Republic of China has been very important in the international communist movement—at first to add numbers to the movement and enrich its ideology and later to raise more and more pressing questions; the split between advocates and opponents of the Chinese "theses" has profoundly divided the states, parties, and major forces of world communism. The Chinese way is no less important for the Third World, since China itself is of the Third World. In attaining a reasonable standard of living for an enormous population, in accomplishing spectacular gains in agriculture, industry, and medicine, in establishing itself as a major world power, China broke the "infernal circle of misery" that has held back so many countries that had nominally been given independence. In addition, the Chinese way is a challenge to the West; beyond the concrete differences in the two societies, the original approach of the Chinese Communists in areas such as popular medicine, the relationship between school and society, and the "productive" manual work done by the cadres and intellectuals, are a direct challenge to glaring problems that exist in Western society and culture today.

However, the Chinese way has never been offered as a mechanical model that can be exported to other countries. Attempts to use Chinese formulas have proven inadequate and have had little effect. The Chinese way remains the specific expression of one people and one country.

The Chinese Approach to the Contradictions Between Accumulation and Socialism

In 1949 the peasants and rural artisans (90 percent of the Chinese population) lived at bare subsistence level. Through feudal tenant farming a small number of landowners controlled a small, unproductive agricultural surplus. The countryside was little more than a vast reservoir of cheap labor, the base for industrial exploitation and the great profits made by foreign and national industrial capitalism. But because of the excessive concentration of revenue (due to the weakness of the interior market) and the complete technical dependence of the West, industry was confined to a relatively small number of consumer goods and certain mining products for export. Given these conditions, how could a regime so anxious for independence and development in 1949 begin a process of widespread and clearly defined accumulation that could free the country of its dependence and misery?

The most fundamental task was to use the economic surplus to enlarge the base of national accumulation instead of squandering it or letting it go abroad. The agrarian reform and the nationalization of large-scale commerce and foreign capital in 1949–1952 (see Chapter 2) eliminated the parasitic classes responsible for economic stagnation as well as the basis for the unequal exchange with the West (primarily materials and financial profits against manufactured products). All the tendencies within the CCP agreed at the time on this productive use of the existing economic surplus. But serious differences gradually emerged over the expansion of the surplus necessary for accumulation—which were differences over basic choices—and before long there was a revisionist line and a leftist line.

The revisionist line

The revisionist line is based on orthodox Marxism and an a priori ideology: the party is considered the unique and all-powerful instrument for bringing about the transformation of social relations. Because the party is in power, socialism is a basic and irreversible fact. The fundamental contradiction is now between the advanced, socialist form of social relations and the backward, underdeveloped state of the forces of production.

Absolute priority has to be given therefore to the development of the forces of production in order to achieve the economic basis for socialism. As long as the party is in control of this policy, the means used to implement it do not matter.

In this way, if the private capitalist sector were subordinated to the fixed planning goals of the CCP, it could be a useful instrument in increasing accumulation and developing the forces of production. In the same way the rich peasantry could contribute usefully to the growth of agriculture and thus help bring about the surplus agriculture necessary to industrialization. The support of industrialized countries—first socialist countries and eventually capitalist countries as well—with their equipment, experts, credits, and technology, would also help lead to industrialization.

This classical development strategy is based on accelerated industrialization, which is considered the only way to develop the forces of production. Priority therefore has to be given to the industry of the goods of production—which alone is capable of expanding the range of basic industries—and to the production of infrastructure (transportation, communications, energy production). The sector of consumer goods has to be subordinated to the goods of production and must help finance them rather than the other way around: the mechanization of light industry is not a priority.

In the same way, the heavy-industry sector can only give very limited support to agriculture. The transfer of resources must work the other way: the agricultural surplus must increase for the purpose of industrialization; agriculture is a reservoir of labor and primary materials. If attention has to be paid to agriculture, it is only so that it will not slow down industrialization and its priorities.

This is a very economist conception of development. It is dominated by Stalinist ideology, which placed primary importance on heavy industry and was based on the sequence of modernization = industrialization = urbanization: these ideas influenced many progressive Third World economies and dominated Western theory during the fifties and sixties.

A whole series of potential contradictions stems from this general attitude, centering on the confusion between rapid accumulation and the socialist path of development. The superiority of socialism over capitalism is defined by its ability to maximize economic surplus and minimize unproductive uses of things—which would therefore guarantee a more rapid development. Everything is based on the need to increase surplus: the choice of priority areas, production techniques, planning and management, and the regions in which to establish pilot projects.

Whether these choices block the emergence of socialist political relations is hardly an issue, since this growth is accomplished under the strict control of the party. From the first Five Year Plan to the technically oriented projects of Deng Xiao-ping, this revisionist line has not changed in its basic conceptions.

The revolutionary line of development

The revolutionary line considers that if the transition to socialism has to be accompanied by rapid accumulation, there is still no question of subordinating the transformation of social relations to this objective. They both should be accomplished at the same time, each drawing support from the other. During the period of transition, the nature of socialist society is not independent from the nature of social relations. Socialist society is necessarily a society of classes that are defined not only by the laws of property but by their actual control of production and surplus. If a minority exercises control through the state or party, then new social relations of domination are established. The state and party are not socialist by nature.

Among the different forms of property during the transition period to socialism (state or people's property, collective property of the cooperatives and communes, and the remnants of individual property), the exchanges have to be organized in the form of "business relations." An increasing portion of production is destined to be exchanged and comes from salaried work (workers, employees) or from quasi-salaried work (rural work points); there is thus an objective expansion of the sphere of surplus value and surplus labor. On the other hand, the price of these goods is most often fixed according to the cost of production, depending on certain economic variables. Only a small part of production escapes this law of value —the goods distributed by the state sector according to the principle "to each according to his needs." The price of these goods is set by a political decision, without any margin for profit or loss, since these are necessary goods.

But beyond this limited area exchanges are based on the law of value. The nature of economic relations is not fundamentally different from that under capitalism. Private ownership of the means of production has disappeared, but a great inequality in the various types of ownership remains: on the one hand there is the state sector, and on the other hand there are the small and middle-size rural and city collectives opposing it on the socialist market. And the state sector is much better equipped with modern means of production. This is the reason for the transfer of surplus value to this sector from small industries that are less well equipped and especially from agriculture. The normal course of accumulation leads to an unequal exchange, to a transfer of surplus peasant labor to the modern sector through prices. The development of a state sector is therefore not necessarily a step toward socialism. If these tendencies are not corrected, it could even lead toward a monopolist sector, draining the surplus created by the other forms of ownership. If at the same time business relations are allowed to develop in the countrysides within the framework of the state plan—as the revisionists would have it—the transition toward socialism would lead to a worsening of social antagonisms similar to those under capitalism. In fact, optimal conditions exist for the creation of surplus value (differentiation within the peasantry, the increasing poverty of the great masses), and the state sector possesses all the instruments for attracting it.

This tendency toward state capitalism increases with the very successes of accumulation controlled by the state sector. The margin separating costs from prices is probably not kept by the productive enterprises, since that has been centralized by the state plan; but even so it is nothing else but surplus value, which can be prevented from being turned into a profit only by a political regulation of prices. But if prices are fixed on an economic basis, it is profit that becomes the economic basis of development. For investment decisions depend on economic criteria and the maximization of the surplus rate, and no return can be lower than the average rate established for the sectors as a whole. Such a criterion would be rational and would bring growth and efficiency to socialism.

As seen by the revolutionary line, these positions are totally incompatible with real socialist development. They would wind up reestablishing profit as the principal agent for development. The efficiency of socialist development cannot be measured by technical instruments such as the maximization of the rate of profit and the realization of an average profit rate, which are the classic constraints of capitalism. The economic and social relations stemming from this type of accumulation would necessarily be very close to those under capitalism because of unequal development. If everything is subordinated to development, then this growth would tend to be concentrated in the regions that were already the most advanced, where investments were most profitable; techniques and products that maximize surplus would be chosen at the expense of employment and social consumption. This would lead to increased disparities among regions, between cities and countrysides, and between advanced and backward rural areas; and also between workers and peasants, between manual and intellectual work, and between cadres and workers. The centralization of economic surplus in a society in which most regions are backward can only reinforce bureaucratic and technocratic management by special elites.[1]

This revolutionary line was emphasized in the criticism of revisionist management (in 1955–1956, 1962–1966, and 1972–1975) and by offensives such as the Great Leap Forward and the Cultural Revolution.

Economic and political strategy of the revolutionary line

This strategy is based on two fundamental challenges: it calls into question the relations between the economy and society and the relations between the state sector and the rural sector.

On the one hand, this line shows confidence in the masses, in their ability to mobilize and in their creativity. It rejects the pessimism of the revisionists for whom the technical and cultural backwardness of the Chinese people is the main obstacle to modernization. The vanguard and the masses must cooperate in struggling against misery in the same way they were capable of fighting against Japan and the Guomindang. In order for this to happen, the cadres must understand the masses, help them to take initiatives, and know how to coordinate these initiatives rather than sterilizing the people's creativity. The bureaucratic peril must therefore be eliminated through measures that guarantee the participation of the masses in public affairs. At the same time, the ideology of the old ruling classes must be rooted out, since it has survived on an economic level even though those classes have disappeared: particularly the acceptance of elitism, the hierarchy of powers, and inequality as rational facts. A revolutionary class consciousness must be developed. These are the fundamentals of the great ideological campaigns that have been waged by the revolutionary line over the past twenty years and the meaning of one of its basic watchwords: be red and be expert.[2]

Confidence in the masses also means a refusal to define development solely on the maximization of economic surplus, centralization by the state sector, and price controls. Transfers of funds from the rural areas to finance industrialization must be kept to a minimum, and the state sector could easily handle the financing for

[1] See document 1 at the end of the chapter.
[2] See document 2.

the necessary maximization of economic surplus. Exchanges between sectors and fiscal policy should allow the rural collectives to take in the major portion of income. In this way they could raise their level of consumption, make productive investments, and mobilize resources and men more effectively on the local level than the state could. The central sector maximizes surplus; the local sector maximizes production and employment.

These two objectives are not incompatible when directed by complementary sectors. The leftist line in this way overcomes the false dilemma between the maximization of growth and investment and the maximization of employment and consumption. For the economy as a whole does not depend only on accumulation in the modern state sector. Local resources are mobilized *at their level* without waiting to reach the average rate of return demanded by revisionist theories on "profitable" state investments. Disguised unemployment can therefore gradually be avoided, as well as the rural exodus and underconsumption, a stumbling block in the Third World resulting from resources remaining unused in the economic plans concentrating on the modern sector.

A better balance must therefore be maintained between the modern sector and local collectives, between consumer industries and industries for the goods of production; and the development of small base units must be encouraged. The industry for the goods of production must serve agriculture better so that agricultural growth will increase. This is the principle of "walking with both legs": *both* sectors have an essential role. Through their initiatives the local collectives will best be able to use men and resources, both for local equipment and consumption needs and for selling to the state sector certain surplus local products. The basis for the national process of industrialization would become more solid and diversified. Consumption by the base, employment, and the modernization of local forces of production would develop without slowing down central accumulation. Social and political relations would change simultaneously: from then on local collectives would be in control of their own development and would participate in economic decisions instead of passively waiting for the state sector to act. An organic, cellular, and decentralized model would thus replace a vertical and hierarchical model.[3]

This was the direction of the Great Leap Forward in 1958,

[3] See document 4.

which saw the establishment of people's communes and increased
planning initiative taken by the municipalities, districts, and
provinces. After a tapering off in 1961–1965, the Cultural Revolution emphasized decentralization, popularizing the models of Dazhai
and Daqing as examples of development that conformed to the
leftist line and giving a greater role to the revolutionary committees
in management and in the democratic control of the production
units.

The conflicting development of the two lines

The two lines are not simply schools of thought. They are embedded in contradictory interests and in the basic political options
of specific social groups; they are a manifestation of class struggle.
On one side are the new elite of the regime, the technocrats who are
in a powerful position because of their expertise; the remnants of
the old ruling groups who were traditionally tied to foreign countries in the modern cities; the workers who have benefited from
the policy of bonuses, as well as the wealthier peasants from advanced rural regions who have been tempted by the profits that
could be made in business dealings; and finally certain young people
who reject manual work and the rigors of politics. On the other
side are the low-ranking party cadres and the militants from the
base, the young and old workers from the largest enterprises, the
poor peasants, and the majority of the young people. But these are
only the basic tendencies, the broad outlines: Chinese society is
not abstractly divided in two. The social base for revisionism is
perhaps smaller than that of the leftist line, but the solid support
the left has received from the base does not mean it has always been
in control of the situation, has always taken the initiative, or that
it has unlimited popular support. The adherents of the two lines are
difficult to identify precisely, and they vary greatly depending on
the concrete situation. The policy of readjustment after the Great
Leap Forward and the policy of restoration after the Cultural
Revolution—to which the left resigned itself for a time—no doubt
corresponded to a widespread desire for stability and a political and
economic détente, especially in the cities.

The same asymmetry characterizes the origins of each line. The
revisionists have always been sustained by outside influences (even
if at the same time these influences have expressed the interests of
precise social groups): first the Stalinist tradition, and then Khrush-

chev's liberalism and the attraction of advanced Western technology; from this point of view, Liu and Deng represent two distinct periods of Chinese revisionism, one still linked to the Stalinist five-year plans, the other more influenced by the opening toward the West during the seventies. The leftist line has never benefited from such influences. Its Yanan experience was useful only in general political terms, and it has done considerable groping about. It relies on Marxist principles, but just as much on concrete practices (the Maoist technique of conducting investigations at the base, whereas the management experts prefer to remain in their offices), and also on the rigorous criticism of the other line, even if the leftist criticism of the Five Year Plan was never made public (see Chapter 4).

The differences between the two lines only gradually became apparent. The principal differences probably emerged at the end of the Five Year Plan. But the dialectical relationship between the two lines (and thus between the political and social groups that are associated with them) is not a mechanical kind of balance. At each stage when one line can dominate the other, there is nevertheless always a complex and conflicting relationship with the opposite line; there were thus economist and political versions of the Great Leap Forward, of the readjustment policy of 1960–1962, and of the relative stabilization after the upheavals of the Cultural Revolution. The conflict between the two lines is a permanent reality, and the course of Chinese socialism cannot be defined, as some Western sinologists have done, simply as an alternation between hard phases necessary for advancement and moderate phases necessary for giving some breathing room—even though China has in fact gone through advances and retreats, depending on which side could tip the balance of power. The rather large role played by free rural markets supplied by private plots (as opposed to private plots for family use only), the importance of the militia in relation to the regular army, of factory directors in relation to collective delegations from the base, and the politicized repertories of the Opera all represent examples of these advances and retreats.

The struggle between the two lines is not fought at the abstract level of theoretical concepts; it is not directed from above by wise and charismatic leaders or by eminent experts. In multifarious ways it includes all aspects of the economy and society—daily life and the political principles behind it, the giant-slogan posters on street-corners, and the basic decisions behind the organization of productive work. It has gradually become more refined, to the extent that both sides have come to the same conclusions about certain matters, such as the principle "be red and be expert" and the differences with the Soviet Union.

The example of the agrarian question

The agrarian question clearly illustrates the complexity of the conflicts between the two lines. Between 1953 and 1955 the leftist line worked against the extensions of the agrarian reform, which had been influenced by revisionist principles; on the theoretical level it criticized the polarization of political relations in the countrysides and the subordination of agriculture to the industrial sector controlled by the state. Among the people it worked vigorously for the development of cooperatives.

Its offensive came with the Great Leap Forward, the creation of the people's communes, and the rearrangement of the relations between agriculture and industry. But the difficulties that were encountered allowed the revisionist line to launch a counteroffensive, which, while it could not completely undermine the Great Leap Forward, did manage to change its direction: new priorities were accepted (agriculture as the base and industry as the dominant factor), but they were stripped of their political content. The decentralization supported by the left by means of the communes created well-structured collectives at the base which controlled agricultural surplus and decided on its distribution according to political priorities and in the interests of accelerated socialization. The revisionist version of decentralization, on the other hand, led to the dismantling of the commune as the center of political and economic decision making, leaving the surplus to smaller units— the team, or even the family. At the same time it stimulated business relations, the spread of private plots, and individual profit; and thus it reopened the way for capitalist relations in the countrysides.

In 1962 the revolutionary line reacted with the Socialist Education Movement in the villages; it offered as an example the collectives at the base which actively practiced the principles of the Great Leap Forward: mutual aid and solidarity, "self-reliance" (Daqing, Dazhai). The movement came up against sabotage attempts by the revisionists, but its base was considerably expanded during the Cultural Revolution; great importance was given to the people's communes in that they were collectives at the base managed democratically and capable of centralizing the surplus at a level that would allow for large local investments in agricultural water projects, industry, and infrastructure equipment. The consolidated commune was able to equalize the living conditions and contributions to the common progress by the different teams and brigades, which were initially at very different levels.

Between 1969 and 1974 the revisionist line, without formally challenging the consolidation of the communes, worked for a policy of selective modernization, in an attempt to increase production in certain rural areas that were considered best able to maximize the profits of the investments made with state aid. This policy, whose principles were not really very different from those of the "green revolution" devised by Western experts in the Third World, no doubt led to increased yields, but it also widened the gap between the advanced and backward rural areas. It also led to a certain degree of dependence on foreign technology. It was these negative aspects that the leftist line criticized after 1974; it demanded that the main effort be concentrated on the least advanced agricultural areas, that local resources be better mobilized, and that the experiments in simple local technology made at the base (rather than "advanced" technology) be made more widespread: such as the work by the Shashiyu brigade which cleared away piles of stones to make fields and orchards by methods accessible to everyone.

Economic Transformations

These changes have been based on an original coupling of the productive sectors: "take agriculture as the base and industry as the dominant factor." This principle, which has informed economic policy since 1958, has nevertheless caused considerable controversy over the way it has been applied.

Industry is the dominant factor. Its growth has been the most rapid (an average gain of 14 percent per year since 1949), it represents 70 percent of the gross national product, but it employs only 20 percent of the working population (mines and factories included), and only 3 percent of it is modern industry. Agriculture holds the opposite position: 30 percent of the gross product, 70 percent of the working population.

The agricultural sector must therefore be taken as the base since it includes the majority of Chinese and its productivity is very low. If it were left to itself, its backwardness would only worsen, as has happened in the capitalist countries of the Third World; this would lead to further disparities between production and income, the stagnation of the industrial sector—which would remain an island of modernization—as well as widespread and chaotic migrations of the unemployed rural workers to the cities. General development and the transition to socialism would become impossible. "Take agriculture as the base" thus means that the rural sector requires a special effort, even if it does not become the most important sector: the whole work force in this sector must be employed productively and production must be raised without waiting for these tasks to be automatically accomplished by the industrialization of the modern sector.

The modern sector must support this independent effort by the rural sector with specific kinds of help. And the policy of the re-distribution of income in the two sectors must be independent of the differences in production; if this were not the case, the differences in income between the cities and countrysides would only get worse—which would hurt the peasants.

Evaluation of agriculture since 1949

Food production has been stabilized and diversified, a fundamental if unspectacular achievement. Little by little China has managed to break the cycle of famines and shortages that were so frequent in the past because of uncontrolled natural conditions and the feudal system of exploitation. The population as a whole has been given a decent and relatively diversified diet. This represents a radical break from conditions in China in the past—as well as in Third World countries today. Astonishing amounts of work, organization, and creativity have been mobilized to achieve this—in spite of a paucity of materials available in the beginning.

The available figures do not show extraordinary performances. The yields have been moderate: 17 hundredweights per hectare in 1957 and 30 in 1974 for rice (30 percent of cultivated land), which was half the yield of Japan or North Korea, although some more advanced regions have matched the highest foreign figures. But the efficiency of the enormous quantities of collective work sunk into the land for the past quarter century cannot be judged only by yield. The thousands of hours of work have materialized in small and large dams, irrigation and drainage canals, hydroelectric works, immense retimbering projects along roads and fields, and anti-erosion works. These projects have therefore led to the regulation of agricultural production all across China, and the losses they have avoided have been gains in productivity, which are reflected in a slow but steady growth. The expansion of cultivated lands (perhaps a 20 percent increase since 1949) has also helped to con-

SOME FACTS ON THE OVERALL AGRICULTURAL SITUATION IN CHINA

	1949	1952	1957	1965	1970	1974
Cultivated lands (millions of hectares)[1]	100					127
Irrigated lands (millions of hectares)[1]	20					40
Active agr. population/hectare[2]			2.2	2.3		2.4
Cultivated lands with high and stable yield (% of total)[3]			7%			31%
Chemical fertilizer production (1000 tons)[4]		0.1	2	7	14	30
Pumping stations (power in millions of CV)[3]			0.7	7		32
Tractors (1000)[3]			20	100	±200	±500
Production of grains and cereals (millions of tons)[5,6]	108	154	185	220	240	275
Cotton (millions of tons)[5,6]			1.6	2.1	2.4	
Refined sugar (millions of tons)[5,6]		0.4	8.6	15		
Available cereals per person (kg. per year)[7]			280	300		340

Sources:
[1] F.A.O. Report on Chinese Agriculture, 1974
[2] R. Dumont, *La Révolution culturelle*, Paris, 1974
[3] A. L. Erisman, *China Agricultural Development*, Washington, 1972 and B. Stavis, "Grain Production in China," *China Quarterly*, March 1976.
[4] Jung Chao Liu, *Journal of Farm Economics*, November 1965 and Kang Chao, "Chemical Fertilizers in China," *China Quarterly*, December 1975.
[5] T. Rawski, "*Recent Trends in Chinese Economy*," China Quarterly, March 1973.
[6] J. P. Peemans, *La société et l'économie de la Chine en 1971*, Louvain, 1972.
[7] J. P. Peemans, "L'économie chinoise à la lumière de la Révolution culturelle," *Revue du Centre des pays de l'Est*, Brussels, 1969.

solidate the agrarian base through the efforts of the peasant collectives as well as the young students who have come from the cities since the Cultural Revolution.

The efforts to modernize and increase yields (soil improvement, natural and chemical fertilizers, deep plowing, double harvests, and more frequent plantings) have led to continued great differences between communes and brigades. The number of workers per hectare remains high and has hardly decreased. The productivity per hectare has increased, but not the productivity per worker, since the number of hours worked per year has risen sharply. Rural income remains low (one-third that of worker income, 200 *yuan* per year as opposed to 600, on the average) and this hides great disparities, for incomes in rural areas range from 50 to 600 *yuan* per year, meaning that some people earn twelve times as much as others. The increase in rural income through the diversification of more profitable activities (fruits and vegetables, fowl and pork) has been noticeable, but nevertheless it has been quite modest.

Unequal development of different types of people's communes

In the backward communes (in mountainous or infertile regions and in regions far from the centers) there is little control over population growth, and therefore any progress in production is immediately swallowed up. The small surplus does not reach the level of the commune and remains within the production units; productivity is low and the shift to nonagricultural activities is difficult. Income is low (50 to 100 *yuan* per year). There is no way to finance investments except in manpower.

The moderately advanced communes either were better equipped in the beginning or have been better able to move out of poverty through a more effective mobilization of men and resources. The growing surplus is productively used at the brigade and commune level to place a part of the working population in small industries, which increases local consumption—which has thus been diversified —and helps meet agricultural needs. The small fertilizer factories (8,000 to 10,000 tons) and the factories for agricultural material reduce the work on the land and create an organic link between agriculture and industry. Productivity and average income have risen. In these communes (24 percent of cultivated land) the average income is 200 to 400 *yuan* per year.

For the revolutionary line the principal aim is to transform the backward communes into relatively modernized average communes. A good indication of this was the increase in the number of small fertilizer factories during the Cultural Revolution: an increase of 300 percent between 1964 and 1970 as opposed to a 10 percent increase for large factories. But this tendency was reversed between 1970 and 1974, since the production of the small factories increased no more than 50 percent as opposed to 200 percent for the large factories.

The advanced communes are found particularly in fertile river areas and near large cities. Their surplus is great enough to allow for the development not only of social consumption but also large agricultural and industrial investments: electrification of pumping stations; increased mechanization and particularly an increased use of chemicals (fertilizers, fungicides, and pesticides); quarries, mines, and factories based on local needs; and larger production units integrated into the state plan after a trial period by means of subcontracts. Work productivity is high, and the income of the workers (500 to 600 *yuan* per year) is almost the same as that of the average industrial worker in the modern sector.

It is this third type of commune (a little less than 10 percent of cultivated land) that the revisionist line wants to emphasize; industrial production from the state sector for agriculture should primarily help to raise the production and productivity of the advanced communes. It provides them with cultivators (100,000 per year) and tractors (100,000 per year out of a fleet of only 150,000 in 1968). It especially provides them with fertilizer and equipment purchased abroad. In 1974 the large modern state factories provided them with 16.5 million tons of fertilizer out of a total of 30 million tons (in 1970 they provided only 5.6 million tons out of 14 million). In 1973–1974 twenty-six large factories were bought from foreigners for 500 million dollars. The forecast for 1980 is 75 million tons of fertilizer, a 150 percent increase over 1974. Half this increase will be due to the foreign factories, 40 percent to modern Chinese factories, and only 10 percent to the small local factories that were so active between 1965 and 1970. The economist tendency is most interested in advanced factories, while trying also to raise the level of those factories of the second type that seem most capable of increasing their yield.

This tendency has led to increased production, but the differences among the three types of communes have widened, and heavy debts to foreigners have built up. And since agriculture provides the major portion of Chinese exports, it thus tends to be doubly dependent on the international market and its economic fluctuations (the law of value). This strategy, completely opposed to that of the revolutionary line, was at the heart of the political struggles of 1973–1976: on which of the three types of communes should the main effort be made and by what means—political (*shashiyu*) or technological? The strategy that gave a special place to the advanced communes and made them dependent on Western technology and the world market was denounced as comprador in 1976.[4]

The industrial sector

With industry the question is not one of consolidation, as it is with agriculture, but of one of the highest growth rates in the world (14 percent a year from 1949 to 1952, 12 percent a year since then). In this tightly constructed system, the sectors of equipment, intermediary goods, and consumer goods depend on and support one another. The development of Chinese industry, on the other hand, is based not only on growth criteria but on employment criteria as well. State industry (a strong source of capital) and the industries of the base collectives (a weak source of capital) have developed simultaneously; China is opposed to the industrial performances of Brazil and India, for example, where rapid growth has gone hand in hand with a disequilibrium among sectors and dependence on foreigners (technology, capital, and market). China has developed a complete industrial system.

The first Five Year Plan paid special attention to the development of the intermediary goods of production (steel, coal, electricity, cement) with imported techniques and equipment—especially from socialist countries. In 1958–1965 intermediary goods became more diversified (especially chemicals and fertilizers); this improved balance helped consumption at the base (food, clothing, household goods), the production sector of the base developed (machine tools and other industrial equipment), and this effort was supported by equipment imported from the West. The range of the goods of production expanded during the Cultural Revolution to include even the most sophisticated ones (computers, data

[4] See document 3.

BASIC FACTS CONCERNING THE DEVELOPMENT
OF INDUSTRIAL PRODUCTION

	1949	1952	1957	1965	1970	1974
Industrial production in billions of *yuan* at 1952 prices[1]	14	34.3	78.3	151.1	257.4	351.6
Price index of same[1]	100	245	559	1093	1836	2508
Coal (millions of tons)[2]	32	67	130	220	300	390
Oil (millions of tons)[2]	0.1	0.4	1.4	10.6	26.4	63.6
Natural gas (billions of cubic meters)[2]			0.3	11.3	16.0	35.0
Electricity (billions of KwH)[2]	4.3	7.2	19.3	42.0	60.0	108.0
Steel (millions of tons)[3]		1.5	5	11	18	
Cement (millions of tons)[3]		3	7	13	19	
Synthetic fibers (millions of tons)[3]			2	20		
Cotton cloth (billions of tons)[3]		4	5	6	8.5	
Trucks (1000)[3]			7	25		
Machine tools (1000)[3]	1	13	29			
(price indexed according to 1952 prices)			100	236	350	
Distribution of industrial products[4]						
(a) by sector in %:						
Fuel and energy		12	13	16	17	
Industrial materials		20	27	33	34	
Machinery		13	16	19	20	
Light industry		56	45	32	29	
(b) by regions in %:						
Coastal regions		68	64	56	55	
Interior		32	36	44	45	

Sources:
[1] R. M. Field, "Industrial Output in China," *China Quarterly*, September 1975.
[2] V. Smil, "Energy in China," *China Quarterly*, January 1976.
[3] J. P. Peemans, *La société et l'économie de la Chine en 1971*, Louvain, 1972.
[4] R. M. Field, *Joint Economic Congress*, Washington, D.C., 1972.

processing, television, and automation); the production of durable consumer goods was developed: bicycles, watches, sewing machines, transistor radios; the equipment for middle-range technology was diversified and improved, which increased productive potential of the communes and neighborhoods. On the other hand, this middle sector leveled off in 1970–1975 in relation to advanced state technology. During this period the growth of durable consumer goods was remarkable, but it was the goods of production for advanced technology that led the way, both those made in China and those that were imported. Between February 1973 and August 1974 China signed contracts with the West for 56 factories (worth 2 billion dollars).

As in agriculture, the recent tendency has been technological advancement in order to establish a solid core of industries with the most modern techniques, and it is around this core that the entire Chinese industrial system is structured. This choice was made easier by the promising prospects of oil exports to improve the commercial balance. But doesn't this choice in favor of advanced technology imply a certain retreat from leftist principles: "to walk on both legs," "to rely on one's own strength"? The acceleration of modernization in industry, as in agriculture, runs the risk of concentrating growth in special agricultural and industrial areas, with increased dependence on foreign countries (imports and exports) and a worsening of regional inequalities.

The conflict between the two lines therefore started up again in the seventies, within the new framework of the gains of the Cultural Revolution and the new level of development and political consciousness. Both the future of accumulation and the nature of Chinese socialism depend on this dispute. Because China has opened itself more broadly to the world capitalist market (credits, techniques, primary materials, and industrial products), new constraints on accumulation threaten to weigh on the state sector—which has a monopoly on the access to this world market—and thus threaten to reinforce its hegemony over the collectives at the base; either it will slowly realize that the economy as a whole does not obey its logic of accumulation, or else it will treat regions that need to be developed as "regions supported by aid," but without integrating them into the strategy of advanced technology. Once again, in the face of this new situation, the leftist line has begun by criticizing its adversaries, at present feeling its way toward its own strategy. It does not reject technical progress and industrialization, or the usefulness of making overtures to the outside. But it perceives the dangers and contradictions of these things.

Transportation and exchanges

The infrastructure has undergone considerable development. River travel has been improved by drainage, the building of canals, and the repairing of the banks. Many railroad lines were built (24,000 km in 1949, 52,000 in 1963), expanded, or finished by enormous work projects such as the Nanking and Wuhan bridges over the Yangzi. Modern roads (70,000 km in 1949, 200,000 km in 1960) have expanded contacts between large and small cities. Civil aviation now serves all the provinces. And this modern network is organized around a traditional sector that still remains very large (small transport boats, animals, human labor, baskets, carts, and backs) and contributes to full employment while compensating for the insufficiencies of the modern sector. These traditional means of transportation have also benefited from modernization (rubber tires for carts, small concrete barges).

In a quarter century this system of transportation has considerably expanded the distribution of agricultural and industrial products. Entire provinces such as Sichuan, Guangxi, and Fujian have been taken out of their isolation. A unified national market has been created based on the state commercial companies and the state stores. But the small cooperative businesses remain important.

The progress made by transportation and commerce has led to the growth of the tertiary sector (including cultural, social, and medical services). This has offset the opposite tendency to reduce administrative personnel, for example after the Cultural Revolution. Through the campaigns of political education and manual work there is no gulf between all these employees and the peasants and workers who use these services.

DOCUMENTS

1. CRITICISM OF THE CADRES IN A SHANGHAI BOILER FACTORY

Source: *Vent d'Est*, no. 2, 2nd quarter 1976 (excerpts from a collection of 1974 investigations in Shanghai factories.

. . . The Shanghai boiler factory cadres have also learned that while their own function has changed with the development of the revolution, the nature of the working class has remained the same. Once you become a cadre, you must never stop correcting your vision of the world. To accept the control of the masses is to wage revolution on the ideological level. In a general way it is rather easy to accept the opinions of those involved in production. But when one touches an individual's ideological problem, then things get hot, it is no longer the same!!! A new cadre, originally a foundry worker, had a leadership job in a factory and no longer participated in manual work. The workers in the foundry then tacked up a poster which said that not to participate in manual work is to be on the path toward bureaucratism. The cadre was very irritated when he read this poster. He felt that even though he was in the leadership, he had spent a great deal of time in manual work, although not in the foundry workshop.

Under these conditions isn't it hard to swallow an accusation of bureaucratism? After reading the poster, the secretary of the party committee explained to him that the criticism of the masses is a help and a support to the cadres, which is why the cadres should go back frequently to their original factories and participate in manual work as a way of accepting this control and support of the masses. On the advice of this old cadre, he went back to the foundry for a while. The first day happened to be the "manual work day for the cadres," so the workers thought that he had come just for form and some even said, "You're here because it's manual work day for the cadres, eh?" The next day he came back and worked with a team that was doing very hard work. This time several of the workers spoke to him and said with kindness: "This is very tough work and you've been away for a long time. Be careful you don't get tired." The third day many of the workers were convinced that he had really come to work in order to get the opinion of the masses, and they warmly shook his hand, saying: "If we put up a wall poster, it was not because we had anything against you or because there weren't enough workers. But you used to be a worker like us and now that you're on top, we only see you at official assembly meetings! We didn't want you to forget the workers here." An old worker added: "When someone becomes a cadre it should not be for honors or so that he will never have to go back to work. If you don't use a hammer anymore, you will change!" These words deeply moved the new cadre and made him understand that the masses were really trying to educate him politically. How could he have taken these sincere words as ill-intentioned?

2. THE EXPERIENCE OF THE PEASANTS IS USED IN WEATHER FORECASTING

Source: *Serving the People with Dialectics*, Peking, 1972, pp. 19–25.

. . . The poor and middle-poor peasants welcomed us. An old peasant of seventy said: "In the old society I wasn't bad at weather forecasting, but I couldn't give away my methods because the landowner would have profited from it. Today I am working for the revolution, and I will tell you everything I know." He gave us more than fifty points on weather predicting. The poor and middle-poor peasants gave us some 340 pieces of information, not counting the plain good sense of the popular sayings. We learned how the peasants interpret the sky and how, for example, a foggy morning can turn into a sunny day, and how to make forecasts based on the movements of insects. We learned how to observe ants move their ant colonies, worms crawl from the earth, and dragonflies fly close to the ground. . . .

On May 15, 1969, for example, there had been three straight days of moderate rain followed by hot days and cold nights. We compared our facts with the old popular saying that went: "When the days are hot and the nights cold, the sea in the East is drying out." We also observed that in general between May and September a period of rain followed by differences between the day and night temperatures greater than ten degrees means that a period of dryness is coming. We were thus able to predict the coming dry spell correctly. The members of the commune made water reserves. . . .

When the typhoons hit the province of Guangxi, our district can undergo diluvial rains accompanied by strong winds, wind gusts with no rain, or nothing at all. We studied the weather patterns of the past twelve years as well as the long experience of the peasants and discovered that the effects of the typhoons was determined by local weather factors, primarily the humidity. In July 1969, for example, while our district was fighting against drought, the regional weather service predicted medium to heavy rains in South Guangxi approaching in the wake of a typhoon. But in our district the humidity was not high, which meant that no rain would be coming. We thus did not predict any major rains and the struggle against the drought continued.

3. CRITICISM OF DENG XIAO-PING'S IDEAS ON IMPORTING "ADVANCED TECH-NOLOGY

Source: *Vent d'Est*, no. 3; 3rd quarter 1976.

This document takes a look at Deng Xiao-ping's principal economic theses ("several problems relating to the acceleration of industrial development") and the critical remarks made by a "brigade of worker-theoreticians" from Shanghai; it was published in Shanghai in April 1976 in the magazine Xuexi yu pipan [Studies and Criticism], *no. 4, 1976.*

(Original text) "We must strictly apply the principle of study linked with independent creation. We should study with modesty all the remarkable and advanced things from abroad, import advanced foreign techniques according to a plan with certain priorities so that they will help us to accelerate the rhythm of the development of the national economy. We must still of course count on our own strengths, be independent and autonomous, fight the philosophy of servility to foreigners; however, we should not be presumptuous and proud and practice a 'closed door' policy and refuse to study the good things that come from abroad.

"We must oppose servile imitation; on the other hand we should not plunge into innovations without having studied first."

(Criticism) Chairman Mao teaches us: "Rely principally on your own strength, take outside help only as a backup." It is necessary to import advanced foreign technology, but we must essentially rely on our own strength. Countries that rely on others to develop their economy are incapable of controlling their own destiny. As a socialist country we should keep an independent economic system and follow our own path for developing industry. Everything proves that our people is fully capable of equaling and even surpassing the highest world levels in science and technology. Nevertheless, Deng's "20 points" are excessive in their praise of the "extreme efficiency" of foreign technology, underlining that we unilaterally must "as quickly as possible," "modestly," and "rapidly" "study the good things that come from abroad." But consider: it is clear that "we have built a cargo of 10,000 tons with 10,000 tons of energy," that we have more and more boats of the highest quality, while they think only of spending millions of dollars to import those "dazzling boats" that the foreign capitalists do not want anymore. It is clear that for a long time we have been able to build advanced equipment such as turbine generating plants with double internal cooling systems, while they still want to accept outmoded generators from the '40s and '50s from the Soviet Union. They constantly look abroad, holding out their hands to foreigners and begging with great sighs for "advanced techniques." Isn't this the same thing as wanting to attach the future of our industry to the coattails of the foreign capitalists?

Chairman Mao says: "Seriously study the good experiences of foreign countries, but do not forget to study the bad experiences as well and learn a lesson from them." We must apply the principle of "one divides into two" concerning foreign technology. The technical projects of the capitalist countries are based on the search for superprofits by the capitalist monopolists: thus they bear the incontestable stigma of class. Is it possible for us to use them without distinguishing between the "white cat and the black cat"? According to Deng Xiao-ping, if it is "foreign," it is "good." Whoever wants to criticize and transform the negative aspects of what is foreign is angrily scolded by him for "presumption and pride," accused of practicing a "closed door" policy. He decrees: we are forbidden from "plunging into innovations." This only reveals his reactionary servility to foreign countries.

4. Planning methods after the Cultural Revolution according to a French expert

Source: "Decentralized Planning in China," by J. Attali, Le Monde, May 15, 1973.

The author visited China in 1973 with his students from the École polytechnique.

. . . The basic direction of the economy therefore is handled through the annual plan, which is put into practice in a very interesting way. First, the division of responsibilities in this plan is very clear: in June and July each provincial administration writes up a first draft of an annual plan for the people's communes and enterprises located on its territory. (Some very large enterprises are under the direct control of the central administration or are under both provincial and central control.) Then it goes on to a macroeconomic analysis for the coming year: production forecasts for imports and exports, the structure of production by sector. To work out this plan the provincial offices use a very simple economic theory . . . . In September they send their production plan to the various sectoral ministers, who have also made their own independent predictions. At the beginning of the fourth quarter the regional and sectoral plans are analyzed by the National Planning Commission. This central organization, which was recently reconstructed, has the task of making sure that the large-scale strategic objectives are respected. In November there is a final conference of the provincial and ministerial leaders.

Once approved by the commission, the annual production plan is still not final. The production units, which until now have not been consulted on the plan being developed, receive a very detailed proposal for the coming year: production quantity, quality, manufacturing costs, productivity, use of primary materials, labor needs, profit. The revolutionary committee and then the workers of the factory discuss the proposal: can it be accomplished? Can more be done with the same means of production?

At this stage the provincial and national authorities have not yet determined the distribution of primary materials: there is still some margin (5 to 10 percent of the total) for giving resource supplements to the most dynamic factories while the projects are being centralized. For example, the proposed plan for the Shanghai machine tool factory called for the production of 2,400 grinding machines in 1971. The factory said that it could produce 2,500 with the same primary materials. This goal was written into the plan. 2,570 were produced.

In the numerous discussions we had with workers we learned that this self-management phase of Chinese planning has not been completely successful: we were told that workers in numerous factories had trouble giving advice on the projects presented to them, since they were often too complex to be analyzed at the factory level. On the other hand, they were very much in favor of the monthly meetings that dealt with work on the plan in progress and determined how much could be accomplished. Very rarely did they decide to surpass what the plan called for. . . .

Conclusion

The Problems and the Stakes of the Chinese Way

The "ten major relations and contradictions" that Mao defined in 1956—but did not try to solve—have continued to weigh heavily on the development of Chinese society and Chinese socialism.

Leaders and led

Starting in the sixties the seriousness of the contradiction between leaders and led has been openly admitted. The struggle between the two lines has deep roots in the society, but even so, at each stage it has crystallized and been resolved on the level of the leadership. To what extent have the masses had at least partial control of the development of the society? The revolutionary line has emphasized the establishment of systems that work "from below": the independence of management and planning of local collectives, the creative initiative of villages and neighborhoods, technical inventions by workers, and responsibilities assumed by the base, as during the upheaval of 1976. The principle of "self-reliance" has often come into play, as has "dare to revolt": one example was the crisis in education in 1972–1975, and another is the fact that the power of the cadres in factories, cities, and provinces is often subjected to critical *dazibao*.

But when the masses take charge of themselves it is mainly on the level of base production, local structures of society, and daily life. As one ascends the hierarchy there are more and more limits and counterbalances to this independence. The led are very aware of the real power of the leaders, and they show strong tendencies to be passive and resigned. Delinquency and the rejection of collective priorities reappeared, for example, during the disturbances of 1976.

In fact, the cadres and the party are quite powerful. The mass line consists of bringing together the cadres and the workers (through base investigations and manual labor), but does not question their essential separation (as embodied in certain Maoist metaphors: pianist and piano keys, white page and brush, plant and humus). Many cadres live very simply, but the upper-echelon leaders travel around in the privacy of their limousines with curtains drawn. In China, the leader-led duality is still very conspicuous. The CCP is an avant-garde endowed with an a priori mandate and a special status (as far as information, responsibilities, and decision making go), even if its concrete administration is always vulnerable to unexpected shake-ups.

The power of the cadres and the party is ideological rather than mechanically coercive. "Where do correct ideas come from?" asked Mao in the sixties. To what degree is the dominant ideology imposed from above, as Peking's enemies allege? To what degree, on the other hand, is it *produced* by a deep movement of society working through certain intermediaries?

Mao himself was one of the main intermediaries. "Mao Tsetung's thought" is the supreme, unanswerable authority in China. Mao identified with the leftist line on crucial occasions (in 1958 and 1966, for example) and he played a considerable personal role into the seventies. Certain people in the West as well as liberal Soviets compared him to Stalin. Yet apart from the personal importance of the two Communist leaders, their orientations were very different. The economic break in 1958 was a break with the Stalinist model of society. Stalin insisted on order, continuity, and hierarchy; the restless and turbulent themes of Mao's poems were completely foreign to him—winds and storms, waves and tempests, the high ridge road and the defiance of the elements.

Stalin could never have said, as Mao did, "Let us not be afraid of troubles; the more troubles there are, the better for us . . ." Mao was immensely powerful; he dominated China's whole politics. Yet in several decisive situations he deliberately tried to invite trouble and allow crises to happen, so that the social order, the authority of the party, the authority of the state, and consequently his own authority would all be called into question. After his own fashion and within certain limits, he tried to leave room for the forces from below as a necessary counterbalance to the weight from above. Few statesmen of his standing have taken that care.

Men, women, and children

Three very strong periods attest to the fact that there has been a vigorous women's liberation movement: the Great Leap Forward, when the women enthusiastically helped organize a collective life which freed them from domestic duties; the anti-Confucian campaign in 1973, with its emphasis on the emancipation of women; and the period in which the housewives took initiatives in managing neighborhoods and creating small workshops. These periods confirmed the destruction of the feudal status of the family. The Cultural Revolution also reaffirmed the positive role of the young people: "The world is yours," Mao told them. But this liberation was limited: how many women rose to positions as cadres or became more highly qualified? More generally, the family model has not really been attacked, and a burdensome conformism seems to weigh on the whole issue of sexuality—which is regressive in comparison to Yanan and sometimes even in comparison to current laws. There is pressure in favor of late marriage, discouragement of divorce, rejection of premarital and adulterous relations, and an absolute condemnation of homosexuality.

Naturally these tendencies are explained by the priorities of the economy, the need to involve all the most vital forces in it. Besides, the nuclear family guarantees for the most part the caretaking of the old people, which the collective is not yet equipped to handle. What is more, an attack on the family unit, which provides so much security, would pose profound ideological questions which China does not seem ready to confront, as is shown by its total rejection of the contributions of psychoanalysis. There is another aspect of the struggle between the two lines: should the economic function of the family, especially the rural family, be exploited, therefore retaining this authority structure; or should the enormous productive forces of "half of Heaven" be freed, which would also mean freeing the women themselves? At least the question has been asked.

Regional disparities

The regional maps of agriculture and industry have changed radically since 1949. High-yield crops, which until then were confined to the warm and fertile river basins in the South, have extended toward the North; the limit of double-harvest rice is now the basin of the Yellow River, and that of rice followed by one other crop is now the plateaus of the Northwest. Industry, which in 1949 was confined to a few remote centers in the Northeast and Southeast, has extended into the interior on a large scale, with major centers like Lanzhou, Xian, Baotou, Daqing, Zhengzhou, Wuhan, and Peking itself, which has changed from a consumer administrative metropolis to a large production zone, especially in metallurgy, electro-metallurgy, and textiles.

But this new distribution of economic activities, which was envisaged at the time of the first Five Year Plan, has displaced and increased the regional disparities rather than absorbing them. There are still great contrasts—they have even increased—between advanced economic sectors and the great majority of rural districts or small provincial cities. The growth of industry, especially around very large towns and generally around provincial capitals, has directly stimulated the agriculture of neighboring regions: there is a better system of roads, an improved supply of durable goods and finished products, and a more favorable market for food and industrial crops. Already in 1965 and again in 1970–1975 there was a strong temptation to concentrate on these agro-industrial centers which were already so rich, to make "pilot" zones out of them along the lines of the differential tactics popular in capitalist Third World countries. Among these centers were the Lower Yangzi, the Canton region, and central Henan. The revolutionary line, on the other hand, apparently advocated the equalization of the different regions through giving priority to the most disadvantaged areas (even if the progress they made would not help to increase growth rates as fast). The pilot regions in this case would be of a different sort—these poles would serve as *political* examples, like Shashiyu, Daqing, and Dazhai, and people from all over the country would visit and study them.

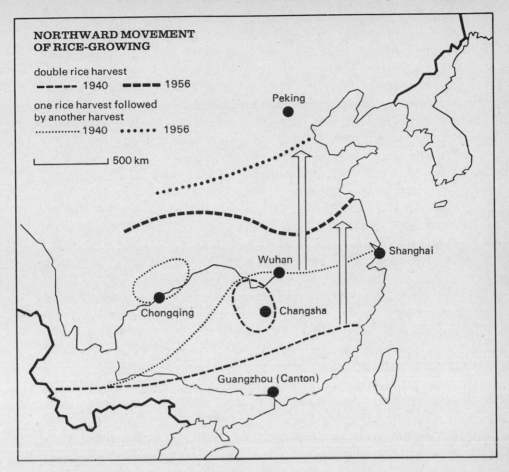

NORTHWARD MOVEMENT
OF RICE-GROWING

double rice harvest
━━━━━ 1940   ━━━━ 1956

one rice harvest followed
by another harvest
············· 1940   •••••• 1956

|————————| 500 km

Peking

Wuhan

Shanghai

Chongqing

Changsha

Guangzhou (Canton)

Demography and employment

By 1953 the population of China had already reached 583 million (as opposed to a previous figure estimated at 400 million), and by about 1975 it had undoubtedly reached 800 or 900 million. This jump in population has had the effect of lowering the average age of the country (perhaps 50 percent of the population is under twenty), which is an important political factor. It is a result of the fact that the birthrate has remained very high, especially in the villages, while the death rate has been radically reduced by improved hygiene, medical care, and nutrition.

Here the healthy condition of agriculture, which assures all Chinese a decent and relatively equal amount of food, becomes really meaningful: we are talking about a population that has doubled in twenty years. The growth rate of food crops has more or less kept up with the population growth. But barely. This is why China, going against the tradition in socialist countries, has instituted a policy of birth control, both for economic reasons (to relieve the pressure of food consumption on agriculture) and for social reasons (to reduce the social, medical, and educational costs that a very young population imposes on the collective and to reduce the burden on families). Birth control was begun in 1956, abandoned for a time in the midst of the enthusiasm of the Great Leap Forward, and systematically resumed in 1960: there is contraception, late marriage, and pressure to limit the size of the family to two children. But there are ideological obstacles in the form of certain Confucian ideas (the social prestige conferred by having many children and particularly sons), and these remain powerful in the villages, where birth control is less readily accepted.

The growth of the population also governs the question of employment. Disguised forms of rural and even urban unemployment caused by economic stagnation have persisted for a long time, and the selective development of the first Five Year Plan did not really help. At the same time, the ideological choices of the left concerning development are based on a realistic appreciation of the demographic situation: its aim is to ensure full employment in an expanding population, even at the expense of profitability and productivity priorities. Manual work has been mechanized as little as possible, while at the same time made less arduous; the work pace has not been pushed up to an international level; and the latent rural unemployment is absorbed by vast programs of large-scale hydraulic works and road and forestry work.

Cities and rural areas

Urban growth has been very rapid since 1949 in the very large cities and perhaps even more in the middle-sized cities. It has the same negative effects as in many other Third World countries: longer distances, overburdened transportation systems, extended work hours, greater need for provisions, and the risk of the society crumbling because of the monotonous way of life in the new residential areas. As has often been true of other issues, there are two attitudes toward this issue in China. Sometimes this growth is welcomed as a good thing just because it is "modern"—any repercussions it may have are secondary and temporary; for example, it was this tendency toward modernist urbanism that caused the Peking walls to be destroyed in 1960–1964. At other times attempts are made to counteract unlimited growth by systematically slowing it down: since the Cultural Revolution, for example, the population of Shanghai has dropped from 11 million to 9 million. There are also attempts to give the urban fabric a new quality, to make it more highly structured, less dispersed. Neighborhood committees encourage productive activities and social or medical mutual aid in residential units, especially with the help of old people. Around the large factories more independent and viable "industrial campuses" have been organized, the true descendants of the brief urban communes of 1959: they contain housing, shops, cultural and social equipment, and even market gardens.

In the countrysides, where the immense majority of Chinese still live, the rural landscape has been radically changed by the reforestation of roadsides, hills, and field borders; by the laying down of new roads and the implementation of large-scale hydraulic works; and by the construction of community buildings (granaries, offices, workshops, social and educational centers, and machine sheds), which have been integrated into the ancient fabric of small individual peasant dwellings.

There is still a fundamental imbalance between the cities and the rural areas. On the average, the standard of living is three times higher in the cities, and this also exerts a cultural attraction: the cities implicitly represent a model of social superiority to many people. The spontaneous exodus from rural areas increased into the sixties; sending large numbers of young students from the cities into the rural areas, a movement that started in 1970, fulfilled a need for sociological balancing as much as for political education. The ill will with which some people react to being transferred is a sign that the cities still have a good deal of prestige and also that the young people do not all adhere to the mass line. Another clear sign of the imbalance between cities and rural areas is the fact that whereas for the peasants of Shashiyu a great deal of labor is needed to bring one *mou* of land under cultivation, what is that *mou* worth, when it is cultivated in the suburb of a large city to be included in the borough area of an administrative or industrial unit?

In the cities as in the countrysides, priority continues to be given to progress in production, consumption, and material needs (equip-

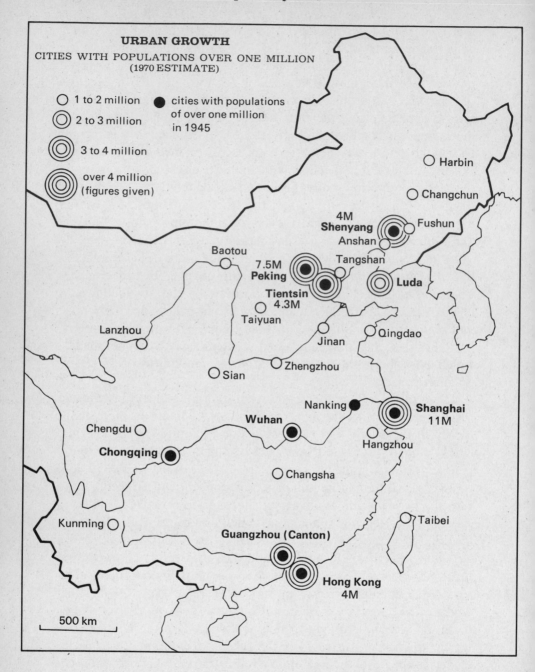

URBAN GROWTH

CITIES WITH POPULATIONS OVER ONE MILLION
(1970 ESTIMATE)

○ 1 to 2 million   ● cities with populations
◎ 2 to 3 million   of over one million
◎ 3 to 4 million   in 1945
◎ over 4 million
    (figures given)

Harbin

Changchun

4M
Shenyang   Fushun
Anshan

Baotou   Tangshan

7.5M
Peking   **Luda**

Tientsin
4.3M
Taiyuan

Lanzhou   Qingdao

Jinan

Sian   Zhengzhou

Nanking   **Shanghai**
11M
Chengdu ○   **Wuhan**

Chongqing   Hangzhou

Changsha

Kunming ○   Taibei

Guangzhou (Canton)

Hong Kong
4M

500 km

ment, housing). This often poses a threat to the balance of nature: there is an excessive use of chemicals in agriculture (in the form of weed killers, pesticides, and chemical fertilizers), the air in large cities is polluted, and small streams in towns are turned into open sewers. These pollution problems are taken very seriously, but essentially from the point of view of waste; a great deal of ingenuity is used in trying to have as many waste products as possible. But the truly ecological aspects of industrial development and man's relationship with nature as such are confronted less often. Other matters take precedence.

The international situation

The establishment of the Chinese way depended heavily upon the international situation. Economically, China had to fit into the international system of the circulation of raw materials, rates of exchange of currency, complex commercial exchanges, banking equalization—a system whose rules and constraints were imposed on China even though they were the product of an economic system that China rejected. Even in the Third World, China has to deal with the West, which has always been dynamic and still is— especially where technology is concerned—and therefore still exerts a strong attractive force. The temptation is always present, then, to enter the same orbit, to define oneself according to the same references, to try to attain an international level instead of taking a qualitatively different path: this possibility has had a profound influence on the struggle between the two lines, especially since China's entry into the United Nations, which provided greater opportunities for relations with the West.

Politically, China is confronted with an international community organized on an interstate basis; "We live in a world of nations," Zhou En-lai said without optimism in 1970. The People's Republic therefore *puts up with* the need for a state structure with its considerable negative burdens. Its state diplomacy necessarily favors relations with other states, in spite of its ongoing efforts to give some support to other popular movements throughout the world. Its army is very expensive and constantly poses the threat of forming an independent political force with its own requirements: Peng De-huai and Lin Biao were descendants of the old warlords and represented profound tendencies on the part of Chinese political society. Yet this army has to be maintained and properly equipped because of very real international imperatives, especially on the Sino-Soviet frontier.

China's national territory is very spread out and particularly vulnerable, since the regions that are hardest to defend and most thinly populated also contain the largest groups of minorities (see Chapters 1 and 3). And should priority be given to promoting the independence of these national minorities, especially those in Mongolia, Xinjiang, and Tibet, combating tendencies to Greater Han chauvinism and assimilation? Or should priority be given to national defense, keeping close watch over the risks of infiltration from outside and of dissidence? China's policy toward the national minorities is particularly delicate and uncertain, particularly marked by the contradictions in the international situation.

But where does temporary acceptance of these state, diplomatic, military, and territorial constraints—imposed by an international system whose terms China did not choose—end, and where does voluntary adherence to the state as a permanent structure in order and power begin? The weight of China's twenty-five centuries is particularly heavy in this context, as is the ancestral belief in the uniqueness of the Middle Kingdom.

How do people live in China?

Because of material conditions in China, life is frugal but contains few crises or uncertainties. Everyone can be assured the same stability, including the stability of the *yuan* (about fifty cents in 1975), and prices are lowered more often than raised (they are lowered when a product reaches the stage of being mass produced and is therefore less expensive to produce). The typical family budget is very small: 10 to 50 *yuan* per month for the peasants, and 30 to 120 for the workers. A meal in the communal dining room costs .2 *yuan*, a blue cotton jacket 7 *yuan*, and in the city rent is always calculated at 5 percent of the family income. Yet quite a few people own watches, bicycles, and transistor radios, which cost from one month's to several months' salary. Also, the family budget is not the only indication of how well off the people are, since there are many public services: for example, any working woman is freely allowed to take her young children to the factory for the day; there they will be looked after for her. Disparities in living standards are also limited by the authorities: for example, neither cars nor motorcycles are available as private consumer goods.

Yet there is a fairly wide range of salaries. Not only between city and country, but also within urban society. The employees of the tertiary sector and the lower cadres hardly earn more than the most humble workers—30 to 40 *yuan*. But factory technicians earn as much as 200 to 240 *yuan*, and there are some very highly paid people (300 to 400 *yuan*) who are either leftovers from the past— for example, former national capitalists or old university teachers whose original salary has been guaranteed for life—or part of the privileged hierarchy, like certain high cadres in economy.

In this society, the community certainly comes before the in- dividual. Television, for example, exists all over, but is collectively owned. Each individual has very little space for himself physically, politically, and culturally—especially in the cities. A person's destiny is not defined in terms of himself or his family, his region or his corporation. The potential economic progress of a particular individual or a particular social group is in some sense absorbed by the delays and inequalities of the country and the people as a whole. To live in China is to live in solidarity with all of China. Chinese society is highly politicized, highly political in the true sense of the word. Its dynamics emphasized the common destiny over the destiny of the individual.

Should China be compared to the West, where so many live in comfort and where there is nominal respect for the individual, yet where everyone is also secretly frightened by the instability and economic insecurity of his living conditions? Or should it be com- pared to the other countries of the Third World, pursuing models of development that are increasingly inaccessible to more and more countries—and being sucked down into a descending spiral of misery, as was true of the land of the Han for such a long time?

Glossary of Chinese Terms and Names

bangong banxue	半工半学	dazibao	大字报
Beida	北大	Deng Tuo	邓拓
Beidaihe	北戴河	Deng Xiaoping	邓小平
Beifa	北伐	dizhu	地主
bixueganbang	比学趕帮	Ding Ling	丁玲
Bo Yibo	薄一波	dousipixiu	斗私批修
cai	才	dujunzhuyi	督军主义
changzheng	長征	duoquan	夺权
Chen Boda	陈伯达		
Chen Yi	陈毅	Fanshen	翻身
Chen Yonggui	陈永贵	fan youpai yundong	反右派运动
Chen Yun	陈雲	Feng Ding	馮定
		Feng Youlan	馮友兰
Dagongbao	大公报		
Daqing	大庆	ganbu	干部
Dashijie	大世界	ganxiang gangan	敢想敢干
Da Yuejin	大跃进	Gao Gang	高岗
Dazhai	大寨	gaochao	高潮

gongzuodui	工作队	*kaimen banxue*	开门办学
gongzuozu	工作组	Ke Qingshi	柯庆施
gugan	骨干	Kuai Dafu	蒯大富
guanliaozhuyi	官僚主义	Lei Feng	雷峰
Guangming Ribao	光明日报	Li Fuchun	李富春
Guo Moruo	郭沫若	Li Jingquan	李井泉
Hai Rui	海瑞	Li Xiannian	李先念
Han	汉	Li Xuefeng	李雪峰
helihua	合理化	Li Zuopeng	李作鹏
hezuo yiliao	合作医疗	*Lian Si*	联四
heiliao	黑料	Liang Shuming	梁漱溟
Hongqi	红旗	Liao Shen	辽沈
Honglou Meng	红楼梦	Lin Biao	林彪
Hou Wailu	侯外卢	Lin Liguo	林立果
Hu Feng	胡风	Liu Bocheng	刘伯承
Hu Shi	胡适	Liu Lantao	刘澜涛
huzhuzu	互助组	Liu Ningyi	刘宁一
Huang Yongsheng	黄永胜	Liu Shaoqi	刘少奇
Hui	回	Lu Dingyi	陆定一
Jian Bozan	翦伯赞	*Lushan*	卢山
Jiang Qing	江青	Luo Ruiqing	罗瑞卿
jiefang	解放	Mao Dun	茅盾
Jiefang Ribao	解放日报	*maodun*	矛盾
jinbiaozhuyi	锦标主义	Mao Zedong	毛泽东
Jinggangshan	井冈山	*Mao Zedongsixiang*	毛泽东思想
jiuguo	救国		

minbing	民兵	sanjiehe	三接合
		sanzi yibao	三自一包
Nie Yuanzi	聂元梓	Shashiyu	沙石圩
paoda silingbu	炮打司令部	shengchan dui	生产队
Peng Dehuai	彭德怀	sidaminzhu	四大民主
Peng Zhen	彭真	sijiu	四旧
pi Lin pi Kong	批林批孔	siqing	四清
putonghua	普通话	sitong	四同
Qi Benyu	戚本禹	Tan Zhenlin	谭震霖
qingguan	清官	Taoyuan	桃园
Qinghua	清华	Tao Zhu	陶铸
Qiu Huizuo	邱会作	Tian An Men	天安门
quanguo	全国	Tianqiao	天桥
quanguo zonggonghui		*tiaozheng*	调整
全国总工会		*tufa*	土法
qunzhong luxian	群众路线		

Rang liang tiaotui zoulu		Wang Guangmei	王光美
让两条腿走路		Wang Hongwen	王洪文
Rao Shushi	饶漱石	Wang Li	王力
ren	仁	*weida duoshou*	伟大舵手
renminbi	人民币	*wendou*	文斗
Renmin Ribao	人民日报	*wudou*	武斗
renmin gongshe	人民公社	Wu Faxian	吴法宪
sanfan	三反	Wu Han	吴晗
sanhai	三害	Wu Song	武松
sanhe yishao	三和一少	Wu Xun	武训

Wufan	五反	Yu Gong	愚公
wuqiyi	五七一	yundong	运动
wushi	五史	Zhang Qunqiao	张春桥
wutoulong	无头龙	Zheng Weishan	郑维山
		zhenglihua	整理化
xiafang	下放	zhiduhua	制度化
xian	县	Zhongguo	中国
xiang	乡	Zhonghua	中华
xin cheng wu	新成物	zhongyang	中央
Xinhua	新华	zhou	州
xiuyang	修養	Zhou Enlai	周恩来
Xuanji	选集	Zhou Gucheng	周谷城
		Zhou Yang	周揚
Yanan	延安	Zhu De	朱德
Yanshan	燕山	Zhuge Liang	諸葛亮
Yang Chengwu	楊成武		
Yang Xianzhen	楊献珍	zhuang	壮
Yao Dengshan	姚登山	zichanjieji faquan	资产阶级法权
Yao Wenyuan	姚文元	zili gengsheng	自力更生
Ye Jianying	叶剑英	zongpaizhuyi	宗派主义
Ye Qun	叶群	zongluxian	总路线
yibiandao	一边倒	zouzipai	走资派
yiguandao	一贯道	zu	组
youhong youzhuan	又红又专	Zunyi	遵义

Index

Abbreviations: CCP = Chinese Communist Party
CR = Cultural Revolution
GLF = Great Leap Forward

About the Author

Jean Chesneaux, one of the world's leading Sinologists, is a professor at the Sorbonne. Director of this three-volume modern China project, he is the author of innumerable other works, including *The Chinese Labor Movement, 1919–1927, Peasant Revolts in China, 1840–1949, Secret Societies in China,* and *The Political and Social Ideas of Jules Verne.*